Identity & Security

Identity & Security

A Common Architecture & Framework
For SOA and Network Convergence

Rakesh Radhakrishnan
Sr. Principal IT Architect

Futuretext Ltd.
London, England

Identity & Security
A Common Architecture & Framework
For SOA and Network Convergence
by Rakesh Radhakrishnan

Issue Date 15 May 2007

Published by
Futuretext
36 St George St
Mayfair
London
W1S 2FW, UK

Email:info@futuretext.com
www.futuretext.com

ISBN: 978-0-9544327-9-9

Foreward

We are at a juncture today where many Industry Organizations are studying the many possibilities of protecting the Internet and the Services and Content offered via the Internet to the respective legitimate users in a secure way. Identity System which originally focused on user life cycle management and their access to services has now formed the foundation with which many traditional security tools and techniques are reinvented. Startup companies are specializing in Identity enabled Firewalls, Gateways, XML routers, NAC appliances, Devices and more. Along the lines of these developments traditional Identity Systems such as AAA, HLR, RADIUS, TACACS and many more are redesigned around a Federated Identity Systems, as well. User Centric and URL based Identity models are evolving today and Device centric Identity System standards are also integrating with Federated Identity Systems. Rights Management models are being reinvented around the user and being device and network agnostic for the Web 2.0 world and the Read/Write Internet. Many, industry standards bodies are aligning themselves to inter-work with each other including OASIS, Liberty, TCG, OMA and more.

Even with all these developments the Identity Systems in the Network are fragmented and still require Vertical Integration from Devices, to Users to Access Networks, Core Network and the Services and Content the user's consumer to ensure that the Network acts like a Computer and to form the foundation for a Pervasive Policy Paradigm that ensures end to end Security.

This book nicely recaps all the developments as of 2007 and probes into the future to see how the Identity Space will evolve to offer User's contextual, cohesive, convenient, consent based and controlled Network of Services. I agree and echo with what the reviewers have stated:

- It is a great work of synthesis,
- a good collection of IP,
- with a prolific treatment: of how to leverage Identity Management,
- one that, highlights the thought leadership in this very critical area,
- and I'll add that its an excellent piece of work on "Integrated Identity Infrastructure"

Enjoy

Cheers

Ajit Jaokar
Futuretext

Contents

Index of Figures

1. Introduction and Overview

This book is based on the author's experience working at Sun Microsystems as an IT Architect specialising in Identity System Integration with Telecom Customers and Cable Customers along with Sun's NEP (network equipment partners) and integrating Sun Identity System with ISV (independent software vendor) partners. It also includes the author's understanding of market developments in the Identity space and potential future, based on the developments that have taken shape in the last five years (2002 to 2007). The objective of this book is to explore the strategic significance, market requirements and all the potential possibilities of leveraging Standards based Identity Systems for an Enterprise IT environment (& Enterprise Architecture) and Telecommunication environment to provide a pragmatic view for the future in network convergence and converged services based on Service Oriented Architecture. This book also looks into the alignment and functional integration offered by an Identity System as a Common Security Framework for Enterprise Services (such as ERP, SCM, CRM Services based on SAO), Web Services, DRM Services, Telecom Services (Data, Voice and Video), Enterprise Networks and Telecom Networks (including Sensor Networks, Programmable Networks, 4G Networks and IMS Networks).

In the early years of this decade we saw the proliferation of Services to Cell Phones and Mobile Devices over 3G and 2.5G Networks—wherein a Cell Phone/Mobile Device evolved into a more complex device that handles TV, email, SMS, IM, Games, Pictures, Videos, Video mail, News and more. In the later part of this decade in conjunction with the deployment of 802.11 (WiFi), 802.16 (WiMax), BPL (broadband over power line) and other access networks along with the evolution into 4G network where seamless traversal between all types of wireless networks is made possible. Identity enabled Service Delivery is even more promising, especially from a mobile user perspective (users on the move—which includes almost all the user population). We can expect to see more adoption of these multi-media and multi-modal services and mass acceptance and consumption of such services, moving forward. All locations such as airport lounges, hotels and conference facilities, retail locations such as Starbucks, Regional Malls, McDonalds, have rolled out these networks. Along the same lines, it should be noted that both Wire-line and Wire-less Communication Service Providers (CSPs) are seeking new ways to expand into delivering data services securely with offerings in broadband access networks ranging from DSL to Cable Modem, as well. In many cases they are forging partnerships as the delivery of Voice, Video and Data is made possible with the reach of IP (internet protocol) as the foundation across all networks.

Imagine mobile services that allowed you to get information based on your specific need. For instance, every morning at 6:30 A.M. you want to see the top ten sports highlights from the day before (based on your preferred set of sports activities), check the weather for the specific location you are in and see a traffic report for your commute to work. The Network had the intelligence to sense that these services are something you used every day and could offer up an on-the-fly bundle that included these things before you even got up in the morning. You pick up your mobile device and a new icon appears with your name on it with these customised services. With one push, you are offered the services you want and now have a totally customised service offering specifically designed to meet your individual needs. This is based on your preferences, service profiles, network profiles, location, subscription information, your entitlement information, your presence and more.

Services today are not only user centric but also utilize voice, data and video (multi-media) to deliver more complex and advanced services such as Context sensitive delivery of Entertainment, which implies orchestration and choreography of multiple data services with voice and video services. The overarching goal is to transcend all types of access networks and access devices and deliver User Sensitive (preference, profile and policy based), Location based, Context driven Services with true Service Mobility. That goes beyond user and terminal mobility. Different dialects of XML are used here, including, SAML/SPML, MOML/MSML, CpML, XKMS, VXML, XRI/XDI and more. In the early years of this decade many software vendors have addressed the need for an Integrated Security framework that addresses Security requirements with extension of their solutions to Network Identity Systems (such as Sun's Java Identity System), including Oracle, SAP and other business software vendors designing and developing B2C, B2B and B2E services, essentially Identity enabling all the business services that an enterprise will need, customer, supplier and employee facing. Since 2004 more of these Independent Software Vendors (ISVs) have either developed new Identity based services such as a Device Reputation service (that tracks the history in terms of behaviour of these devices), Device Policy Services (that pushes policies onto devices based on location, context, and more), XML gateways, firewalls, routers and accelerators (essentially augmenting a Service Network with an Enterprise Service Bus with security mechanisms), Identity based DRM disintermediation services (abstraction layer between multiple content protection mechanisms) and more developments are geared towards addressing nine specific challenges that an Identity System can potentially solve.

What will I get by reading your book?

This book is intended for Systems Architects, Network Architects, Software Architects, Security Architects, Enterprise Architects, CSO, CTO and other IT professionals who work in the Identity and Security space, both in the CME (communications, media and entertainment) Industry and Enterprises as well. This is the first book on the market that talks to the end-to-end spectrum of Identity enabled Networks and how an Identity System acts as a Core Building Block for Enterprises building their Architectures based on SOA and evolving IP Network that require a common security platform. This book talks about the value proposition of an Identity System for Web 2.0, Mobile Web 2.0, 4G Networks, Sensor and Programmable Networks, IMS networks, DRM, Devices, Computing, ILM and Web Services. It recaps all the major developments in the past five years and projects the potential developments that can take place in terms of Vertical Integration in the next five years as multiple Billions of Dollars gets invested in the NG Network Architecture and Enterprise Architecture based on SOA. This book explains how an Identity Centric Architecture (as the Security, Policy and Control Stratum), helps align SOA (the service signaling stratum) with NGN (packet handling stratum).

What's the value of the content?

Using the content of this book readers are expected to add value to their Enterprise from the following perspectives:

- Align a Common Identity System as the linchpin for major security initiative (more as an eigenvector)
- Leverage an Identity System to address Regulatory compliance issues
- Develop Secure Services as Web Services, Telecom Services and Mobile Services
- Understand and apply the significance of an IDS for NG IN and OAM&P Services
- Understand and align the Enterprise Architecture with the evolving 4G IMS based network
- Align User Centric Services to Events in the Communication Network
- Align User Centric Services to Events in a Sensor Network
- Align SOA to Programmable Active Grid Networks
- Understand and apply an Identity System for Open Service Delivery Platforms
- Understand and apply an Identity System for Open Content Delivery and Open DRM Architectures
- Understand and align an Identity Lifecycle with the Information Life Cycle and Service Lifecycles
- Understand the value proposition of an Identity System for Trusted Networks and Trusted Computing
- Understand the alignment between an Identity System and Web Services, ESB and Service Registry
- Understand and apply the alignment between Identity Standards

such as Liberty, SAML, Open-ID, XACML and more

The real measure of the value of this book is for the readers to go through the Content and use it on their jobs to Architect and Align System Solutions around a Common Open Standards based Security Architecture and Framework.

1.1 The Nine Potential Pain Points

There are nine potential pain points or challenges that are presented by Accenture (see reference URL http://www.sun.com/events/horizons2006/sessions-track1.jsp) to ensure "mobility" in SOA (a topic key for Telecom SOA as well).

They are:

- Seamless Integration of different Access Networks
- Secure and Controlled integration of external service providers
- Integrated registration and customer service support
- Common view of the static and dynamic data of the customer
- Access control and content filtering
- Flexible and convergent charging
- Integrated environment for VAS development and management
- Integrated environment for multi-device support
- Management of internal and external content and DRM policy support

An Identity System implementation and integration leadership in this space stems from the fact that in the past half decade or more the foundation work has been accomplished which paves the way for Vertical Integration of horizontal identity systems in multiple layers, thus, in the next few years, in essence creating a meta layer that allows for users to have secure and controlled access to "any service", "any content", from "any network" or "any device" at "any time" from "anywhere" -you have (IP –internet protocol –based) connectivity with a Policy and Control layer that takes into account QOS and SLA.

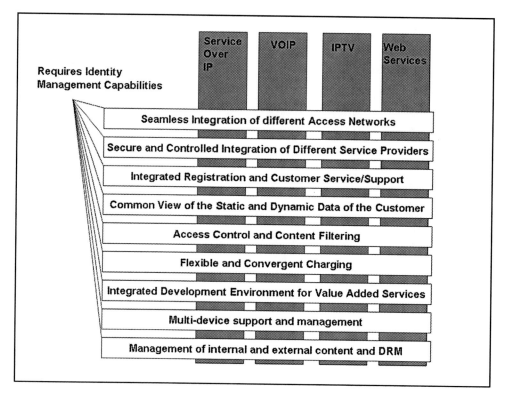

Figure 1.1 Nine Potential Pain Points

The 12 chapters following this introduction, namely;

- Identity enabled Sensor Networks
- Identity enabled Programmable Networks
- Identity enabled WiMAX & Wifi (4G and NG) Networks
- Identity enabled IMS Network and Network Services
- Identity enabled Enterprise Networks (NAC)
- Identity enabled IN Services
- Identity enabled OAM&P Services
- Identity enabled Web Services
- Identity enabled ESB Services
- Identity enabled DRM Services
- Identity enabled ILM
- Identity enabled Devices

discuss how these nine potential pain points can be addressed with the notion of a simple nine step methodology that can be achieved with the concept of "Vertical Integration" of individual disparate identity systems, by aligning network facing Identity Systems (that are device centric, network equipment centric, (trusted) computing centric, access network centric, etc.) with Service centric Identity Systems (that are Service centric, Enterprise network centric and content centric).

1.2 The Nine Step Methodology for Identity based Security

There are **Nine (R) Steps** that an enterprise (including telecom companies) needs to take in order to sustain an Identity Centric Security Architecture. Here is a brief look into each of these steps:

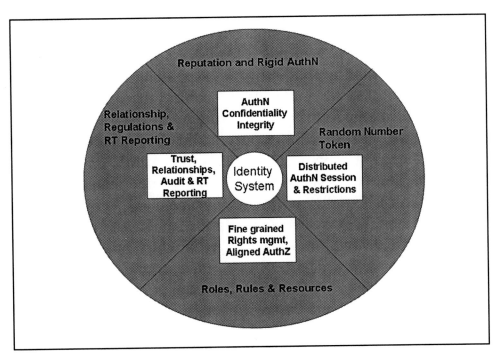

Figure 1.2 Nine Step Process

Step 1: Reputation—Before you admit someone from a client device into your network and allow access to services you want to ensure that the User's and Device's reputation is good or excellent. This includes checks for <u>patches, security fixes, updates, worms, viruses, thefts, and attacks (like spyware and phishing)</u> on the client device (whether a PC, workstation, handheld, cell-phone or a Set top box). A user gets added (provisioned) into a system only when his reputation is cleared (valid identity, credit checks, etc.). Some NAC companies specialise in NAC (network admission control) that includes reputation checks. Some firms like iOvation specialise in it as well. This step1 is described in more detail on the chapters on Identity enabled Enterprise Networks (NAC) and Identity enabled Devices.

Step 2: Rigid Authentication—This includes multi-factor authentication, strong authentication, bio-metric, certificates and more based on the sensitive nature of the content and services that are expected to be accessed. Some firms like Authernative specialise in this space. Strong authentication is important not just to validate the identity of a user and/or a device but is also important to establish confidentiality and integrity (a secure communication channel with the user and his or her device). Strong Authentication (AuthN) is one of the core functionalities performed by an Identity System, along with sharing the AuthN context. The AuthN levels and context drive the alignment with Authorisation (AuthZ) and distributed AuthZ –which in turn has an impact on roles-rule-resources and rights as described in this introductory chapter. The reach of an AuthN environment in the form of access management and federation management is described in the Chapter on Identity enabled 4G Networks. An Identity System is typically agnostic to AuthN mechanism, i.e., it can support several hundred ways with which one can authenticate a user and/or a device. SAML, for example, support associated XML schemas for: Internet Protocol; Kerberos; Password; Password; Secure Remote Password; Smart Card PKI; Smart Card; Previous Session and many more. Other standards for AuthN include Higgins and OpenID which use URI validation, .NET which uses Kerberos or tickets (similar to a guard standing at the door with a clipboard and you ask if your name is on the clipboard before being permitted to enter). At this stage both password construction and maintenance also play a significant role (mostly handled by password management logic).

Step 3: Random numbers/token generation—The next step is to establish an Authenticated Session—wherein the authentication and level of authentication are only relevant and valid for a given Session and there are restrictions applied within the session as well. This is typically accomplished by Access Management solutions, which handle the full life cycle of a Session. These session tokens are relevant for federated access as well in the form of distributed session management. At this juncture OpenID like initiatives can be linked back to an IDSP (Identity Service Provider) using SAML extensions. Aligning the Assertion Artifacts as part of a Session allows multiple context data to be shared over and above AuthN context, such as presence, location, payment, digital rights and more.

Step 4: Roles—Roles based Access Control (RBAC) can also be viewed as User rights management. In this step role engineering, role mining, role discovery and mapping, role alignment etc. take place. This is the first in the 3 steps (roles, rules and resource) that is part of Authorisation). Firms like <u>Vaau</u> specialise in this space. Rights management (both Enterprise RM and Digital RM) are nothing but fine grain levels of RBAC that require mapping and an abstraction layer (between back-end services such as licensing services, content protection services, entitlement services and more). This is discussed in detail in the chapter on Identity enabled DRM and ERM (digital rights management and enterprise rights management).

Step 5: Rules—Rules and restrictions are typically applied via policie—that link users, devices, access networks, QOS/SLA metrics and services. Firms like Bridgestream, Trustdigital and I-log specialise in rules engines and rules can be executed within an access manger (web or ejb container) in a distributed manner as well. Rules can also be viewed as a mechanism that links roles to one or more resources (services) and the combination of roles2rules2resources is offered as a Realm within an Authenticated Session. Rules as policies can be resource/service centric, device centric or access network centric residing at the edges of the network as well (set top box, handheld, base stations, access controllers, head-ends and more). Rules as polices can also be enforced in the Service Networks that run an ESB and Orchestration engine similar to the ones offered by Reactivity. This is further explained in the chapter on Identity enabled ESB, Identity enabled OAMP/OSS and Identity enabled Enterprise Networks. These policies and rules also help address the Governance (SLA and QOS) aspects of an SOA and the NGN.

Step 6: Resources — Resources, in most cases, are Services and from a SOA perspective these resources are defined in a Service Registry (in a Registry Repository). A number of digital artifacts are secured and stored in this tool. Through SPML only provisioned services can be accessed by users. Steps 4, 5 and 6 can be viewed as authorisation after the establishment of a successful authenticated session that ensures access to services and content is provided. Identity enabled ESB is significant for access to Services, Identity enabled DRM is significant here for access to content and Identity enabled ILM is significant here for access to Information and Data. Mapping policies (authorisation in the form of RBAC — role based access control) to entities is critical in steps 4, 5 and 6 and this is covered in the chapter on Identity enabled Web Services (section on policies).

Step 7: Relationship — This is the step wherein all kinds of relationship are validated beyond an enterprise network where traditional AAA takes place. This is where XRI like abstracted mapping, federation (SAML), virtual maps (GUP/ENUM), multi-domain provisioning, linking identifiers, XACML, etc. come into play wherein the user traverses beyond the first original network destination. A whole new set of **roles-rules-resource** scenario would apply within a circle of trust or within federated parties with trust relationship. It can take place with multiple (more than two) parties as well. Federation Manager plays a key role here. Here, distributed authN sessions are established with a single (macro) token so one can get single log out. The significance of Federation is more relevant in the chapters on Identity enabled IMS (core network), Identity enabled ESB, Identity enabled XML Firewalls and others.

Step 8: Regulation — Beyond AAA and federation (or trust relationship establishment) all events have to be logged and tracked — logs from provisioning, logs from reputation checks, logs for authN and authZ, roles-rules-resources logs, relationships and more need to be tracked for financial regulations, privacy regulations, government regulations, international regulations and more. Identity Provisioning and Management as well as Identity enabled ILM plays a major role here.

Step 9: Real-time Observe-ability—When you have identity enabled everything and can view what is going on in the network (near) real time you are sure to sustain the security model established. Logical/ Physical correlation, security event models, RT visuals all come into play here. For example, Security folks and operations staff can view an employee's activation of a device, accessing a specific access network, authN level, current presence and location, active usage of services, trail of service and content accessed, session specific parameters and more. This implies that Identity enabled OAM&P and NG IN Services are important.

Note: It is important to have traces from the provisioning cycle back to the phase at which 'credential issue' takes place. We tend to take 'authentication' as the 'be-all and end-all' of identity verification, where actually it is not. Authentication is the process of validating that the person/entity presenting the credentials to you now is (probably) the person to whom they were issued at some prior point. When you look at it in those terms, a couple of things become clear:

1. If the credentials are trivially easy to forge or 'pass on', then essentially you may have proved nothing. Bob told Alice his password, or Mallet did an exhaustive attack on Bob's password file.
2. If the credential issuing process was flawed, then you may have issued credentials which assert that the user is "Bob", where in fact s/he is Alice.

Some customers segment this phase into "Registration, Validation and Enrolment", where the data subjects assert the data they wish to be registered, the IDP validates that data through more or less rigorous processes and then 'enrolls' the data subject by issuing credentials which 'encapsulate' some set of attributes of the user.

1.3 Validating the Value Proposition of Vertical Integration of Identity Systems

The fundamental value proposition of Vertically Integrating disparate and fragmented Identity system is the fact that it addresses the lack of links between multiple layers of Identity System. Lately (last few years) there is this heightened awareness in the market that debates the topic of network centric identity systems (RADIUS, AAA, X.500, etc.) or NAC versus service centric identity systems. There are five articles in this space: TNT blog on security services offered in each layer, Eric from DIDW discussing the value proposition of linking the two, an article at Network World discussing the momentum and the need behind this linking, another blog on the significance of roles (dynamic) in integrating these layers beyond identifiers and a five part series written by Phil Becker on the Network perspective. In my role as an Identity Integration Architect—this is exactly the space that I have been working on during the last five years with Sun's NEP (network equipment providers) partners, such as; Alcatel/Lucent, Motorola, Siemens, Ericsson, Nortel, Cisco and others. Additionally ISV (software partners) who specialise in this space (such as Bonsai, Pronto, Openwave, Location-net, and more) integrating what is a Service Centric Security framework (Identity Systems) with Network facing Identity Systems such as AAA Servers, RADIUS, HLR/HSS, ENUM/GUP, TACACS, NAC, TS69, X.500, Service Controllers, Access Controllers, Base Stations, and more not just from an Enterprise Network perspective, but also from an Access Network perspective (integrating with Wifi, Wimax, BPL -broadband over power-line- and more), Sensor Network perspective, Programmable network perspective and a Core Control network perspective. Long awaited discussion and debates on this topic are good to see taking shape now. Both the network centric and service centric layers need linking with identifiers and integration with roles and policies.

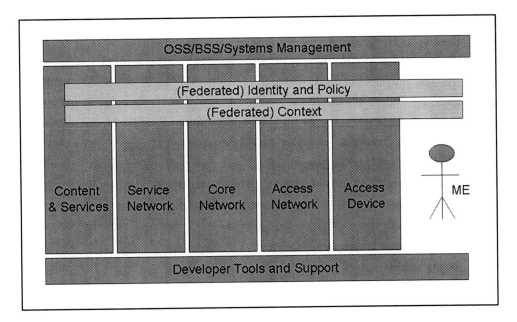

Figure 1.3 Identity Transcending Networks, Devices and Services

To achieve this target state (as depicted in the picture above) an Identity System (with the **five integration models**) has to be integrated:

1. With the User (the "me") : User Centric Identity Systems (URI/XRI based, extensive profile, preferences and policies—defined by the user—with the users consent and control)
2. With the Access Devices (such as TS69): Device Centric Identity Systems (for device profile, machine authentication, virus checks, client side firewall updates, sensor devices etc.)
3. With the Access Networks (such as BPL): Network Centric Identity System (for context, QOS capabilities of access networks, session traversals, mobility etc.)
4. With the Core Network (such as IMS): Network Centric Identity System (for controlled invocation, federation, secure choreography, OAM&P, NG IN, Single Sign-off, auditing, etc.)
5. With the Service Networks (Enterprise Networks that offer Services): Service plus Network Centric Identity System (for NAC, RBAC, Service orchestration, ESB, programmable network elements, service profile, context, etc.)
6. And the Content Networks (such as DReaM based): Content Cen-

tric Identity System (for disintermediation of DRM, entitlement, content protection, content profile, content context etc.

This implies Vertical Integration with non-IDP centric (liberty enabled solutions are also user centric since they allow for user consent and control as well) Identity Systems (such as OpenID), device centric Identity Systems (such as a DRA –device reputation authority), to integration with multiple types of Access Networks (such as BPL-broadband over power line, WiMAX, Wifi and more) and linking multiple federated IDP (Identity Service Providers) with IMS core control layer, the NAC (Network admission control) implementations on the Enterprise Networks and DRM implementations of different content networks, as depicted in the figure below.

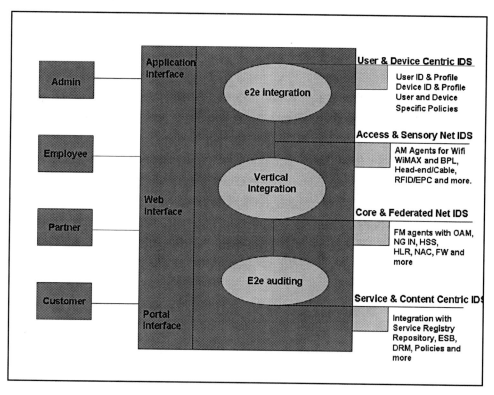

Figure 1.4: Vertical Integration

This vertical integration in the majority of cases is accomplished with the federation model—wherein, fundamentally user identities from multiple service providers are linked by an Identity provider. For example, the Device Reputation Authority, although it is a device centric Identity System is mapping device identities back to user identities, that in turn can be offered as a Service of an Identity Service Provider (IDP) that federates with multiple Service Providers. This could be true especially with IDPs that federate with a lot of security sensitive services that require device reputation validation along with user authN. One of the most important value propositions of an Identity System for any enterprise, which is mostly an after thought, is the value proposition that an Identity System has to offer as an Instrument for Intelligent Integration. Within the Industry there needs to be more discussions around an Identity System based intelligence in the network:

1. about users (profile and context),
2. about services (profile and behaviours,
3. about device (profile and reputation),
4. about content (profile and drm), and,
5. about data (meta-data/ILM) etc.

This intelligence actually need not be fragmented; it can be integrated through;

1. Consolidation (virtual mapping, virtual directories, generic macro profiles etc.),
2. federation (linking identifiers and identities, trust relationships etc.),
3. correlation (linking based on policies, policy based control, correlation within a session etc.),
4. aggregation (using it as a core reusable SBB/IDSP within an EA), and,
5. trailing (indexing, reputation, references etc.).

Vertical Integration allows for the de-fragmentation of this intelligence and ensures a security framework within which intelligence data is shared within a common security framework and context.

1.4 Business Value of Vertical Integration of Identity Systems

This vertical integration of an Identity System addresses the three dimensions for boundary-less information flow and business interaction; in terms of Improved Access to Services leading to improved business opportunities, reduced costs in terms of operations, development and integration of Services (based on Service Oriented Architecture) and at the same time ensuring Systemic security against internal threats and external threat via trusted computing, trusted relationships, integration with exiting security tools (Firewalls, Intrusion Prevention and more).

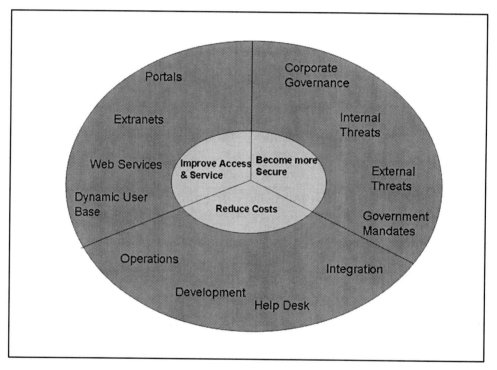

Figure 1.5 Business Value

The majority of the Identity System deployments in various industries stem from addressing either one of these areas:

*   To meet auditing requirements (HIPAA, SOX, etc.)
*   To reduce cost of operation of multiple fragmented Identity Systems

- To offer a common security environment for multiple applications and/or services
- To establish a circle of trust between multiple business entities
- To integrate with existing security tools—i.e. to leverage the AuthN and AuthZ performed for users by an Identity System (IDS)
- To achieve Single Sign On and Single Log out
- To reduce administrative costs
- To automate provisioning
- To introduce Role and Rule based access control
- To reduce integration costs
- To securely share User Profile data
- To securely share Device Profile data
- To securely share Service Profile data
- To securely share location context
- To securely share presence context
- To securely share payment provider information

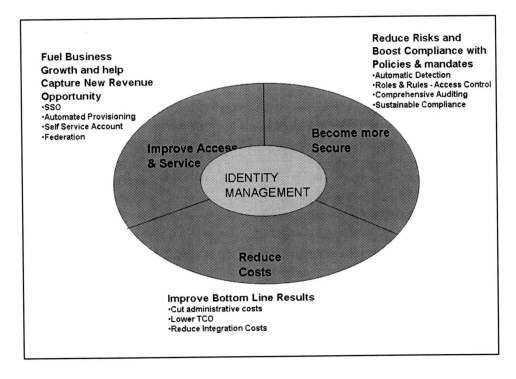

Figure 1.6 Business Value listed out

Typically, projects get started with one or two goals in mind, (such as compliance to a specific integration effort), but later expand to address many other areas. An IDS being a Core Service Building Block for Service on the Network transcends all Enterprise Projects and also acts as a strategic tool for enabling NG Services for the Business regardless of whether it stems from new opportunities around sensor networks/ RFID enabled Business Processes, new business relationships, integrated view of the customer, reach to multiple IP (internet protocol) access networks and more.

1.5 Architecture of an Identity System

First an introduction to Network Identity System is covered, followed by the four perspectives from which an Identity Centric Architecture needs to be looked at.

1.5.1 Identity System and the Four Layers

The generally accepted industry norm today adds four layers to an identity system;

- Access Management layer
- Federation Management layer
- Identity Repository layer (typically a Directory server or a RDBMS)
- Identity Management & Audit layer

1.5.1.1 Access Management

An Identity System software is a standards-based solution designed to help organisations (Enterprises and Telecommunications Companies) manage secure access to Web and non Web-based applications both on the intranet and extranet acting as an Architectural Building Block (ABB). Within enterprises such as Coca Cola, Home Depot and American Airlines this ABB is typically leveraged for Business Services (B2B, B2C or B2E[1]) and within Telecommunications environments it's

---

1. Business to Business, Business to Consumer, and Business to Employee Services.

a strategic ABB that is leveraged for all types of Voice, Data and Video services. From an enterprise perspective, an Identity System provides more financial, organisational and competitive agility to compete in the marketplace, through scalable access management services that help secure the delivery of business information services, improve the user experience through Web single sign-on and put a federated identity framework in place that helps create new revenue opportunities through enhanced affinity relationships with business partners and customers. It is important to note that an Identity System acts as the Foundation for True Boundary-less Information Flow. From a telecommunication perspective, an Identity system provides more agility through mobility with security that leads to true "service mobility" —meaning any data, voice, video service can be accessed in a device agnostic and network agnostic manner, yet user specific/location specific and preference/profile driven delivery of such services, based on user defined policies, is made possible any where in the globe.

Some of the key capabilities of Network Identity Solutions such as JES Identity Server are:

- *Access Management services:* Securely controls access to Web and non Web-based resources (such as Services delivered via a Service Delivery Platform, devices, roaming partner's network equipments, etc.).
- *Session Management Services:* Ability to offer cohesive/integrated session management, i.e. full life cycle management of a user's session.
- *Policies:* User defined policies for service delivery.
- *Identity Administration services:* Provides centralised administration of identities, policies, and services. Authentication controls including LDAP, RADIUS, X.509v3 certificates, Safe Word token cards, anonymous, and UNIX platform authentication services, Microsoft Windows NT and Windows 2000, resource-based authentication, Online Certificate Status Protocol (OCSP) validation for X.509 v3 digital certificate.
- *Out-of-the-box modules:* To help simplify integration into an existing security framework: Java Authentication and Authorszation

Service (JAAS) technology-based authentication framework. An open standard, flexible, and extensible authentication architecture that enables Organisations to customise authentication mechanisms, for JEE/JAIN based services.

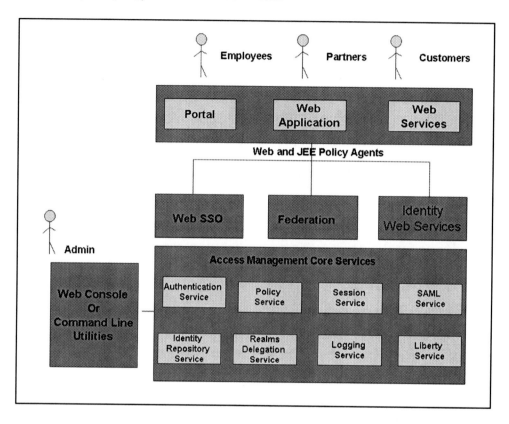

Figure 1.7 Access manager

The above AM Architecture depicted in Figure 1 shows the Central role-played by an Identity System as an Access Manager. **"Managing the Access for Users, from Device over Networks to different Services".**

Core Services provided by an Identity Infrastructure, such as Authentication, Authorisation, SSO,[2] Federation, Policy and Access Control act as a Service Building Block for all Business/Communication Services. This AM role ensures that mobility with security is addressed by providing a Central mechanism to validate and verify Identity of Users,

---

2 Single Sign On

Services, Networks and Devices—end to end. From this perspective an IDEN acts as a distributed firewall that enforces policies around users, devices, services and networks, where a typical policy contains (RULE, SUBJECT and CONDITION—see figure 1.8):

- Action that can be taken against a Service/Resource
- Who, where (location), time limitations etc.
- Conditions—Level of authentication required, schema, IP address etc.

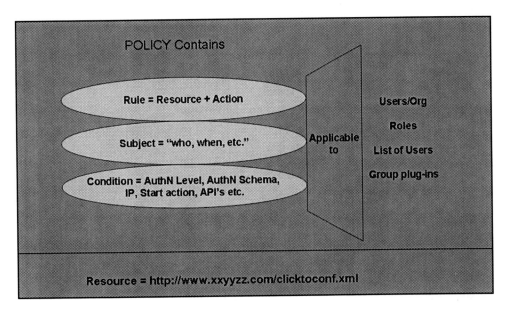

Figure 1.8 Distributed Policy Engine

Access Manager is the layer of the Identity System that integrates with specific hardware components in the network (such as a Wifi access controller or BPL gateway) with an Agent that runs on a JVM redirecting any user request to the Access Manager instance that accomplished AuthN and AuthZ for the user. The access manager policy agent also runs on resources protected by Access Manager within an Enterprises Network so when a user directs a request to access the resource the user session is validated by Access Manager as an Authenticated session with the Authorisation to access such resources. Access Manager also integrates with NAC (Network Admission Control) appliances that specialise in validating and checking for **patches, security fixes, updates, worms, viruses, thefts, and attacks (like spyware and phish-**

ing) on the client device (whether a PC, workstation, handheld, cell-phone or a Set top box- any IP device), before allowing the device into the network. The NAC appliance typically quarantines the device in a secure VLAN while running these checks. Similarly the Access Manager also integrates with XML based firewalls, routers, gateways and accelerators (more on this in the Identity enabled Enterprise Network chapter) and with Policy engines that specialise in switch level security policies. The support for Policy Hierarchy is very significant when integrating with externally policy enforcing points.

Typical Access Manager System Requirements

Operating Systems and Platforms
- Solaris 8, 9, 10 OS (SPARC Platform Edition), including support for zones on versions 9 and 10
- Solaris 9, 10 OS (x86 Platform Edition), including support for zones
- Windows Server 2003, Windows XP (development only)
- Red Hat Enterprise Linux AS/ES 2.1, 3.0
- HPUX 11i

Supported Web containers
- BEA Web Logic Server
- IBM Web Sphere Application Server
- Java System Application Server
- Java System Web Server

Supported standards
- Java Authentication and Authorisation Service (JAAS)
- Kerberos
- Lightweight Directory Access Protocol (LDAP)
- Liberty ID-FF
- Liberty Identity Web Services Framework (ID-WSF)
- SAML
- SOAP
- Secure Sockets Layer (SSL)
- WS-I Basic Security Profile tokens

- XML Digital Signature
- XML Encryption

Data stores
- Java System Directory Server
- Flat files
- Microsoft Active Directory
- Relational Database Management Systems (RDBMS)

Supported authentication modules
- Active Directory
- Anonymous
- Certificate
- HTTP Basic
- Java Database Connectivity (JDBC)
- LDAP
- Membership
- Mobile Subscriber ISDN (MSISDN)
- Password Playback
- RADIUS
- SafeWord
- SAML

Windows Desktop SSO
- Windows NT

Policy agents for Web servers
- Apache Web Server
- IBM HTTP Server (This agent is supported by using the Apache Agent)
- Microsoft IIS
- Java System Web Server
- Java System Web Proxy

Policy agents for JEE™ application servers
- Apache Tomcat Servlet, JavaServer Pages (JSP) Container
- BEA Web Logic Application Server

- JBoss Application Server
- IBM Web Sphere Application Server
- IBM Web Sphere Portal
- Oracle Application Server
- Java System Application Server

Policy agents for enterprise applications
- Lotus Domino
- Oracle
- PeopleSoft
- SAP
- Siebel

1.5.1.2 Federation Management

Federation Manager is the sub system of an Identity System to extend federation to a large number of partners. It establishes and extends trusted domains to include large numbers of service providers as part of a hub-and-spoke architecture. Federation Manager provides secure federated services by allowing spoke partners to more efficiently leverage the core security and identity infrastructures of the hub provider. Because it makes trusted domains easily extensible across vast networks of partners, Federation Manager can create application security mechanisms that are reusable and that enable authentication and access solutions to work together seamlessly across diverse partner environments.

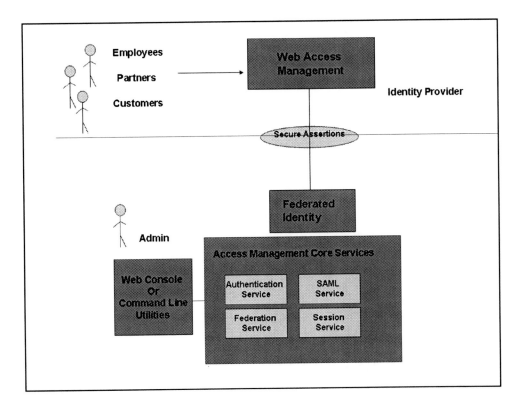

Figure 1.9 Federation Manager

Federation Manager (FM) in many instances is deployed along with the Access Manager (AM). The AM FM combination is deployed for extranet Single Sign-on, Authenticating users (at multiple AuthN levels) and exchanging credentials and security tokens across partners in a Trusted Domain. The FM leverages recognised authorities to identify users and determine which applications and services they may access. Typical FM capabilities include automated Identity Federation, linking user accounts across multiple security domains thus creating a seamless, yet highly secure, user experience in multi-provider service offerings. AM/FM also allows for Single Log-out and manages sessions across Trusted Domains to define when user interactions must be terminated. The basis of FM is the control on how sensitive an application is and matches that control to the trust agreements deployed by partners. Through an FM Meta Data is exchanged, i.e., automatically imports or exports the data required to establish basic federated communications between hubs and spokes.

The FM creates easy-to-manage Trusted Domains across partner networks by organising hub-and-spoke partners and controlling how they share security and user-related information.

Centralises and simplifies administration, management, and control of Trusted Domains, allowing companies to quickly expand their networks of service providers. Via the FM the process of adding providers to an Authentication Domain is possible. SAML support (security assertion markup language) ensures assertion exchange simplifies the mechanisms used to authenticate users across security domains and offers Web Services Development Framework. Federation Manager provides the tools and APIs to quickly develop, register and enable web services.

Many of the Network Equipment providers and ISV (independent software vendors) creating Network facing Identity Systems such as HSS and ENUM integrate with the Federation Manager primarily to ensure seamless access to web services.

Typical Federation Manager System Requirements
Operating Systems and Platforms

- Sun Solaris 8, 9 and 10 Operating Systems (SPARC Platform Edition)
- Sun Solaris 9 and 10 Operating Systems (x86 Platform Edition)
- Microsoft Windows
- Red Hat Enterprise Linux

Supported Web Containers
- BEA Web Logic Server
- IBM Web Sphere Application Server
- Sun Java System Application Server
- Sun Java System Web Server

Supported Standards
- Security Assertions Markup Language (SAML) 1.0, 1.1 and 2.0
- Liberty Identity Federation Framework (Liberty ID-FF) 1.1, 1.2

- Liberty Identity Web Services Framework (Liberty ID-WSF) 1.0

Data Stores
- Flat files
- Microsoft Active Directory
- Relational Database Management Systems (through customer plug-in implementations only)
- Sun Java System Directory Server

Supported Authentication Modules
- Active Directory
- Anonymous
- Certificate
- HTTP Basic
- JDBC
- LDAP
- Membership
- MSISDN
- Password Playback
- RADIUS
- SafeWord
- SecurID
- Windows Desktop SSO
- Windows NT

Policy Agents for Web Servers
- Apache Web Server
- IBM HTTP Server
- Microsoft IIS
- Sun Java System Web Server
- Sun Java System Web Proxy

Policy Agents for JEE Application Servers
- Apache Tomcat Servlet/JSP Container
- BEA Web Logic Application Server
- JBoss Application Server
- IBM Web Sphere Application Server

- IBM Web Sphere Portal
- Oracle Application Server
- Sun Java System Application Server

Policy Agents for Enterprise Applications
- Lotus Domino
- Oracle
- PeopleSoft
- SAP
- Siebel

1.5.1.3 Identity Repository

The majority of the Identity System deployments leverage Directory Server as the Identity System repository; however an Identity System repository in terms of User data and Policies can include a RDBMS, a flat file or other types of repositories as well. The repository typically should be capable of delivering Secure, Highly Available, Scalable, and Easy-to-Manage Data Services. The repository solution provides a solid foundation for identity management by providing a central repository for storing and managing identity profiles, access privileges and application and network resource information. It needs to integrate smoothly into multi-platform environments,and provides secure, on-demand password synchronisation with Microsoft Windows Active Directory and more.

Directory servers are vertical and horizontal in nature, and can be applied in any industry where identities and users need to be managed securely and efficiently. It scales for enterprises from tens of thousands of users to the hundreds of millions found in service provider environments. A few of these industries include government, telecommunications, financial, retail, healthcare, manufacturing, energy and utilities and education. A Directory System is considered to be a good Identity System repository due to multiple capabilities it offers such as Directory proxy or Directory Access router that can route request to multiple instances of directories running and data location, the Virtual Directory Capability that maps distributed identity data in a mapping file, its Replication and Data distribution capability and more. However many deployments of an Identity System leverages more that one repository (e.g., a combination of a Directory System and a RDBMS).

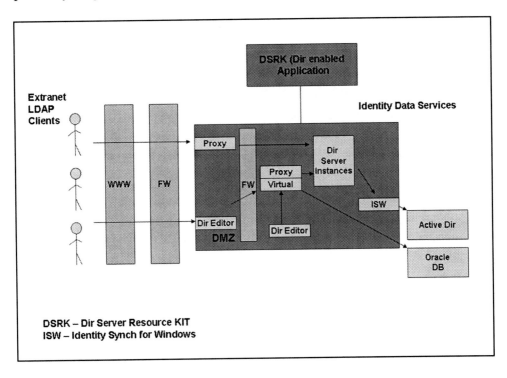

Figure 1.10 Identity Repository

An Identity Repository is generally the Centralised Repository for Identity, Application, and Network Resource Information (in many cases consolidation of NIS like name spaces as well).

A Directory implementation support N-Way Multi-Master Replication that provides a highly scalable and configurable replication framework across global locations along with fractional replication for Wide Area Network and high latency link replication. It can ensure 24x7 update access to data across the globe. Updates can be performed locally to data which is then replicated across locations. This system also allows for portions of a users entry (attributes) to be replicated instead of all data which provides means for privacy compliance and allows for efficient replication over WAN and/or high latency connections by using compression and grouping mechanisms.

The repository technology should potentially support 64-bit environments and multi-threaded multi-core computing with linear CPU scalability which allows access to maximum memory capacity and delivers high performance accommodating extremely large directories.

Through the Proxy Services the Repository Technology prevents denial of service attacks, controls access based on specific criteria and intercepts unauthorised operations. It enables failover operations, allowing directory service to continue when server is offline with load balancing that protects the directory environment from load-related failures and delivers horizontal scalability on reads/searches. It should also provide client compatibility for applications that require specific schema provides and strengthens multi-level security.

The repository should also provide an intuitive web based administration interface for managing users, groups, and organisations and makes key administrative functions readily available and easy to deploy and provides a flexible and quick interface for performing day to day data administrative tasks and basic self service capabilities.

Typical System Requirements

Operating Systems and Platforms*
- Sun Solaris 10, 9 or 8 Operating Systems (SPARC Platform Edition)
- Sun Solaris 10 or 9 Operating System (x 86 Platform Editions)
- Red Hat Enterprise Linux AS 2.1
- Red Hat Enterprise Linux AS 3.0
- Microsoft Windows 2000 Server and Advanced Server
- Microsoft Windows 2003 Standard Edition and Enterprise Edition
- HP-UX 11.i PA-RISC (not Itanium)
- IBM AIX 5.2

1.5.1.4 Identity Management and Auditing

An Identity Management layer is expected to be a solution with a comprehensive provisioning and non-invasive architecture for fast, easy and cost-effective implementation with Identity auditing capabilities to address regulatory mandates, internal privacy and policy initiatives for ongoing and sustainable compliance. Quick, accurate automated provisioning and synchronisation services, adding audit policy to the provisioning process for preventative along with detective compliance is a key strength of an Identity Management layer. Identity controls consistently applied across provisioning and auditing with an automated review and proactive scanning, consistent enforcement and repeatable processes are given feature of an Identity System. Policy violation tracking and expiration capabilities to handle exception are also important.

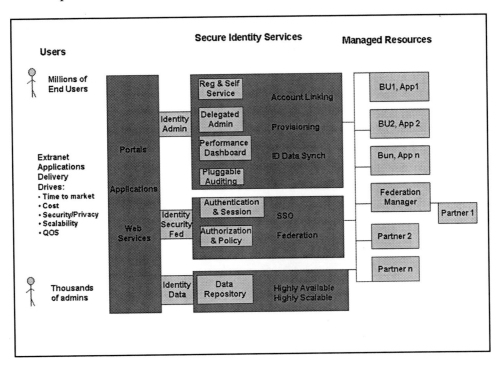

Figure 1.11 Identity Management

The Identity Management layer is the key layer that is leveraged for Integration across multiple legacy Identity systems such as AAA, RADIUS, TACACS, NIS+ and more. The base toolkits are utilised for automated provisioning within an Enterprise and the SP (service provider) edition is used for provisioning across multiple enterprises and therefore is more relevant for deployments of Federation Manager is an Identity Service provider environment. (IDSP).

Typical supported standards and system requirements include;

- SPML v2.0 integration interface support
- Workflow Management Consortium (WfMC) TC-1003 Workflow Reference Model standard for workflow implementation

Operating systems
Solaris Operating System
Red Hat Linux
HP OpenVMS
HP-UX
IBM AIX
IBM OS/400
Microsoft Windows
SuSE Enterprise Linux

Applications
Oracle E-Business Suite
PeopleSoft HRMS
SAP R/3 Enterprise
SAP Enterprise Portal
Siebel CRM
Virsa Access Enforcer
Bridgestream Smart Roles

Directory servers
Sun Java System Directory Server
Lightweight Directory Access Protocol (LDAP) v3
Microsoft Active Directory
Novell eDirectory
OpenLDAP

Databases
IBM DB2 Universal Database for Linux, UNIX, and Microsoft Windows
Microsoft SQL Server
Microsoft Identity Integration Server (MIIS)
MySQL
Oracle
Sybase Adaptive Server

Help Desk
Remedy Help Desk

Message platforms
Lotus Notes
Microsoft Exchange
Novell GroupWise
Blackberry RIM Enterprise Server
Sun Java System Messaging and Calendar Service
Java Message Service (JMS) Message Queue

Security managers
CA-ACF2
CA-Top Secret
IBM RACF
RSA SecurID
ActivIdentity
INISafe Nexess
Passlogix v-GO

Web access control platforms
Sun Java System Access Manager
IBM Tivoli Access Manager
CA eTrust SiteMinder
RSA ClearTrust

Rapid connectivity for custom applications
Generic Database Table Wizard
Generic Database Script Adapter
Generic UNIX/Linux Script Adapter
Generic Windows Script Adapter
Generic Host Access (Mainframe) Script Adapter

Standards
Service Provisioning Markup Language (SPML)

1.5.2 Identity System and the Four Perspectives

The prior section discussed the four layers of an Identity System typically found in the industry. When we extend these layers into an Enterprise IT Architecture and the Network (core, service and access networks), we can also view the four perspectives of an Identity System when Integrated into the Network of Services and Content. While the four layers are meant to understand the working of an Identity System in its' entirety, these four perspectives are for us to better understand how the Identity System in its entirety can be integrated with various Network and Service elements.

1.5.2.1 Identity System – Data Model and Meta-Data

To better understand these four perspectives, the following diagrams and illustrations can be used.

An Identity System's primary role is to ensure that a user's identity/data that is typically distributed everywhere in a SILO nature is synchronised and centrally managed. This includes an identity of a user within an Enterprise's Business System (such as ERP, HRMS, CRM, etc.) and between Enterprises (such as a user's Identity at Amazon, Yahoo and Netflix). A sample Logical Identity Architecture and its functionally decomposed into an ID Grid with ID Management Services, ID Transaction Services, ID Data Stores & Interfaces to Client/Portal/Applications are depicted in figure, below. The majority of this functionality addresses data elements in an Identity Grid.

- Provisioning Users and there Profile data
- Password data Management
- Directory data Management
- User data Management
- Data Transformation
- Data Synchronisation Services
- Data Storage Services

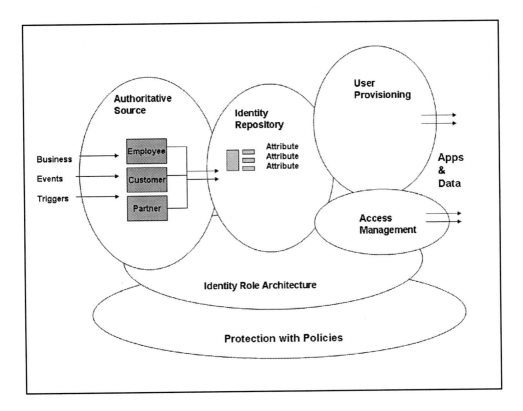

Figure 1.12 Functional decomposition of an IDM

Also from a data perspective a user has a bunch of profile data associated with the services he or she consumes. For example, a user's smart card's profile/pin, credit card profile, travel profile, airline profile, hotel profile etc. T hese profiles that are typically fed into a system are shared through an ID server. Services such as Location, Presence and Payment are ID enabled Services; Mapping of profiles could take place with custom coding and policy enforcements as well.

Generic Industry Profiles (standards based user data models) that are powerful in terms of users Network Identity includes:

- Liberty's WS-PP (personal profile for web services)
- Liberty's WS-EP (employee profile for web services)
- GUP – 3GPP's Generic User Profile (initiative is folded under Liberty WS-PP)
- Common Device Profiles
- Common Service Profiles

ENUM could potentially be an extension of the Personal Profile Services within Identity Services and all Services that require ENUM profile can lookup and re-use (through an ID System).

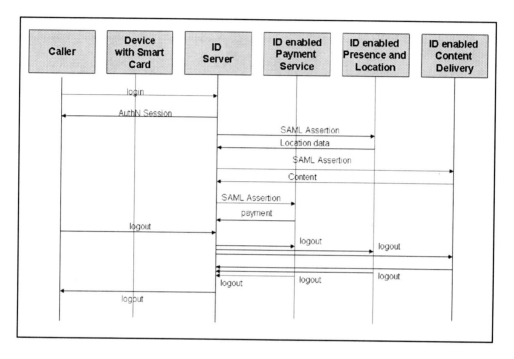

Figure 1.13 In each step a profile is shared – Caller Profile, Device/telephone Profile, Payment Service Profile, etc.

"These data models around a user, device and services and a user's profile/preferences are shared through a common profile management service". This acts as the foundation for not only seamless single-sign on across services and domains (see diagram below), but also ensures all related information/data models associated with a user is shared securely and seamlessly between services that are invoked (primarily through XML). In this case a caller/user using a Smart Card enabled device (such as a PDA/Cell phone) Logs into Identity Server (that seeks the Device profile) and establishes an authenticated Session. Based on the user's profile, ID Server has a list of associated services that the user has access to. The majority of these services are ID enabled, i.e., they do not require re-authentication and the service sessions are invoked via ID Server.

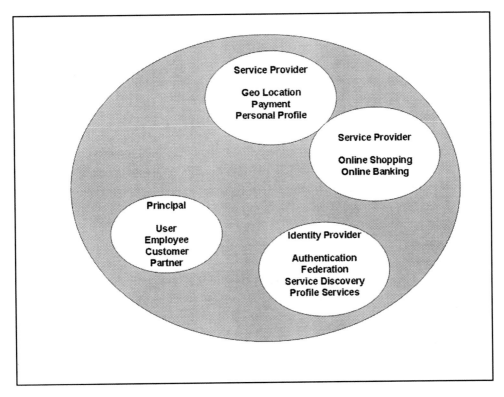

Figure 1.14 Profile Sharing between Services and Domains

More than half a decade of industry efforts has gone into the Liberty Alliance program, that has created standard protocols (liberty, SAML, etc.), for sharing identities. These have been implemented by more than 12 ISVs[3]. The Liberty Alliance membership also ranges in the 200+ corporations (a large number of them are Fortune 500 firms).

1.5.2.2 Identity System — Services

Common Identity Services, (Core Identity services such as Authentication/Authorisation/Auditing, Session Management and SSO Services), can be leveraged by both Communication Services and by Business Services as well as Web Services. *"This makes an Identity System a Core Service Building Block (similar to the potential offered by ENUM Services) for Converged Services".*

---

3 Independent Software Vendors

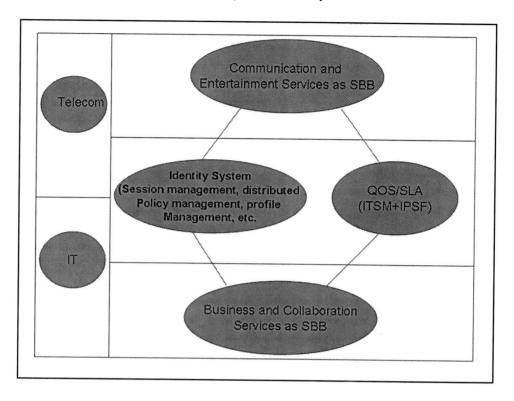

Figure 1.15 IDP acting as a Core SBB for both Telecom and IT Services

Here we see how *"Identity System acts as the central solution that ties devices and services together based on a user's profile and preferences"*. Services that are highly related to a user's identity such as, location, presence, payment, digital rights management, etc. are treated as Service Building Blocks that get reused when building other Customer centric services.

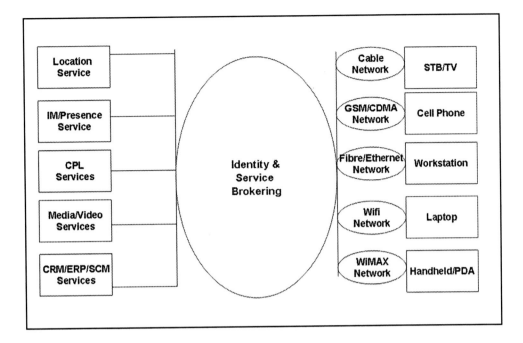

Figure 1.16 Core ID Services—playing a central role between services, access networks, devices and users.

The list of devices can include:
- TV with a STB[4] (with a smart card)
- Cell Phone (with a SIM card)
- Laptop/Desktops
- Handheld/PDAs

The list of Networks (access) can range from:
- Cable Networks
- GSM/CDMA Networks
- Wifi Networks
- WiMAX/EVDO Networks

The list of Identity enabled Services can be categorised into:
- Enterprise Business Services (ERP, SCM and CRM)
- Communication Services (Voice, Data and Video)
- Contextual Services (such as Location and Presence)
- Entertainment Services (such as VOD, Digital Radio etc.)

---

4 Set Top Box

The majority of the Enterprise Business Services and Entertainment Services are Identity enabled (i.e., service access is secured through ID agents), however over and above the Core Identity Services, Contextual and Communication Services are not only Identity enabled, but are also Identity based. As stated earlier, Services from an Identity System perspective can be categorised as:

- Core Identity Services (AAA, Session Management, Federation, etc.)
- Identity enabled Services (Services protected via Agents and extensions)
- Identity based Services (Identity enabled services that also share data/metadata)

It should be noted here as to how an IDEN and the core services of an Identity system compliment the notion of Service Oriented Architecture. Both by Identity enabling services i.e. protecting services as a resource via agents and extensions and Identity based services that are provision-able i.e. services that are not only identity enabled but also share data/meta-data between services via an Identity System.

A good example of an Identity based service that is also a Contextual Service that share user and service profiles and preferences extensively is one where a user specifies that he or she want a message sent to their Cell phone—with a weather report/doppler image for the city they are in every morning at 8:00am (regardless of the time zone). This will involve a user specific policy that works in conjunction with services such as messaging services, location services and weather services and some sort of timing services. So, if I am in San Francisco, California Monday morning I get a weather report at 8:00am PST for San Francisco, CA and its vicinity. If I traveled to Chicago Tuesday night I get a similar report at 8:00am CST for Chicago and so on. This involves sharing a subset of my location profile to the weather service and a subset of the weather profile shared with a Content Delivery service etc. All these services are typically identity enabled (that is the user gets Single Sign On across all these services) first before they tend to become Identity based (i.e.) profile sharing. Also Identity based Services are typically provision-able to users via the Identity System using Markup Languages such as SPML (service provisioning markup language).

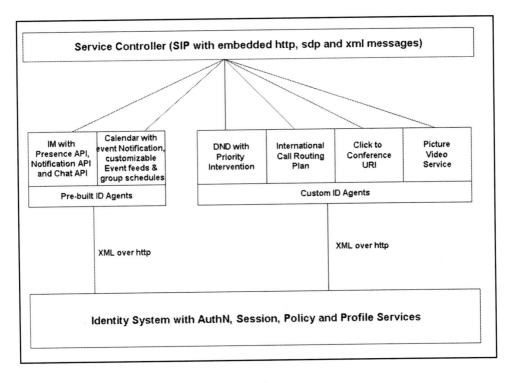

Figure 1.17 ID based Communication Services

1.5.2.3 Identity System—Networking

An identity system extends to all types of access networks (including DSL, Cable, 3/3.5G, wimax (802.16, 802.20), Wifi (802.11) and more) from the Services Network and the Core Network, all the way to different types of devices (both client devices and network devices). This makes service mobility possible at both the access networks and access devices making the delivery of service client device agnostic and access network agnostic – with session state maintained all the way through. From figure 10, we see that Content and Services are Identity enabled (i.e. they use an Identity System as an Architectural Building Block for AAA, Session Mgmt etc.), in the Service Network is where IDP and SP run their services (IDP-Identity Service Provider and SP—Service Providers that offer identity enabled and identity based services), in the

Core Network, networking devices and voice stack/services are identity enabled and identity based, Access Networks run Access Controllers (such as a Wifi Access Controller or a Cable/DSL controller) that extend to an IDP for establishing authenticated sessions when the user accesses the network and Access Devices can have specialized client side authentication mechanisms that are mandated prior to authenticating with a IDP (such as SIM card or client side certificates).

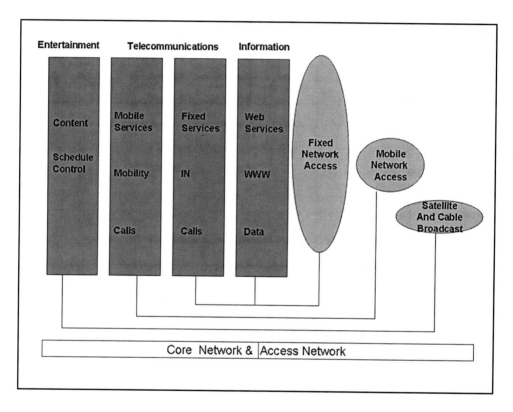

Figure 1.18 Silo Nature of today's Networks

This problem space depicted above ("silo nature of networks/devices/services) is beginning to be addressed with a standards based Core Service Building Block (ID System) that transcends all networks to offer user centric Services—"ME", as depicted in Figure 1:19.

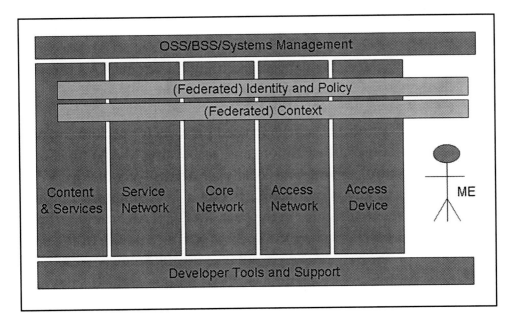

Figure 1.19 Identity in all Networks, Services and Devices

In the telecommunications world this is even more significant, since consumers are seeing a convergence in Devices, i.e. a Laptop is TV/ DVD player, a TV can accept Calls via a STB (set top box) and a Cell phone has enough resources to call it a computer with mobile TV services. Essentially consumers expect all services to be accessible from all these devices, especially since these devices are evolving into pure IP devices and content (voice/data and video content) is digitized. Enterprises like Blockbuster and Netflix are looking into offering VOD, Cable Operators are offering not just TV, but high-speed Internet Access and SIP/VOIP applications. In all these advances the user is lost, i.e. his or her experiences are not shared between access networks and access devices. However, with an IDEN, what is delivered is a set of comprehensive, cohesive services that are user centric. A good example of Access Network and Device Agnostic delivery will be, one where a user accesses a VOD movie while flying from the east to the west coast—via a Wifi LAN after authenticating with an IDP via an embedded device in a Plane, he or she, pauses the movie half way and works on something else. After reaching home in California he or she switches the TV On and LOGS IN—the TV prompts him if he wants to continue and finish watching the VOD movie that he/she paused in a plane. This implies that both the access networks Wifi in a plane and the cable network from home are identity-enabled networks (IDEN) and the user's service session is tracked. This type of an Architectural Solution can be achieved only by augmenting traditional AAA services with Liberty based ID Services as described below.

Today, RADIUS protocol is a widely used protocol for performing network authentication, authorisation, and accounting (AAA) functions. It is used to control remote and local user access—via dial-in, VPN, firewall, LAN, or any combination. It was a key component of any network security architecture in the past. RADIUS Architectures have depended on users connecting to a specific port on a device from a specific location on the network and is not user aware. Subnets, ACL[5] and COS[6], for example, are defined on ports of routers and switches and IT staffs very often manage a user's connection via the physical MAC address on the desktop device.

However, in a wireless environment (802.11, 802.16 and 3G/4G networks) devices and location can no longer be the control point since the user can be anywhere in the network (or any access network) and can attach to the network using any device. If we take into account the fact that NETWORKS exists to provide services to USERS, a user's identity is the best foundation. *"Identity enabled Networks (IDEN) revolutionises the model for Network Service Delivery making it Access Network Agnostic, Device Agnostic—yet USER centric (profile/ preference driven delivery of Services".*

While considering an Identity System some of the key value propositions of a RADIUS implementation have to be leveraged, such as,

Role-based Firewall/VPN Security
RADIUS plays a key role in enabling role-based network access security for firewall/VPN devices. True role-based network access security relies on tuning user access privileges with business policies and a device's vendor-specific attributes.

---

5 Access Control Lists

6 Class of Service

VPN User Authentication

In a VPN environment, RADIUS One can manage both user authentication and tunnel authorisation, allowing you to reduce total cost of ownership by managing credentials from a central location.

Firewall Administration

RADIUS One can be used as a single, consolidated user database for firewall administrators. Centralising authentication of firewall administrators reduces the chance that a failure to synchronise authentication data manually will cause a security problem. In fact, RADIUS One can simplify authentication for a wide variety of network access and policy-enforcement devices.

All these three key features can be extended and/or integrated to an Identity System. Taking this into account an Identity Platform's support for RADIUS as the data repository (along with LDAP/Directories, NIS, etc.) is also critical. An Identity Platform also supports PKI like features and Certificate/Signature based Security features — that force chained higher-level of authentication for users before more security sensitive services are accessed. For example, additional levels of restrictions can be applied to accessing certain services based on not only user's authentication level, but also the domain/network from which the device is attached to, and more (through written policies). Fundamentally RADIUS was a solution created to meet the needs of more rigid non-mobile — non-service centric environments. However — the challenge of today is to address mobility with security in a highly Service centric environments. Mobility involves user mobility, device mobility and service mobility — which directly forces the requirements for a distributed firewall like network identity solution. Key capabilities, found in an Identity System that is not addressed in a RADIUS solution includes;

- Single sign-on (SSO)
- Centralised authorisation services
- Centralised Session Management services
- Federated Identity support
- Comprehensive APIs
- JEE/Java Support

- Enterprise-class scalability and reliability
- Real-time audit

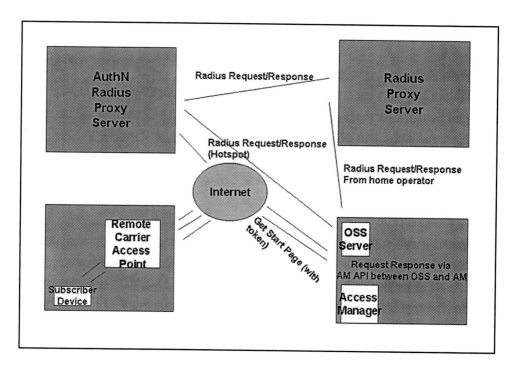

Figure 1.20 Role of RADIUS and IDEN

The above figure depicts a scenario where a user roams from one Wifi hotspot to another and accesses different services (such as a business tools and listing services).

Also from a Telecommunication Next Generation Network perspective, Identity Management Framework lays the foundation for a highly agile Services Architecture. For a highly Agile Service Architecture, which enables services to be built as a SBB (service building block) that are reusable, replaceable and accessible by users from any device and access (IP) network. The fundamental idea here is the fact that Service gets defined, built, integrated, tested and delivered in the network, once and can be packaged and consumed in many different ways. This also highlights the significance of IDEN for NG OSS Solutions as proposed by TMF (telecommunication management framework) and their eTOM initiative.

1.5.2.4 Identity System—User Centricity

Of all the perspectives from which one can view an Identity System, the most important is the User perspective. The ID system provides the basis for a user centric "Service Mobility", i.e. services as accessible for users from any device and access networks, in a context sensitive manner. It is well known that consumers are seeking the following (regardless of the underlying technology):

- **Convenience**—seeking access to services any time, anywhere
- **Consolidation**—seeking an optimised cost structure resulting in lower bills and lower number of bills
- **Coherence**—seeking customer centric coherence—profile, preference, policy driven services
- **Control**—having an option to define what they want, what gets shared (consent), opting-in to trust circles, privacy protection, and last but not the least; addressing
- **Complexity**—seeking simplicity and not being overwhelmed with complexities, no silos

(Note: If we take these as the criteria for User Centric IDS –URI based solutions such as OpenID addresses only a partial list)

As per Robin Wilton from Sun Microsystems "A clear illustration of the notion of 'consent' can be found in the use of RFID chips embedded inside objects such as garments, passports and (if the conspiracy theorists are to be believed) banknotes. It is practically impossible for a consumer to know whether or not a given object contains an RFID chip, what data might have been encoded onto it (for instance, at purchase time) and when that data is being read off the chip. In fact, as a 'passive' device there's a general consent issue about the person carrying it never knowing when an RFID chip may be 'beaconing' information about them." Here Identity System plays a major role in capturing users profile, preferences and personalisation elements—to deliver Services in a context sensitive manner (who, what, when, where etc.).

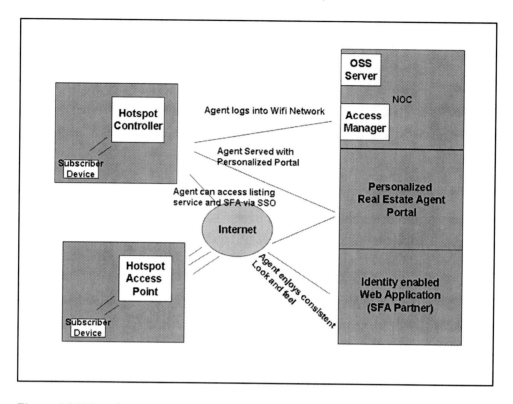

Figure 1.21 User Centric Service access (Roaming between hotspots and accessing location specific services)

The Identity System acts as a conduit (with the consent) that shares information and data between identities based services such as location, presence, payment, digital rights management, content delivery etc. There are restaurants in Boston (Harvard square area) that have an embedded flat panel in each table. The guest identifies the number of members in the group in the table and orders dinner via the digitised menu. This is 2004— extrapolating the same a few years from now with an IDEN, the restaurant's network (wireless) identifies individuals (using retina scan, thumbprint or a simple id/credit card swipe) welcomes them byname, and generates a custom menu based on preferences and time of day (such as vegetarian breakfast or seafood dinner etc.). Preference and Profile driven services are further customised based on location, weather etc. Applying the same concept to the communication world, one scenario could involve the cancellation of a meeting a few hours before, due to unforeseen weather conditions. The notification of the cancellation could be via a beeper, email, sms, voicemail, instant message etc. based on presence of the individual users and the service they are actively using, so that notification is sent via the appropriate service, that the user is actively using at a given point in time. Customer Centricity also involves contextual affinity. Especially when customers have signed up with promotion programs such as earning frequent points at a Best Buy, earning Miles from United or free night stays from Marriott etc. Through an Identity System, users can opt into combining their program points and consume benefits in a very cohesive manner. This is made possible by Liberty based Identity Systems and its federation capabilities across two or more service providers. This capability makes it easy for two or more companies to collaborate with each other. A good example of this is a promotion like "fly twice with United and get a free Hertz one-week car rental for the third trip". By leveraging the identity system and data sharing between users United Airlines frequent flyer program and Hertz Gold program, the consumer enrolls and is automatically provided that benefit by Hertz when a car is rented the third trip (without coupons, membership ID, promotion code, etc.), without even the customer asking for it, ensuring true consumer convenience. From a communication services perspective one relevant scenario is feeding in one's international calling card profile into the identity system provided by the local, long-distance carrier and every time a customer makes an international call from a specific number, the calling card company's service is invoked. This implies that the consumer does not have to dial a specific 800 number, plug-in a 10-digit code, 4-digit pin and then the destination number. Similarly a user can define a few numbers as priority numbers in his/her profile and even when DND (do not disturb) is turned on, incoming calls from the spouse or boss go through.

"The idea here is that the user is offered an option to define how he/she wants the services to behave under varying conditions, is conceptually very powerful. Offering the user this capability will be a competitive edge, to begin with".

1.6 Identity Centric Architecture

This section essentially aligns Architectural approaches such as SOA (for Service Oriented Architectures) and EDA (Event Driven Architectures) with the approach *centered on Identity*—known as **Identity Centric Architecture.** In the past decade or so there have been many Architectural Approaches recommended by practicing Architects as a guiding principle for building Enterprise Systems Architectures. Typically these approaches are further solidified based on support from major IT Vendors (such as IBM, HP and Sun) and other Industry bodies (such as OMG, ITU, TOG and more) offering thought leadership in this space. The majority of these Architectural Approaches are Open and Technology Neutral and they address the Challenges faced by Enterprise IT Architects via techniques and tools prescribed within such an approach. One such approach to Architecting Enterprise Solutions that has received a lot of attention and traction lately by Industry groups and IT Vendors as well as IT Consumers (the Enterprises themselves) is SOA for Services Oriented Architecture. In this chapter the author attempts to highlight the true value proposition of SOA as an Architectural Approach that builds upon other prevalent approaches that existed in the past, complimenting, augmenting, extending, supplementing and supporting SOA. We identify five Architectural Approaches that have received major attention as an approach with their respective techniques and toolsets and align these Architectural approaches to SOA. These five Architectural Approaches are (other than SOA): **MDA** for Model driven Architecture, **EDA** for Event driven Architecture, **CBA** for Component based Architecture, UCA for Utility Compute Architecture and **ICA** for Identity (User) Centric Architecture. This conceptual conundrum of architectural approaches and its respective techniques and tools, aids in the process of leveraging a virtuous cycle of synergistic benefits that lead to "Agility" in all layers of an Enterprise Architecture, including Business Architecture, Information and Data Architecture, Applications and Services Architecture and the Technology and Infrastructure Architecture.

De-coupling Presentation Logic from Services offers Abstraction from Client Devices

Modeling Data Resources from Services offers Abstraction from Data Resources

Modeling Network Events against Services offers Abstraction from Network Complexities

Modeling such as PIM allows for Abstraction from the Development Technology

Virtualized environments (such as a JVM) provides Abstraction from the hardware and OS (end-to-end)

De-coupling the Security Logic with a Security SBB (such as an Identity System) allows of Abstraction of Services from changing Security Constraints

Figure 1.22 Abstraction in All Layers

1.6.1 Alignment for Agility

It is interesting to note that Abstraction from all dimensions ensures Architectures that can accommodate changing requirements. *"Align able Architectures enable Business Agility—what enables Align ability in Architecture is Abstractions through layering and modeling"*. When an Organisation is moving from an As-is Enterprise Systems Architecture to a Target Enterprise Systems Architecture, wherein an Enterprise System is a System of Systems that covers all the facets of the Enterprise's Architecture, including its Business Architecture, Application Architecture, Information and Data Architecture and Technology Infrastructure, the Enterprise Architect's start with:

- Architectural Principles (for e.g. Agility as the primary goal or Global Reach as one amongst the goals etc.)
- Architectural Approaches (such as SOA and MDA)
- Applicable Reference Models (such as ITU ODP-RM, TOGs TRM and IIIRM, OMGs CWM, and in Reference Models)
- Industry specific Domain Models
- Along with a given Methodology that the Enterprise has embraced (such as ADM for Attribute Driven Methodology proposed by SEI and ADM for Architecture Development Methodology proposed by TOG), or a custom methodology that the Enterprise uses.

Using these as toolsets the Enterprise develops an Organisation specific Enterprise Systems Architecture that aligns to the Organisation specific requirements and maps out dominant Architectural Patterns and Standards, which would influence the direction taken by the Enterprise in terms of Designing the Solution space.

Architectural Approaches & Architectural Principles
Reference Models and Architecture Methodologies

Organization Specific Requirements and
Enterprise Systems Architecture with
Dominant Architectural Patterns and Standards

Tactics, Techniques & Design Patterns,
Taxonomy of Patterns (SOA Patterns, EDA Patterns, etc.)
Systemic Quality Patterns
(Security Patterns, HA Patterns, etc.)

Figure 1.23 Flow from Architectural Approaches to an Organization Specific Architecture

In the current and contemporary world ONE Architectural Approach, such as, the Service Oriented Architecture or Event Driven Architecture etc. alone will not suffice for "practicing IT architects" to follow. Leveraging an Architecture Development Method one can attempt to build an Enterprise's Target Architecture from an as-is Architecture, with some guiding Architectural principles, such as "Agility". In this process of reaching the target architecture with the usage of the methodology, one also has to leverage the concepts behind popular architectural approaches such as;

- SOA—Service Oriented Architectures—and the notion of highly streamlined interfaces and public registries for all services and re-usable Service Building Blocks (XML/SOAP based)
- MDA—Model Driven Architectures—and the notion of modeling

specific to platforms/technologies and independent of them (PIM/XMI/MOF)

- EDA—Event Driven Architectures—and the notion of user interaction with the network along with correlation (Asynchronous/synchronous/triggers/alarms)
- CBA—Component Based Architecture—and the notion of distributable dynamic components along with functional de-composition, plus instrumentation of code (tiered logic, separation of concern, decoupling SBBs)
- UCA—Utility Compute Architecture—and the notion of dynamic discovery and provisioning of resources, service level based optimization (dynamic grids, storage networks)
- ICA—Identity Centric Architecture—and the notion of user session/state/context traversing anywhere along with service mobility (device, network agnostic access of services)

This section highlights the value proposition that all the benefits associated with differing approaches bring to the table to reach the one goal of more identity and user centric "Agile Architectures" i.e., Architectures that can accommodate all types of Changes and Strategically Maneuverable. Including changes in:

- Business Relationships (consumer facing and supplier facing)
- Mergers and Acquisitions
- Technology Changes
- User Requirement changes
- Government and Regulatory changes

This combined work is also referred to as the "Architecture Reference Model" since all architects start from the meta-architecture phase to a realisable architecture phase and an implementation phase. The figure below depicts the overall "Architecture Reference Model": that can also aid towards building Target Enterprise Architectures.

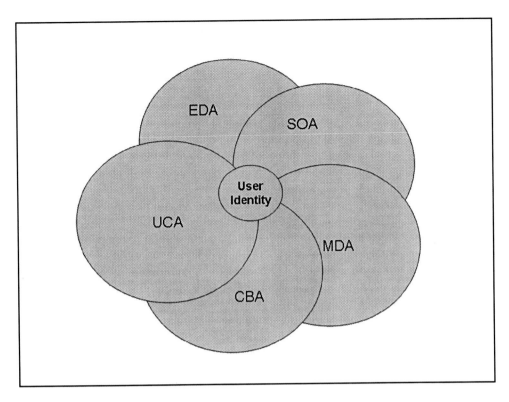

Figure 1.24 An Architectural Refeernce Model that Aligns Architectural Approaches

The table below also depicts the key synergistic value proposition that all of these conceptual architecture patterns bring to the table:

ICA	SOA	MDA	EDA	CBA	UCA
User Centric	Service Centric	Data Centric	Network Centric	Developer Centric	Resource Centric
Security Framework for Trusted SOA	Reusable – Replaceable Service BB	Abstraction of Data from Services and Services from Service Execution (Service Orchestration)	Addresses Network concerns	Component based Development (evolves from OO design principles)	Convergence of Applications and its IT environment
Core SBB for SOA that delivers User centricity	Streamlined Interfaces – Interface driven development	Common Information Model aligns to a Common Services Taxonomy	Takes context into account	Firms the Basis for distribution (DCA)	Utility model –pay per use wrapped with SLA and OLA
Enables federation, integrated with COTS and Cross Domain/Cross Service SSO	Loose Coupling with request response and publish/subscribe models	Platform Independent Execution	Events bridges users, devices and context from the Services from across multiple Service Networks (cross enterprise and domains)	Business/Technical implementation units that are environment/container aware	Component instrumentation and dynamic service provisioning
Profile sharing in a secure manner- profile/preference driven Service delivery	Autonomous SBB – Functionality of Service is used across the Enterprise	Modeling Resource Requirements	Relevant for wireless sensor networks, real-time networks and programmable networks (sense –response)	Decomposes a SBB into multiple, pluggable, distributable parts (Presentation, Business , Integration, Event, Security components)	Virtualization and provisioning of resources

Table 1 Key Synergistic Values

1.6.1.3 MDA enabling SOA (the second dimension)

This perspective looks into the value propositions that MDA and its prescribed techniques have to offer for SOA. The techniques in MDA (such as MOF, CWM XMI, PIM and PSM) in conjunction with CIM (common information model) that provide a common definition of management information for systems, networks, applications and services allow for vendor extensions. CIM's common definitions enable vendors to exchange semantically rich management information between systems in the network (see http://www.dmtf.org/standards/cim/). Some of the key benefits associated with CIM are: Common and versatile model for all information within the system, expressive in nature, capturing quite a bit of semantic, consistent naming scheme that provides global uniqueness, powerful operations set both within the model and within the model managers and last but not the least, adaptable to many protocol types. Based on DMTF (distributed management task force) CIM is comprised of a Specification and a Schema. The Schema provides the actual model descriptions, while the Specification defines the details for integration with other management models. The latest version of the Schema, CIM 2.8, provides new classes for storage and also offers modeling for the Java™ 2 Enterprise Edition (JEE) environment. It also introduces the concept of management profiles, provides support for managing security principals and describing their authentication policy and privileges, manages IPsec policy and resulting security associations and features modeling of the management infrastructure for discovery. One can view CIM as an example of MDA concepts and principles for the management information for systems/networks. This generic CIM (common information model) approach can be extended beyond traditional management information (MIB/SNMP) and leveraged for the integration of information between common services—CSM (common services model—what is also known as pervasive services or service enablers) such as—DRM services (digital rights management services), LBS (location based services), AAA (authentication, authorisation and access control services) etc. For example, a CIM was defined for user profile data for IP based Multimedia Systems by 3GPP (3G Partnership Program) called GUP (Generic User Profile). The data model behind GUP adheres to the specifications and standards proposed by the Liberty Alliance, for Web Service—Identity Personal Profile—ID-PP (through alignment and mapping). This data model behind a user's personal profile can also be thought of as a Common Information Model.

Value Proposition of Meta-Models/Meta-Data (MDA) for Services (SOA):

There are five perspectives from which Meta-models and meta-data add value to services, and they are:

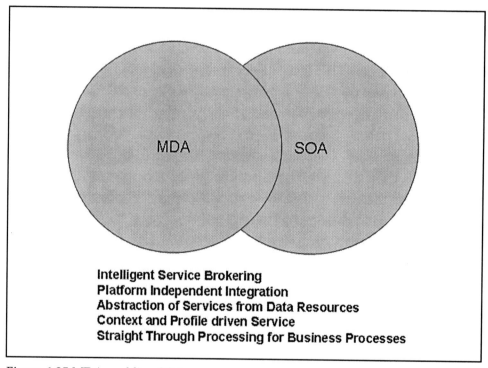

Figure 1:25 MDA enabling SOA

- Grouping, interlinking and coupling services
- Integrating services implemented with multiple underlying technologies
- Building value-added data/information driven services
- Delivering context sensitive and profile driven services
- Total Business Integration and end2end Straight Through Processing (STP)

1.6.1.4 EDA augmenting SOA (the third dimension)

In setting the stage and provide a validating scale to the discussion, the authors first present how EDA completes and compliments the meta-architecture solution space with SOA and MDA. Then they present an architectural viewpoint that will validate while highlighting the value-proposition of EDA for SOA with examples. Firstly, Authors believe MDA, SOA and EDA form an axis of Architecture Strategies that makeup the evolution of any software architecture in the architectural solution space. This belief stems from the fact that three fundamental orthogonal elements of any software are structure, function and data. Authors believe MDA, SOA and EDA are orthogonal concepts that are evolved forms of these fundamental three. MDA addresses structuring through abstractions; while SOA defines functions in chunks and EDA describes the data in context. Secondly, in constructing a validating scale for discussion, authors would like to present similar orthogonal concepts in the architectural concern space. Authors view users, business domain and system builder as three primordial architectural stakeholders whose concerns are usually orthogonal to each other. Users represent the dependency concerns existing external to the system on the system, business domain represent the internal functionality concerns that make up the system and system builder represents the development concerns that exists in evolving the system. Authors believe viewpoints emanating from these architectural stakeholders into the architecture will attain coverage for the discussion, hence validating the supposition that EDA augments SOA.

Value Proposition of Events (EDA) & Modeling (MDA) for Services (SOA):

There are five perspectives from which events and modeling add value to services, and they are:

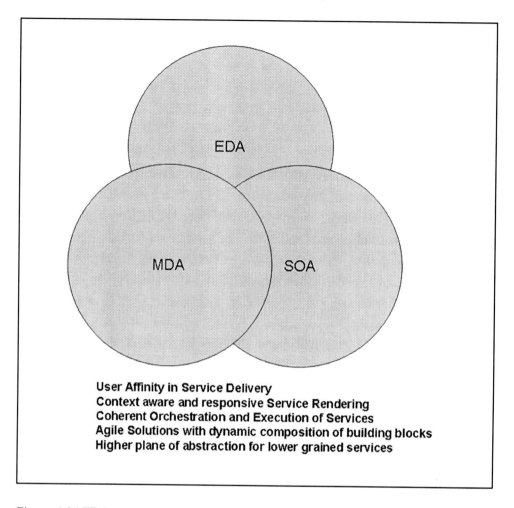

User Affinity in Service Delivery
Context aware and responsive Service Rendering
Coherent Orchestration and Execution of Services
Agile Solutions with dynamic composition of building blocks
Higher plane of abstraction for lower grained services

Figure 1:26 EDA augmenting SOA

- User affinity in Service delivery
- Context-aware responsive service rendering
- Coherent Execution and Orchestration of Services
- Building agile solutions with dynamic composition of reusable services
- Building a higher plane of abstraction using lower-grained Service

1.6.1.5 CBA supplementing SOA (the fourth dimension)

Authors, Alan Brown, Simon Johnston and Kevin Kelly in a Rational Software white paper published in 2002, refer to even C++ as a monolithic application development environment that is not conducive for true component based architectures. There are not many programming paradigms that exist today that fully support Component Based Architectures that leads distributed components under SOA. CBA solution that is built on the Java Technology Platform (that include JEE/JME, RTSJ, JAIN SLEE, JBI, and more) fully supports CBA that supplements SOA, with its support for Java APIs for XMl. If we assume a world where SOA and its fundamental principles around streamlined/simplistic interface design for seamless integration between other services will suffice, then any monolithic application, that is not modular, not-distributable, not-instrument-able, not-extensible to multiple clients etc. wrapped with a XML interface for service interaction is good enough.

However, taking this approach with programming paradigms that do not support a component based development will lead to non-granular set of services that will have disruptive effect on the entire application on change, that are difficult to be distributed and be accessed from multiple networks/devices, that are not instrumented with a boundary for service management and more. What CBA offers in terms of supplementing SOA is exactly addressing these set of issues by taking into account the need for component based design and implementation that support capabilities to:

- Evolve right-grained implementation units
- Remain goal-focused with infrastructure services exported to containers
- Build cohesive, reusable and serviceable units
- Build mobile and distributed logic
- Self-describing components to support instrumentation
- Aggregate component assembly that deliver coarse services
- Mitigate disruption due to change

CBA also aligns well with EDA, MDA and SOA from a holistic approach, wherein, some of the distributed components are actually events in the network, and MDA aids in the space of component instrumentation, to allow for the alignment of Software Architectures with IT Architectures.

Value Proposition of Components (CBA) for Services (SOA):

This is explained further in detail in this chapter. There are several perspectives from different architectural stakeholder viewpoints where components add value to services, and they are:

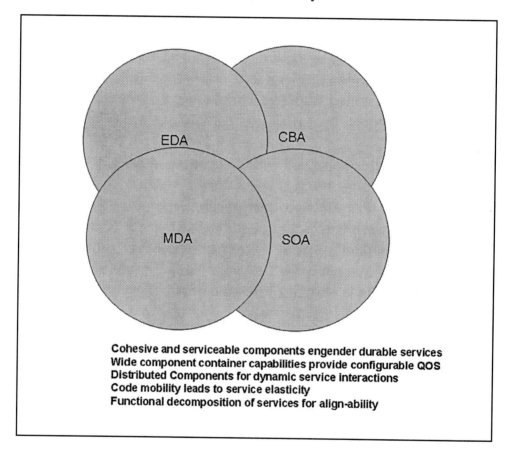

Figure 1:27 CBA supplementing SOA

- Cohesive and serviceable components engender durable services
- Wide component container capabilities provides configurable QoS
- Distributing Components for Dynamic Service interactions
- Code Mobility for Service Elasticity
- Functional decomposition of Service for Alignability

1.6.1.6 UCA supporting SOA (the fifth dimension)

Utility Computing Architectures go beyond traditional GRID Computing Architectures, wherein, web services concepts and technologies are also leveraged for GRID Services (based on OGSA- Open Grid Services Architecture, EGA- Enterprise Grid Alliance, etc.). In the past, GRID computing solutions were meant for Services that were compute intensive and grid-able (i.e., workloads such as batch jobs that were distributable to multiple compute nodes) such as:

- Derivative Analysis (Monte Carlo)
- Protein Modeling (Computational Research)
- Reservoir Simulation
- Electronic Design Automation (Simulation and Analysis)
- Movie Production (and 3D Visualisation) Rendering)

However, lately (with the advent of XML and Java) Services in a SOA built based on CBA are distributable in nature, making common business services (CRM, SCM, ERP and more) as Grid-able (and granular) Services. In a chapter entitled "Building Next Generation Grid-Enabled Business applications with Today's Technologies", the authors, Victoria Livschitz (Sun), Stacey Farias (Sun) and Seth Polansky (Visa), explain how not only 1) Job-oriented applications (e.g., billing reconciliation jobs) and 2) Batch applications (e.g., reporting on Data warehouse) are suitable for Grid computing environments, but also, 3) Transactional applications (e.g., Supply chain) and 4) Session-driven applications (e.g., shopping cart at Amazon) are also a good fit for Grid computing environments making all types of business applications Grid-able. According to the authors these four types are further clarified in the chapter as:

Job-oriented applications—These are traditionally the most common type of grid applications, found far more often in the realm of scientific and advanced engineering computing than business computing. The term "job" stands for a unit of computation that can be carried out independently of other computations. This term in general is used to describe parallel processing environments.

Batch applications—Batch applications constitute a very important part of business applications. Requests for computation are typically accumulated in a "batch" for future processing, where transactions are atomic, and long in duration (typically minutes), key operational metric is the length in the transaction window.

Transactional applications—Transaction applications typically have requests for computation originating from external clients triggered from events outside of applications control, each transaction is processed individually and immediately (typically as threads), transactions are atomic and short in duration, load may fluctuate heavily between peak and average conditions, key operational metric is throughput –transactions per second.

Session-driven applications—These are interactive business applications that are often designed around the notion of a "user session" which forms the relationship between a user and applications, across many transactions. From a grid computing standpoint even though session management and transaction processing are handled by separate application components, the design issues are largely uniform.

Also today's Grids leverage advances in technologies that consolidate and virtualises resources (compute/network and storage) and automates the provisioning of services to virtualised resources. These solutions simplify IT operations by allowing you to manage your data center as if it were a single system. Using virtualisation and automation technologies, these Grids take operational efficiency to new heights. Both hardware and software provisioning enable administrators to effectively manage growing numbers of network services across complex IT infrastructures and also optimise resource utilisation through dynamic workload distribution and fine-grained partitioning of individual servers. By bringing crucial abstraction and automation into the data center, Grids can help lower TCO and improve productivity, service delivery, and corporate "agility" that offer a critical competitive edge. These Grid solutions are built on a common set of architectural principles, setting the stage for the delivery of a single Grid interface for managing an entire enterprise and beyond.

There are many types of classifications of Grid Computing; from a usage perspective they are classified into:

Compute Grids enable you to turn a set of independent systems into a single compute resource that can be employed by large numbers of users to run jobs of many types.

Data Grids consist of distributed storage devices along with the necessary software to provide transparent, remote and secure access to data wherever and whenever it is needed.

Access Grids provide a secure, anytime, anywhere connection to compute and data grids -- yielding a single Web-based point of delivery for services, content, and complex applications (a.k.a. Identity Grids).

From a deployment perspective they are classified into:

Enterprise Grid that are deployed within an Enterprise/Organisation for Inter departmental sharing (e.g., Home Depot and Coca Cola as enterprises deploy GRID computing for enterprise applications and services).

Partner Grid that are deployed within multiple Enterprises across multiple departments as well (e.g., Fannie Mare deploying a Grid computing environment in conjunction with other partner financial institutions).

Service Grid that are deployed using the Utility model supported by xSPs (2003+), wherein the xSP, could also be hosting web services based on SOA (typically these are telecom companies that are hosting services such as sales force automation, payroll services, etc.).

Value Proposition of Utility Computing (UCA) for Services (SOA):

There are many aspects to the evolution of Utility Computing especially when considering how today Grid Computing Solutions leverage concepts behind SOA, MDA, EDA and CBA. By leveraging these concepts the alignment of SOA to UCA is improved extensively. There are several perspectives from different architectural stakeholder viewpoints where utility based computing add value to services, and they are:

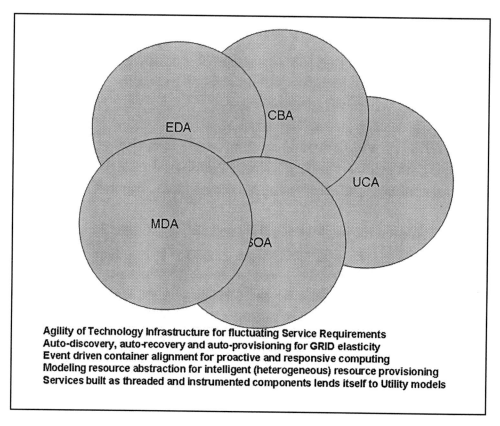

Figure 1:28 UCA supporting SOA

- Agility of Technology Infrastructure for highly fluctuating Service Requirements (for SOA)
- Auto-discovery, auto-recovery and auto-provisioning for Grid Elasticity (CBA for UCA)
- Event driven Container Alignment for responsive and proactive grid computing (EDA for UCA)
- Modeling resource abstraction for intelligent resource provisioning (MDA-CIM/MOF for UCA)
- Services built on instrumented and thread-able Components lends itself to Utility Grids (CBA+SOA for UCA)

1.6.1.7 ICA extending SOA (the USER dimension)

An Identity System is a foundation Core Service Building Block for SOA (and Converged Voice/Data/Video Services) and its central role is managing the Access for Users, from Devices/Networks to different Services. The data models around a user, device and services and a user's profile/preferences are shared through a common profile management service, securely using XSD—XML Schema Definition and its support for tools such as Service Registries makes it important from an MDA perspective, essentially making it a Meta Layer. The notion of an Identity enabled Networks (IDEN) revolutionises the model for Network Service Delivery making it Access Network Agnostic, Device Agnostic—yet USER centric via the Integration of an Identity System with a Core Control & Policy layer (See chapter on Identity enabled IMS) adding relevance of an Identity System to EDA. Trusted computing (see chapter on Identity enabled Computing and ILM) and ILM ensures that all hardware and software components in a Component based Architecture leverage an Identity System for a common security framework. An Identity System captures a lot of information around user's QOS and Service Quality requirements that in turn gets transferred to Services managing a Grid computing environment, adding the value of IDS to UCA. The grid environment also leverages IDS to ensure that secure access to resources from the grid is provided to a user. All this and the idea that the user is offered an option to define how he/she wants the services to behave under varying conditions is conceptually very powerful (control and consent). Offering the user this capability will be a competitive edge, to begin with. This is the primary reason why we have:

- Identity enabled Web Service
- Identity enabled OSS Service
- Identity enabled IMS Service
- Identity enabled IN Service
- Identity enabled Sensor Networks
- Identity enabled Programmable Networks
- Identity enabled Converged Core Network
- Identity enabled Personal Networks

- Identity enabled Telecom Data Models
- Identity enabled Contextual Data Models
- Identity enabled Audit Data Models
- Identity enabled Data Models
- Identity enabled ILM
- Identity enabled Trusted Computing
- Identity enabled Devices
- And more.

Wherein Identity plays a major role as a Core SBB for all types of IP Services and IP networks (including devices) sharing the appropriate contextual data (user context and service context) within a given Session. This makes an Identity System the Central GLUE between Users, Services, Networks and Devices.

Value Proposition of Identity Systems (ICA) for Services (SOA):
An Identity System is also powerful from all the other architectural ap-

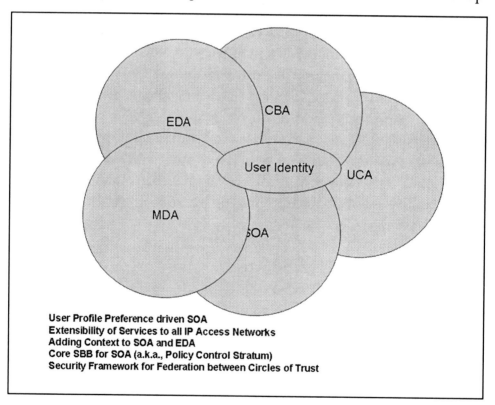

Figure 1:29 Identity Centric Architectures extending SOA

proaches perspective since it plays a significant role in tying together the concepts in these architectural approaches together; Identity enabled Components (Service Components along with Compute and Network Components) enable the unification of Event Driven Architecture and Service Oriented Architecture – more prevalent when we take Sensor Networks into account. An Identity System acts as this Meta-Layer that aligns Model Driven Architecture with SOA – more prevalent with the notion of Service Registries, Identity enabled ILM, Identity enabled Profile sharing,etc. where this meta layer acts as the layer of abstraction between resources and services that access these resources (with the notion of roles, rules and resources). Also the most important value proposition of an Identity Centric Architecture is the role it plays as a Policy and Control Stratum (IPSphere Forum) allows for the alignment of SOA (Service Signaling Stratum) with the NGN —Next Generation Networks (Packet handling stratum).

- User's Profile/Preference driven SOA
- Extensibility of Services to All IP Access Networks
- Adding Context to SOA and EDA
- Core Service Building Block for SOA (as a Distributed Policy Engine)
- Security Framework for federation between Circles of Trust

1.7 Use Case

If the embraced Architectural Approach addresses one or two stake holders' priorities then it could result in biased solutions. By combining these Architectural Approaches and leveraging the virtuous cycle of synergies, wherein, each approach compliments SOA from one perspective or the other, we also address different stake holders' concerns, since each one of these approaches addresses a complimentary set of concerns, wherein:

- Identity is User and Security Centric and hence addresses User and Security (CSO) concerns
- Events is Network and Context Centric and hence addresses CTO/CIO concerns

- Components—Distribution and Extensibility Centric and hence addresses developers and designers concerns
- Model—Abstraction, Brokering and Data Centric and hence addresses CIO and Data Architects concerns
- Utility—Delivery, Support and Resource Centric and hence addresses CIO and Support staffs concerns

Also an Enterprise Systems Architecture has agility only when Architectural Layers (From Business Architecture to Information/Data Architecture to Application/Service Architecture to Technology/Infrastructure Architecture) are Align-able. This combined Architectural Approach Builds one on top of the Other (does not negate the approaches techniques) and is powerful when combined from an end-to-end converged IP Network/Services perspective with true Service Mobility wherein any service can be consumed anywhere (device and network agnostic).

Business Domain Model and Business Architecture

Data and Information Architecture
Application and Services Architecture

Technology Infrastructure Architecture

Figure 1:30 Align-able Layered Architectures

Also one key contribution of the combined Architectural Approach that leverages developments in the past few decades is that it addresses the full-life cycle of Services built based on SOA and the Transition to SOA. That is to move from an As-is Architecture that does not adhere to SOA principles with a number of legacy systems underlying technology platforms, proprietary and closed interfaces to a Target SOA that requires techniques, tactics and tools from the other Architectural Approaches such as MDA, CBA and more.

- Service Creation
- Service Modeling
- Service Dependencies
- Service Integration
- Service Testing
- Service Intelligence
- Service Context
- Service Deployment
- Service Quality (QOS)
- Service Activation
- Service Execution
- Service Calibration
- Service Identity
- Service Management
- Service Brokering
- Service Orchestration
- Service Policies
- Service Security
- Service Delivery
- Service Abstraction
- Service Extensions
- Service Billing
- Service Level
- Service Support
- Service Resource
- Service Retirement

An example Scenario:

Since this example is based on a sample scenario that leverages almost all of the Java technologies, a brief introduction of the same is required (for more details on each of these technologies visit http://java.sun.com, also there are books on each of these topics too). The entire spectrum of Java Technology Platform includes:

- **JEE,** Java Platform, Enterprise Edition (JEE) defines the standard for developing component-based multi-tier enterprise applications.

- **J2ME,** The Micro Edition of the Java Platform provides an application environment that specifically addresses the needs of commodities in the vast and rapidly growing consumer and embedded space, including mobile phones, pagers, personal digital assistants, set-top boxes and vehicle telemetric systems.

- **Java Web services** are Web-based enterprise applications that use open XML-based standards and transport protocols to exchange data with calling clients. Java Platform, Enterprise Edition (JEE) provides the APIs and tools you need to create and deploy interoperable Web services and clients. Java based Web Services are organised into:

    - Java Web Services Developer Pack (Java WSDP)
    - Java API for XML-Based RPC (JAX-RPC)
    - Java API for XML Registries (JAXR)
    - Java API for XML Processing (JAXP)
    - Java Architecture for XML Binding (JAXB)
    - SOAP with Attachments API for Java (SAAJ)

- **Java Card** technology provides a secure environment for applications that run on smart cards and other devices with very limited memory and processing capabilities.

- **Jini** network technology, which includes JavaSpaces technology and Jini extensible remote invocation (Jini ERI), is an open architecture that enables you to create network-centric services—whether implemented in hardware or software—that are highly adaptive to change.

- **JXTA** technology is a set of open protocols that enable any connected device on the network, ranging from cell phones and wireless PDAs to PCs and servers, to communicate and collaborate in a P2P manner.

- **OSS through Java** Initiative ("OSS" stands for "Operations Support Systems") produces a standard set of Java technology-based APIs to jump-start the implementation of end-to-end services on next-generation wireless networks and leverage the convergence of telecommunications and Internet-based solutions.

- The **JAIN** initiative has defined a set of Java technology APIs that enable the rapid development of Java based next generation communications products and services for the Java platform.

- **Java Dynamic Management Kit** (Java DMK) is a Java technology based toolkit that allows developers to rapidly create smart agents based on the Java Management Extensions (JMX) specification. The power of the JMX framework is that it supports multiple protocol access to management information residing in the agent.

- The **JMI** specification enables the implementation of a dynamic, platform-independent infrastructure to manage the creation, storage, access, discovery, and exchange of metadata. JMI is based on the Meta Object Facility (MOF) specification from the Object Management Group (OMG), an industry-endorsed standard for meta-data management.

- **JBI** Developers are adopting service oriented architecture approaches resulting in the need for composite applications, where, the challenges are how to integrate application components and orchestrate application services. JBI provided a system to address these challenges. JBI helps to break the lock-in that exists in the integration industry and enable developers to implement truly open integration solutions.

- The **RTSJ** is the specification resulting from JSR-1, the first specification launched through the Java® Community Process. The specification was approved in January 2002. The first commercial implementation followed in spring of 2003. The second release of the reference implementation (RI) was in Spring 2004 and version 1.0.1 of the RTSJ was released (with updates to the RI and Technology Compatibility Suite) in June 2005. RTSJ is designed to support both hard and soft real-time applications. Among its major features are: scheduling properties suitable for real-time applications with provisions for periodic and sporadic tasks, support for deadlines and CPU time budgets, and tools to let tasks avoid garbage collection delays.

- And few more (such as JTAPI and Java Media Extensions).

Today within Telco environments services such as Identity, Location, Presence, Weather have been implemented as a re-usable service, i.e. the location logic running in a Location service can be re-used for many other services—such as location based weather report, location based mapping, location based retail list etc. Now as an end user I travel to a particular city—such as Seattle for an important meeting the next morning. I setup my alarm for 6:00am on my cell phone and along with my alarm I receive a short weather report and a Doppler image for the specific location that I'm in. The majority of this scenario is made possible due to a Service Oriented Architecture (SOAP/XML). Now by adding the concepts behind Event Driven Architecture, this scenario can get even more interesting. Let us say due to time difference (5:30PST is actually 8:30EST) I actually wake up before the alarm goes off, and access/login to a TV/STB. With my presence in the network now, I only receive a weather report/Doppler image on my cell phone and not the alarm, since an event gets triggered the minute I login stating that I'm present and hence awake (canceling the wake-up call). This could be taken one step further: when I not only access TV/STB services, but I actually view a weather channel report. Based on my consumption of this service another event takes place where the weather report/Doppler image along with the wake up call all get cancelled. (This is user centric!!). At the same time the flight that was scheduled to depart at 2:00pm that afternoon from Seattle is delayed due to a storm in my destination city (Washington DC) and an event is triggered to send me a message notifying the same, with an alternate schedule.

- The Weather Service is itself a simple Web Service, that has a highly explicit and streamlined interface (SOAP/XML/JBI) so that other services can leverage it as a reusable SBB – this is the basis and a good example of a SOA where location service logic refers the location info to obtain location based weather information. Hence here, both JEE/JBI and Java Web Services are used as a component based application environment – that executed multiple modular logic in the form of EJBs and MDBs.

- The alarm setup on the cell phone that is an identity enabled device is based on the JME technology and the components involved are midlets, servlets, etc. JME with its support for protocols such as SIP, OCAP and WAP – runs on multiple identity enabled devices such as cell phones and STB/TVs.

- Logging into the Cable Network via a STB/TV triggers the presence service in the network and event based technology (such as JAIN) is used to cancel a telecom service (such as alarm/notification) and web service (such as the location based weather service). Components involved here include Xlets and JAIN SLEE components and profile/policy services.

- RTSJ may potentially be leveraged when the user makes real time communications with the travel agent to reschedule.

- One add-on to this scenario might include leveraging a P2P service between the STB/TV and the Cell Phone (connected to the network), wherein the weather report is saved on both devices for the day. Jxta components are executed in the network for this extended P2P service to work.

- In this scenario, OSS though Java initiative is leveraged, such as billing mediation, to ensure appropriate billing logic gets executed and mediation occurs between multiple access network providers and the core network provider, as well as the Identity Service Provider and other Service Providers.

- The alarm service in itself could be rendering user centric alarm tones that are played by IP media services, using XML dialects such as MSML and MOML (two related markup languages related to media services). Using techniques from JMI and its support to OMGs XMI, the underlying dialect interchanges can be handled through an XMI repository. Many XML components are involved here including XMI components and other XML components.

- These Services can be hosted in a Jini enabled Grid environment.

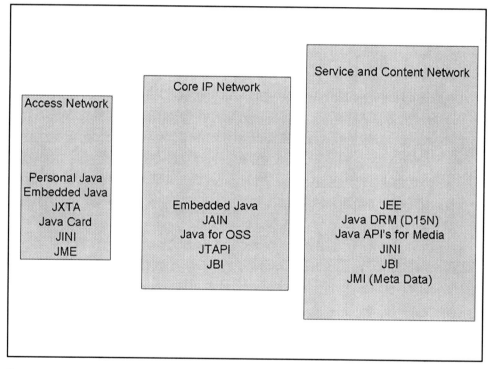

Figure 1:31-B Java Technology Platform as a CBA

- This is an example that highlights the value-proposition that components bring to services. It also highlights the significance of MDA and EDA, along with CBA to enable, augment and supplement SOA in various manners. Jini, J-DMK and component instrumentation also play a significant role here—where SLA and OLA around services are well managed within the Service Grid Networks (UCA). What needs to be noted is that these Java Technologies work in conjunction with IP initiatives such as MobileIP, IPSphere and IPSec as well as XML technologies including SAML and XKMS.

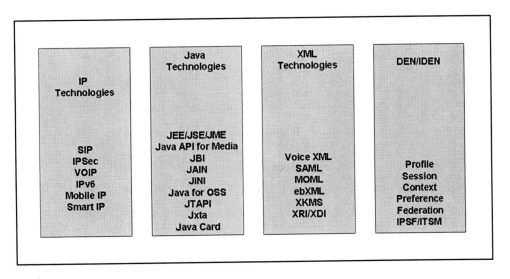

Figure 1:32 Java Technology Platform + IP, XML and Identity Technologies

David Goldsmith from Sun has three use cases that talk to the core value proposition of Federation and Liberty specifications, namely:

- Service Outsourcing
- Supplier Network
- Acquisition or Merger

Each of these use cases are depicted in the following six figures, with and without federation, that illustrate the simplicity and significance of federation for integration and interoperability of services when outsourced to different entities, services stemming from a network of suppliers and constant changing M&A business environments.

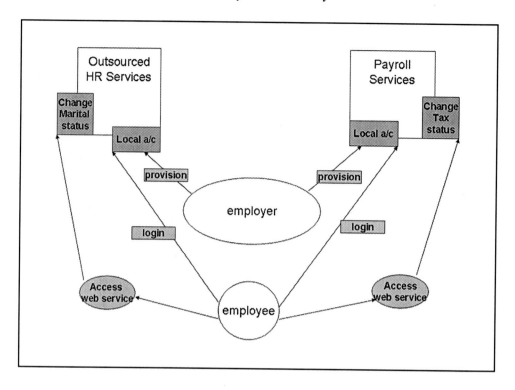

Figure 1:33 Service Outsourcing without Federation

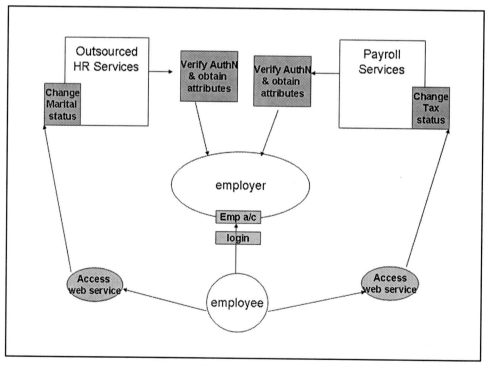

Figure 1:34 Service Outsourcing with Federation

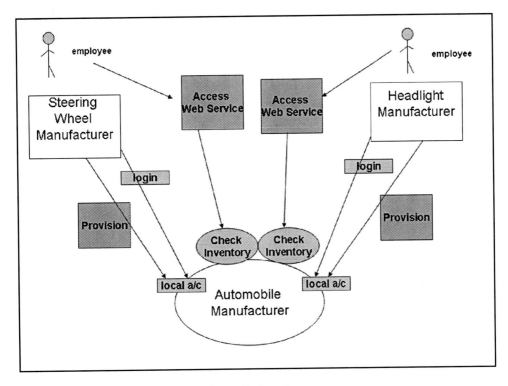

Figure 1:35 Supplier Network without Federation

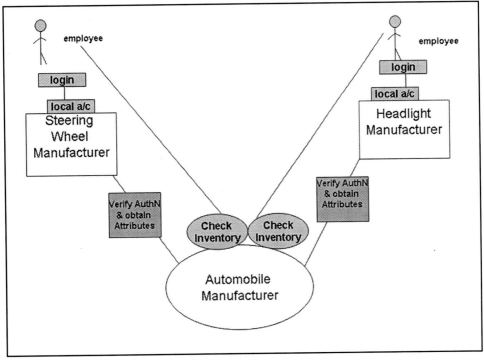

Figure 1:36 Supplier Network with Federation

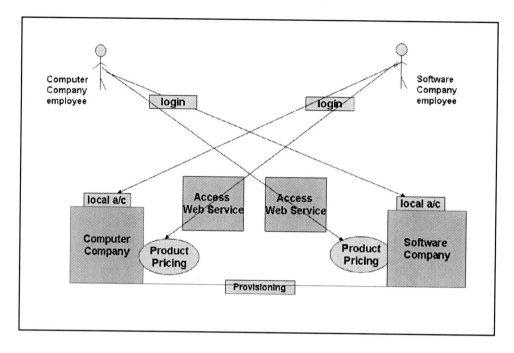

Figure 1:37 Acquisition or Merger without Federation

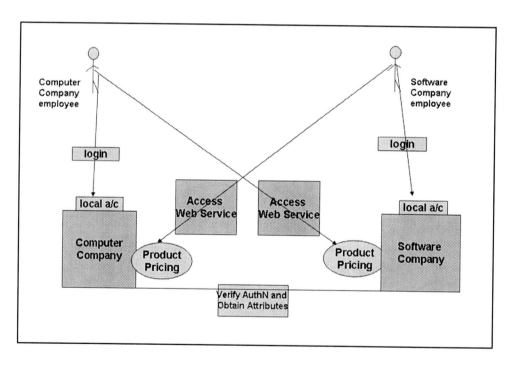

Figure 1:38 Acquisition or Merger with Federation

1.8 Key take-away

The integration of Services, Network elements, Devices and Users data with Network Identity helps set the foundation for context driven/preference based content/service (IPTV, VOD, IP music, VOIP, IMS, Business Services, etc.) delivery to all Access networks and Access devices.

Also the proliferation of wireless networks cannot be stopped and is very strategic for Carriers. The advances in Wireless Metropolitan and Wide Area Networks such as WiMAX, EVDO, etc. compliment the notion of an Identity enabled Network due to performance factors and the requirements around privacy/security. As traversal between LANs and Wireless WANs are made seamless with varying throughput from devices, IdEN enhance the usefulness of related technologies such as Infrared and RFID (sensor networks). The end scenario eventually offers true ubiquity for end users accessing, not just networks, but also Services from all other types of networks. These developments along with standards such as SOAP, SAML, XKMS, RFID, also extend the capabilities of Identity Solutions to validate not just web users, but validate identity of web devices, web services, web sites and web applications.

Key Strategic points highlighted in this chapter are;

- "Identity Systems central role is managing the Access for Users, from multiple Devices/Networks to different Services."

- "The data models around a user, device and services and a user's profile/preferences are shared, securely, through a common profile management service."

- "Identity System is a foundation Core Service Building Block (similar to the potential offered by ENUM Services) for Converged Services."

- "Identity enabled Networks (IDEN) revolutionises the model for Network Service Delivery making it Access Network Agnostic,

Device Agnostic—yet USER centric (profile/preference driven delivery of Services."

- "The idea that the user is offered an option to define how he/she wants the services to behave under varying conditions is conceptually very powerful. Offering the user this capability will be a competitive edge, to begin with."

- "The four layers and the four perspectives of IDS are instrumental for the Vertical Integration of multiple functional IDS that focus on specific areas."

- "An IDS also acts as the Core SBB that aligns concepts put forth by EDA, CBA, SOA, UCA and MDA – when viewing the "Network as a Computer."

- "The nine pain points are addressed when the nine step methodology of Identity based Security is addressed in conjunction with the Vertical Integration proposed."

- "The business value of an IDS implementation can be derived for years after an implementation from a SOA and Converged Network perspective (ICA Aligning SOA with NGN)."

1.9 Organisation of the Book

The 1st chapter (this one) is the **Introduction chapter**—that lays the foundation and framework of Identity Centric Architecture and also has a description of the content in the book. This introduction covers the (pain points typically faced in SOA for NGN (Service Oriented Architecture for Next Generation Networks), the nine Step Methodology to address Security with an Identity System, the four Layers of an Identity System and the four Tiers of the Identity System. It also talks about the significance of Vertical Integration and the overall Business Value of an Identity System to an Enterprise.

There are six chapters on identity enabled Networks & Network Services: Although these chapters are relevant for telecommunication companies such as Vodafone in Europe, Telstra in Australia and Sprint in the US, plus the Network equipment providers, such as Alcatel/Lucent, Motorola and Ericsson, they are equally important for any business, including large corporations such as Walt Disney, Coca cola, Home Depot and small business entities, since these advances in the Telecom space make it possible for business to operate anywhere and anytime, employees, customers and suppliers/partners alike.

Chapter 2 on Identity enabled 4G Networks talks about the evolving nature of the 4G networks and its wide scale deployment via standards such as 802.11, 802.16 and 802.20 that can again leverage an Identity System. This chapter also talks about the integration approaches and alignment that can take place between multiple access networks and a Session aware Identity system. It also highlights the significance of Standards for 4G Networks and the role an Identity System plays via Alignment of these standards.

Chapter 3 on Identity enabled Sensor Network talks about the relevance of RFID/EPC based networks and services that get impacted by them including supply chain, logistics, distribution, retail etc. and the relevance of an Identity System, in this context. RFID Repositories and Service Registry Repositories are secured with an Identity System that acts as the glue between objects and things (any entity) and user entities.

Chapter 4 on Identity enabled Programmable Network talks about the relevance of today's dynamic programmable networks and the alignment between these networks and its events with Services leveraging an Identity system. Programmable Networks are highly evolved Service Network Grids that adapt to the real-time demands and requirements of users, sensor networks (as users) and compos-able applications.

Chapter 5 on Identity enabled IMS Control Network talks about the integration approaches between an IMS environment and SOA based Services as well as, highlights the value proposition of an Identity System to a Control Network in terms of secure profile sharing (for Services such as VOD, IPTV, Video Conferencing, etc.). An IMS network is envisioned to act as the common control layer for 3G and 4G networks that can deliver value added multi-media services.

Chapter 6 on Identity enabled NG IN (Intelligent Network) Services talks about how an Identity System is the GLUE that ties multiple fragmented Intelligence Services such as IN, AIN, NGIN, Web-IN, WIN, etc. that were originally developed for PSTN networks or 3G cellular network or the Internet can now be integrated for an IP network end to end and how intelligence aids in convergence as well.

Chapter 7 on Identity enabled OAM&P Services talks about Identity enabled OSS/J Services for these NG Networks and the relevance of Identity Systems for operations, administration, management and provisioning as well. As the network evolves into a 4G network with an IMS control layer and a transcending IN layer, OAM&P solutions have to take into account this network evolution and the SOA based OSS services that are required. It also talks about the alignment between Services and NGN that can take place with a Common Policy and Control Layer for QOS and SLA.

Chapters 8 to 10 talk about the relevance between Identity and Services/SOA, ESB and DRM as a Service Building block. Chapter 8 on Web Services and IDS talks about the integration that exists between Identity Systems and Web Services as well as SOA and is the contribution of five Sun employees (as a paper on Identity enabled Web Services). It also talks about the distributed policy functionality of an Identity System for Services and Entities.

Chapter 9 on Identity enabled ESB (orchestration and choreography) discusses the specifics between the functional alignment between an ESB plus Service Registry and an Identity System for SOA. Security concerns in composite application integration environment (that is loosely coupled) are also discussed here.

Chapter 10 is on ID enabled DRM (trusted content network) Services and its implications in terms of delivering content in an agnostic manner. This is a chapter that highlights the linking and value proposition of disintermediation for DRM.

Chapter 11 on Identity enabled IP Devices (trusted mobile devices, CPE and NE) talks about the latest developments in terms of securing client devices and network equipment, taking into account SOA and the evolving Network.

Chapter 12 on Identity enabled Service Containers (trusted computing) discusses the recent development in TCG (trusted computing group) and provision-able service and its relationship to identity systems, as well as trusted computing infrastructure.

Chapter 13 Identity enabled information life cycle management (ILM) and Data Management talks about the strategic significance of aligning identity systems with ILM, data management and storage network services.

The last **14th chapter** on Conclusion discusses several integration points of an Identity System, the identity 2.0 concepts, the future and how integration between multiple identity systems acting as a source of intelligence can take place via five approaches namely, virtual mapping, federation, correlation, workflow/provisioning and indexing.

2. Identity enabled NG Networks

According to Wikipedia, **4G** (or **4-G**) is; short for **fourth-generation** communication system. There is no set definition to what 4G is, however the features that are predicted for 4G can be summarised in a single sentence. The 4G will be a fully IP-based integrated system of systems and network of networks achieved after the convergence of wired and wireless networks as well as computer, consumer electronics, communication technology and several other convergences that will be capable of providing 100 Mbps and 1Gbps, respectively, in outdoor and indoor environments with end-to-end QoS and high security, offering any kind of services anytime, anywhere at affordable cost and one billing.

The WWRF (Wireless World Research Forum) defines 4G as a network that operates on Internet technology, combines it with other applications and technologies such as Wi-Fi and WiMAX, and runs at speeds ranging from 100 Mbps (in cell-phone networks) to 1 Gbps (in local Wi-Fi networks). 4G is not just one defined technology or standard but rather a collection of technologies and protocols to enable the highest throughput, lowest cost wireless network possible.

The objective here is to cater the quality of service and rate requirements set by the forthcoming applications like wireless broadband access, multimedia messaging, video chat, mobile TV, High definition TV content, DVB and minimal services like voice and data at anytime and anywhere. The 4G working groups have defined the following as the objectives of the 4G wireless communication standard:

- Spectrally efficient system (in bits/s/Hz and bit/s/Hz/site)
- High network capacity
- Nominal data rate of 100 Mbps at high speeds and 1 Gbps at stationary conditions as defined by the ITU-R
- Data rate of at least 100 Mbps between any two points in the world
- Smooth handoff across heterogeneous network
- Seamless connectivity and global roaming across multiple networks
- High quality of service for next generation multimedia support (real time audio, high speed data, HDTV video content, mobile TV etc.)
- Interoperable with the existing wireless standards
- All IP system, packet switched network

In summary, the 4G system should dynamically share and utilize the network resource to meet the minimal requirements of all the 4G enabled users. *The 4G Network has characteristics of programmability, sensors, convergence, intelligence and Identity embedded in it.*

First generation: Almost all of the systems from this generation were analog systems where voice was considered to be the main traffic. Some of the standards are NMT, AMPS, Hicap, CDPD, Mobitex, DataTac.

Second generation: All the standards belonging to this generation are commercial centric and digital in form. Around 60% of the current market is dominated by European standards. The second generation standards are GSM, iDEN, D-AMPS, IS-95, PDC, CSD, PHS, GPRS, HSCSD, WiDEN, CDMA2000 (1xRTT/IS-2000), and the 2.5G standard GPRS.

Third generation: To meet the growing demands in the number of subscribers (increase in network capacity), rates required for high speed data transfer and multimedia applications 3G standards started evolving. The systems in this standard are basically a linear enhancement of 2G systems. They are based on two parallel backbone infrastructures, one consisting of circuit switched nodes and one of packet oriented nodes. Currently, transition is happening from 2G to 3G systems. Some of the 3G standards are EDGE and EGPRS (sometimes denoted 2.75G), W-CDMA or UMTS (3GSM), FOMA, 1xEV-DO/IS-856, TD-SCDMA, GAN/UMA, 3.5G - HSDPA, 3.75G - HSUPA. The ITU defines a specific set of air interface technologies as third generation, as part of the IMT-2000 initiative.

Fourth generation: According to 4G working groups, the infrastructure and the terminals will have almost all the standards from 2G to 3G implemented. The infrastructure will however only be packet based all-IP. The system will also serve as an open platform where the new innovations can go with it. Some of the standards which pave the way for 4G systems are WiMax, WiBro and the proposed 3GPP Long Term Evolution work-in-progress technologies such as HSOPA.

With this idea of 4G networks we can understand the developments in the form of proliferation of Wifi (wireless LANs) that caught on like wildfire between 2000 and 2005, and we are seeing the same with the proliferation of WiMAX (wireless MANs) in the world today (2006 and above). The wireless LANs are now available in conference facilities, retail locations, airports, and more over and above several million Wifi deployments in homes and offices. This trend is augmented with comparatively high speed wireless MANs and WANs by Carriers such as Sprint and Verizon. At the same time both the wire-line (including cable) and wireless communications providers are seeking new ways to expand there offerings in terms of data services and video services over and above voice services, with the convergence of wireless and wireline. Another new entrant to the broadband arena is the Power companies with BPL (broadband over power-line) technologies. ATIS as a standards body also talks to how IP (internet protocol) can reach out to all cellular networks (2G, 2.5G, 3G, and more), such as CDMA, TDMA, GSM, GPRS, EDGE, EVDO and more. With this proliferation of cellular networks, Wifi networks, Wifi mesh networks, WiMax networks, BPL and more pundits expect 4G networks to be a combination of all these LAN, MAN and WAN technologies along with smart clients that can traverse all these networks seamlessly, based on location and signal strength through a control layer. This is true even with

Quad Band devices that are available today, for example, ones that can transcend from GSM/GPRS to CDMA/EVDO to Wifi/WiMAX as well as traditional IP based wire-line connections.

Identity System software vendors have teamed up with ISV Solution partners (Corinex Networks, Reactivity Networks, Pronto Networks and others) to deliver solutions and technology that enable next generation service delivery platforms, that has the capability to reach out to all IP end points. Most of these third party solutions are a combination of Hardware and Software (with specific Access Control Appliances) and solutions that are written in JEE™.

Utilising the most scalable operating environment, application technology and hardware platforms available, these partners have integrated both their access management and service management technology. This combination of Linux/Solaris hardware and 3rd party software creates a fully integrated "out of the box" Wifi or WiMAX or BPL solution. Lately these software vendors have also addressed Integrated Security requirements with extension of their solutions to Network Identity (such as Java Enterprise System Identity Server). This chapter takes an in-depth look at the approaches to integrating these technologies (Wifi, WiMAX, BPL, etc. and Network Identity) and the value proposition of doing so. First an introduction to common Wifi and WiMAX Architectures and Network Identity Solutions are covered. The following figure illustrates the multiple overlay architecture of a 4G Network with support for Sensor/RFID capabilities, Personal Networks and DVB/DAB (Digital Video and Audio Broadcasting) support.

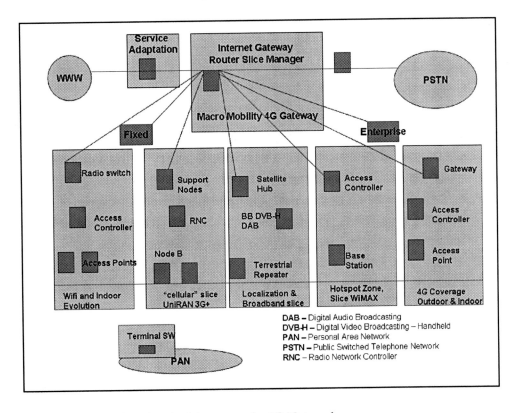

Figure 2:1 Multi Overlay Architecture of a 4G Network

2.1 Value Proposition of Integrating of WiFi & WiMAX with Identity

The synergies of integrating Wifi & WiMAX Solutions with Network Identity are strategic in nature. As Communication Service Providers (CSPs) deploy and rollout several thousands of Wifi and WiMAX networks across the globe in Europe, Asia and the Americas, there are concerns and issues around security, user-identity management, common service provisioning models, centralised session management (across multiple converged services and domains), single Sign-on across multiple Wifi and WiMAX networks etc. The extension of these Wifi and WiMAX solutions to a Network Identity Platform addresses all these issues and lays the foundation for profile and preference driven Services Delivery. Benefits of this integration include:

- Common Identity Management Service—leads to Common Identity Broker Architecture that allows for Integrating with other Enterprise Applications Authentication Mechanisms (Siebel, Oracle, People soft, SAP etc.)—resulting in Secure Single Sign On and Single Sign Off.

- Scales with the business from a few thousand to millions of subscribers (all managed in a centralised manner), lays the foundation for a profile/preference driven Services Delivery—this leads to context driven delivery of services on demand.
- Common/Centralised Session Management and Tracking of user Sessions—this leads to straight forward integration with service session management and call session management.
- Identity Services are reusable/replaceable Architectural building block—with open interfaces, to other building blocks such as Location and/or Presence Services.
- The foundation, to group several hundred/thousand Wifi and WiMAX deployments, to be aggregated into a Virtual WAN or Virtual MAN (in conjunction with VPN technologies).
- Supports client-free and client-based authentication/authorisation techniques (finger print, retina scan, user id/password, token card, java card, MAC address etc.).
- Federated Identity management can lead to setting the base foundation required for roaming between Wifi LANs from the same provider and between Wifi and WiMAX between providers (ensuring the validation of identity of network/roaming devices).
- Over and above the value proposition of integrating with Network Identity—some of the core capabilities of Wifi and WiMAX solutions themselves includes:
- Co-branding with venue owners (such as Starbucks, McDonalds, a Mall, an Airline, Airport etc.)
- Reporting to manage your subscribers, footprint and business
- Variable service and rate plans that can be easily customised for different customers
- Highly scalable and fault tolerant (Nebs compliant) access manager that can be installed at the network edge, switch POP, DSLAM or carrier NOC
- Integrating with existing OSS/BSS solutions for single bill and uniform authentication, allowing Wifi accounts and profiles to merge

with existing systems such as ISP authentication servers

- Combining billing mediation with existing billing systems
- Interfacing with network management and trouble ticketing for better technical support
- Having extensive roaming capabilities that capture revenue from out-of-area visitors
- Ad-hoc subscriber access and "on-the-fly" account creation for existing dial-up, DSL and ISP customers to become Wifi customers
- Built-in prepayment that captures new or visiting customers

2.2 Integration Approaches

In practical terms, WiMAX would operate similar to Wifi but at higher speeds, over greater distances and for a greater number of users. WiMAX could potentially erase the suburban and rural blackout areas that currently have no broadband Internet access because phone and cable companies have not yet run the necessary wires to those remote locations.

2.2.1 Typical WiMAX Architecture

A WiMAX system consists of two parts:

A **WiMAX tower**, similar in concept to a cell-phone tower—A single WiMAX tower can provide coverage to a very large area—as big as 3,000 square miles (~8,000 square km).

A **WiMAX receiver**—The receiver and antenna could be a small box or PCMCIA card, or they could be built into a laptop the way Wifi access is today.

A WiMAX tower station can connect directly to the Internet using a high-bandwidth, wired connection (for example, a T3 line). It can also connect to another WiMAX tower using a line-of-sight, micro-wave link. This connection to a second tower (often referred to as a backhaul), along with the ability of a single tower to cover up to 3,000 square miles, is what allows WiMAX to provide coverage to remote rural areas.

What this points out is that WiMAX actually can provide two forms of wireless service:

There is the **non-line-of-sight**, Wifi sort of service, where a small antenna on your computer connects to the tower. In this mode, WiMAX uses a **lower frequency range**—2 GHz to 11 GHz (similar to WiFi). Lower-wavelength transmissions are not as easily disrupted by physical obstructions—they are better able to diffract, or bend, around obstacles.

There is **line-of-sight** service, where a fixed dish antenna points straight at the WiMAX tower from a rooftop or pole. The line-of-sight connection is stronger and more stable, so it's able to send a lot of data with fewer errors. Line-of-sight transmissions use higher frequencies, with ranges reaching a possible 66 GHz. At **higher frequencies**, there is less interference and lots more bandwidth.

Wifi-style access will be limited to a 4-to-6 mile radius (perhaps 25 square miles or 65 square km of coverage, which is similar in range to a cell-phone zone). Through the stronger line-of-sight antennas, the WiMAX transmitting station would send data to WiMAX-enabled computers or routers set up within the transmitter's 30-mile radius (2,800 square miles or 9,300 square km of coverage). This is what allows WiMAX to achieve its maximum range.

Global Area Network: The final step in the area network scale is the global area network (GAN). The proposal for GAN is **IEEE 802.20**. A true GAN would work a lot like today's cell phone networks, with users able to travel across the country and still have access to the network the whole time. This network would have enough bandwidth to offer Internet access comparable to cable modem service, but it would be accessible to mobile, always-connected devices like laptops or next-generation cell phones.

(*Source: http://computer.howstuffworks.com/wimax1.htm*)

A Carrier grade WiMAX deployment has the following tiered Architecture;

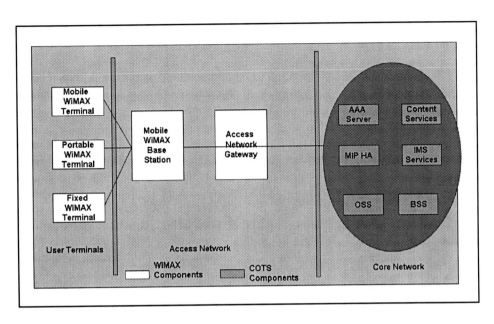

Figure 2:2 WiMAX deployment with AAA Servers

In the Access Network one can find Base Stations and Network Gateways leveraging multiple services from the core service network. Typical AAA deployments in support of a WiMAX deployment is a Secure Network Access Solution that not only handles AAA (AuthN and AuthZ), but also includes NAC (network admission control) like functionality that check the devices for security patches, virus and more. These AAA servers are in many cases integrated with an Identity System for Federation capabilities as well. In essence the AAA server is an Identity System with Access Management, Federation Management and a distributable repository.

One key factor that needs to be noted is the fact that a WiMAX deployment only offers Access Networks across an entire Nation, however there are basic services that would be required for such large scale deployments and connectivity to Service networks via a Core network. Such services include primarily AAA (authentication, authorisation and auditing) services, Identity enabled OSS and Billing if revenue generating services are offered such as content services or if service and content providers are charged for the reach of their services. However, these services are to be augmented with localised services as well, based on local regional requirements in terms of information services, content etc.

Based on this solution architecture, each deployment of a MAN (1000 such deployments can be replicas of the few that gets tested), will include:

- Base Station and/or Radio Access Station (where an AM agent runs)
- Service Network Gateway (where NAC and AM Agents run)
- Redundant AAA Servers (highly distributed identity systems or IDM)
- Redundant OSS/B Servers (ID enabled for Federation)
- Basic Local Services Servers (ID enabled web news app servers – for Federation)
- Switching gear for connectivity to main Link to the backbone
- And WiMax enabled terminals to Test

The majority of the hardware components leverage some software elements from the four layers of an Identity System.

2.2.2 Typical Wifi Architectures

Carrier grade Wifi solutions typically have a two-tier architecture, consisting of the Service Manager (Application Server) and Access Manager (Web Server). These systems are robust, scalable framework with HA capabilities, rapidly deployable (reference-able Architectures) and extensive (built-in interfaces) OSS/BSS integration capabilities.

Other typical features of these solutions include:

- Client Device-free network access
- Support for Virtual Private Networks
- Subscriber- and location-specific classes of service
- Variable retail, roaming and wholesale billing and billing media-

tion schemes
- Extensive revenue assurance and reporting capabilities
- Self- and care-based subscriber provisioning
- Customer session and network trouble ticketing and analysis

Sun's partner products are built 100% in Java and support a wide variety of JEE Services. The result is a highly reliable, interoperable architecture that is easily integrated into the Communication Service Provider's infrastructure. The figures below depict specific integration points:

A sample Logical and Physical Wifi Solution Architecture is depicted in figures, below.

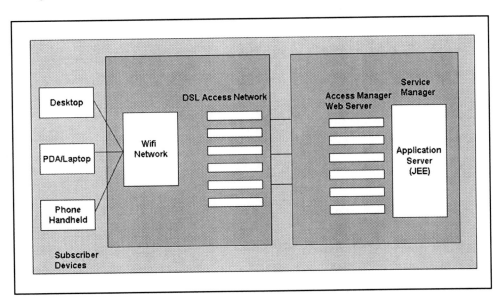

Figure 2:3 WiFi Physical Architecture

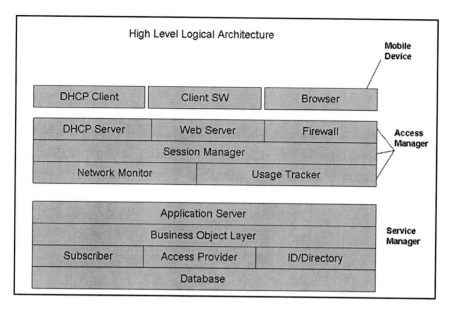

Figure 2:4 WiFi Logical Architecture

Note: Identity enabled NG DNS, DHCP and ENUM Services (such as the solution offered by Nominum) play a strategic role in 4G Networks where the devices are leveraging IPv6 based DHCP addresses and constantly invoke ENUM requests for Service access.

2.2.3 Multi-Tier Network Identity Architectures

At this juncture a logical and physical deployment Architecture of IDS has to be understood. Identity System software are standards-based products designed to help organisations manage secure access to Web and non Web-based applications both on the intranet and extranet. As organisations require more financial, organisational and competitive agility to compete in the marketplace, and they provide scalable access management services that help secure the delivery of business information services, improve the user experience through Web single sign-on, and put a federated identity framework in place to create new revenue opportunities through enhanced affinity relationships with business partners and customers. Some of the key capabilities of Network Identity Solutions are:

• Federation services: Enables shared authentication with affiliate organisation web sites, web applications and web users.

- Access Management services: Securely controls access to Web and non Web-based resources (such as Wifi devices, roaming partners network equipments etc.).
- Identity Administration services: Provides centralised administration of identities, policies, and services. Authentication controls including LDAP, RADIUS, X.509v3 certificates, SafeWord token cards, anonymous and UNIX platform authentication services, Microsoft Windows NT and Windows 2000, resource-based authentication, Online Certificate Status Protocol (OCSP) validation for X.509 v3 digital certificate-based authentication.
- Provides out-of-the-box modules to help simplify integration into an existing security framework: Java Authentication and Authorisation Service (JAAS) technology-based authentication framework. An open standard, flexible, and extensible authentication architecture that enables Organiaations to customise authentication mechanisms.

A sample Logical and Physical Identity Solution Architecture is depicted in figures below.

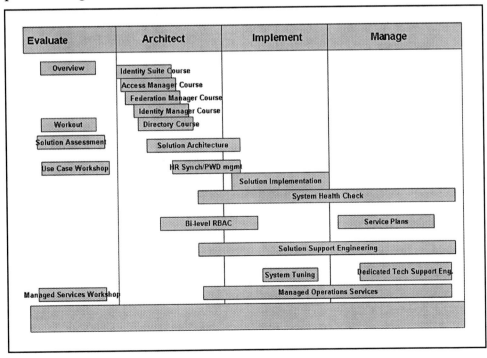

Figure 2:5 IDS Logical Architecture

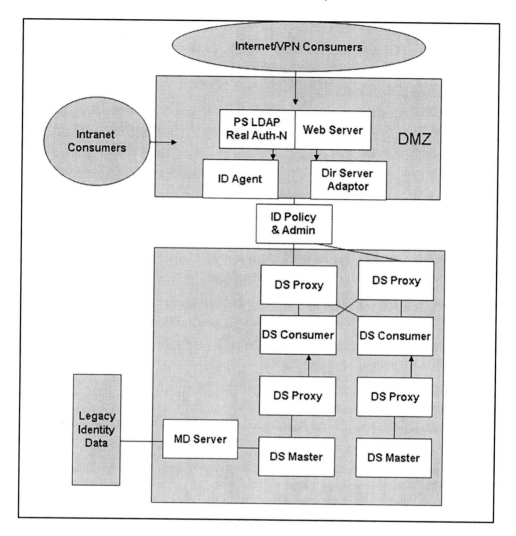

Figure 2:6 IDS Physical Architecture

The above physical sample Architecture takes into account multiple HA and Scaling techniques for the Network Identity Infrastructure. The figure above also talks about how the four subsystems of an IDS (repository, access management, federation management and provisioning) get deployed typically.

2.2.4 Approaches to Integration

With an understanding of the Value-proposition of these two solutions (Wifi/WiMAX and Network Identity) and the synergistic qualities the two bring to the table it is a natural process to see how these solutions can extend and integrate with Network Identity Solutions.

Fundamentally, there are two basic approaches to this integration and extension to Network Identity Solution. In figure above on a logical two-tier Architecture of Wifi solutions are depicted as Access Manager—AM— (running on a Web Container/Server) and the Service Manager—SM—(running on a Application/EJB Container/Server). The same deployment is possible in a WiMAX environment. There are specific policy agents that can be configured for these AM or SM as Web Server Policy Agents (for Web Servers such as Apache and JES Web Server) and Application Server Policy Agents (JES Application Server or Web Logic Application Server). If there are internal authentication mechanisms built into the AM or SM it's possible to add Identity based Authentication as a second layer of authentication. Authentication and Session Management built into AM and/or SM is more geared towards meeting the needs of OSS/BSS integration and metering the usage of the Wifi and WiMAX networks. In many cases this redundancy is not required if OSS/BSS and metering Services are handled as Services that are managed and integrated via an Identity implementation in the back-end core network.

The following five scenarios need to be understood and analysed to go over the pros and cons (analysis) of these approaches:

Note: The WifI LAN 1 can be replaced with WiMAX MAN 1 and so on to extend these scenarios to WiMAX deployments as well.

Scenario A: Multi AM mode

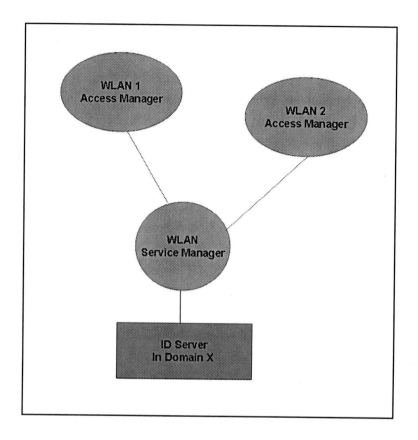

In scenario A the integration approach is simple where the Service Manager of the Wifi Solution validates the credentials of end users with an Identity Server. If the user has authenticated and has an established session with the Identity Server – he carries over his/her session between Wifi LANs (as long as the session has not timed out) that are managed by the same Service Manager. This scenario is relevant when the end user traverses Wifi networks offered by multiple hotspots such as Home Depot and Starbucks all managed with the Mall/Shopping Center's Service Manager.

Scenario B: Multi SM Mode

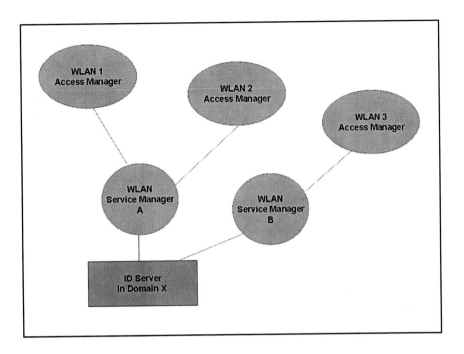

In this scenario, the user is also allowed to roam between Wifi Lans that are managed by different Service Managers. For example a Wifi LAN at the Airport vs. the Wifi LAN at Mall/Shopping Center. Now, as long as the different Service Managers extend to the same Identity Service provider for authentication/authorisation services (as the only ID Service provider or as one amongst a choice of ID Service provider), the user has seamless access between private and public Wifi Lans. However in this scenario the services accessed by the end user are limited to the single domain the ID Service provider has access to.

Scenario C: Multi SM and Multi Service Mode

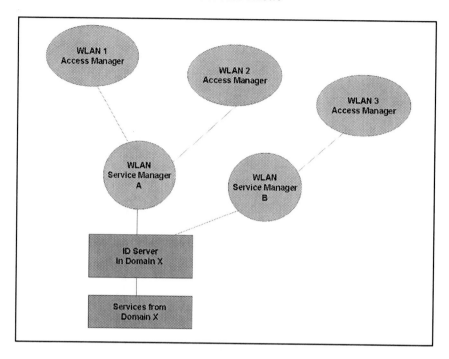

Beyond the traversal between Wifi LANs in scenarios A and B, users also require access to services that the Identity Service manages. For example if your Identity Service provider is Citibank, you could get Single Sign On/Single Sign Off and Session Management capabilities for all types of banking services offered by Citibank.com (including its subsidiaries such as Salomon Smith Barney).

Scenario D: Multi SM and Multi Service Across Domain mode

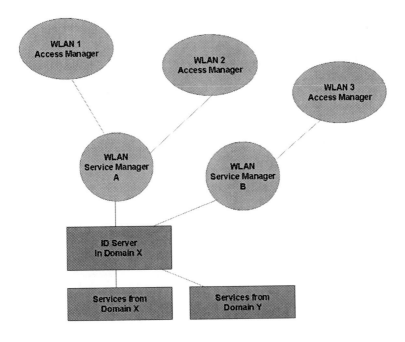

In scenario D since the Identity Service provider has built a circle of trust between its subsidiaries and partner domain/services, the end user can traverse between Wifi LANs and have access to services offered by the ID Service provider's circle of trust. This could include Tax services or Insurance services offered by Citibank's partners.

Scenario E: Multi SM and Multi Service Across Domain—Federated mode

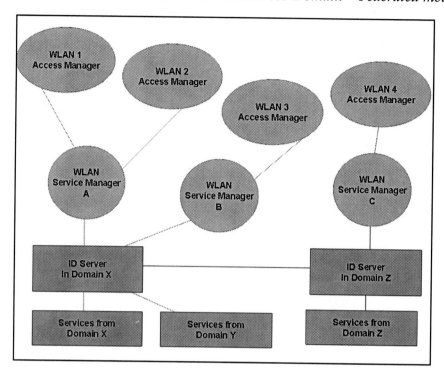

In scenario E the Federated management capabilities of the Identity solution is leveraged and through established relationships between two or more Identity service providers, end users can access services from domains managed by other Identity service providers. This is the full vision of the Liberty Alliance project, where many CSP's (such as Cingular and Nextel) and Financial Institutions (such as American Express and Bank of America) participate.

Note on Heterogeneity of the Architecture: In this conceptual approach the environment is expected to be completely heterogeneous, but based on open standards. The Identity Servers can run on Solaris/Sun Servers, the SM can run on JES Application Servers/Linux Servers, the AM could run on Apache/Linux Servers, the cross-domains can be JES Web Servers (with CDSSO) on Windows 2000, the Access point devices can be Belkin, Cisco, and others, the Identity Server Policy agents used to integrate from the AM for one Wifi solution (Bonsai Networks) and from the SM on the other Wifi solution (Pronto Networks). Access devices ranged from a Motorola Pocket Device to a Dell Latitude Laptop and other such devices.

2.4 Wire-line Access Networks

There are multiple developments in the wire-line networks that offer tremendous bandwidth as well (200MBps and more). These include Fibre to the Home (FTTH), Metro Ethernet, Cat5 Cable, ADSL, BPL (broadband over power-line) and others.

Fibre to the Home (FTTH) or fibre to the building (FTTB) is a broadband telecommunications system based on fibre-optic cables and associated optical electronics for delivery of multiple advanced services such as of telephone, broadband Internet and television across one link (triple play) all the way to the home or business.

A **Metro Ethernet** is a computer network based on the Ethernet standard and which covers a metropolitan area. It is commonly used as a metropolitan access network to connect subscribers and businesses to a Wide Area Network, such as the Internet. Large businesses can also use Metro Ethernet to connect branch offices to their Intranets.

A distinct advantage of an Ethernet-based access network is that it can be easily connected to the customer network, due to the prevalent use of Ethernet into corporate and, more recently, residential networks. Therefore, bringing Ethernet in to the Metropolitan Area Network (MAN) introduces a lot of advantages to both the service provider and the customer (corporate and residential). A typical service provider Metro Ethernet network is a collection of Layer 2 or 3 switches or routers connected through optical fibre. The topology could be a ring, hub-and-spoke (star), full mesh or partial mesh. The network will also have a hierarchy; core, distribution and access. The core in most cases is an existing IP/MPLS backbone. Ethernet on the MAN can be used as pure Ethernet, Ethernet over SDH, Ethernet over MPLS or Ethernet over DWDM. Pure Ethernet-based deployments are cheap but less reliable and scalable, and thus are usually limited to small scale or experimental deployments. SDH-based deployments are useful when there is an existing SDH infrastructure already in place, its main shortcoming being the loss of flexibility in bandwidth management due to the rigid hierarchy imposed by the SDH network. MPLS based deployments are costly but highly reliable and scalable, and are typically used by large service providers.

Category 5 cable, commonly known as Cat 5, is an unshielded twisted pair cable type designed for high signal integrity. Category 5 has been superseded by the Category 5e specification. This type of cable is often used in structured cabling for computer networks such as Ethernet, although it is also used to carry many other signals such as basic voice services, token ring, and ATM (at up to 155 Mbit/s, over short distances).

Asymmetric Digital Subscriber Line (ADSL) is a form of DSL, a data communications technology that enables faster data transmission over copper telephone lines than a conventional modem can provide. It does this by utilising frequencies that are normally not used by a voice telephone call, in particular, frequencies higher than normal human hearing. This signal will not travel very far over normal telephone cables, so ADSL can only be used over short distances, typically less than 5 km. Once the signal reaches the telephone company's local office, the ADSL signal is stripped off and immediately routed onto a conventional internet network, while any voice-frequency signal is switched into the conventional phone network. This allows a single telephone connection to be used for both ADSL and voice calls at the same time. Top bandwidth with ADSL is only 24MBps and 4MBps –upstream and downstream, which could potentially make this an outdated technology for Access Networks (however there are several million ADSL subscriber today all over the world).

Broadband over power lines (BPL), also known as power-line internet or Powerband, is the use of PLC technology to provide broadband **Internet access** through ordinary power lines. A computer (or any other device) would need only to plug a BPL "modem" into any outlet in an equipped building to have high-speed Internet access. BPL offers obvious benefits relative to regular cable or DSL connections: the extensive infrastructure already available would appear to allow more people in more (remote) locations to have access to the Internet. Also, such ubiquitous availability would make it much easier for other electronics, such as televisions or sound systems, to hook up. However, variations in the physical characteristics of the electricity network and the current lack of IEEE standards mean that provisioning of the service is far from being a standardised, repeatable process, and the amount of bandwidth a BPL system can provide compared to cable and wireless is in question. PLC modems transmit in medium and high frequency (1.6 to 30 MHz electric carrier). The asymmetric speed in the modem is generally from 256 kb/s to 2.7 Mb/s. In the repeater situated in the meter room the speed is up to 45 Mbit/s and can be connected to 256 PLC modems. In the medium voltage stations, the speed from the head ends to the Internet is up to 135 Mbit/s. To connect to the Internet, utilities can use optical fiber backbone or wireless link. Much higher speed transmissions using microwave frequencies transmitted via surface wave propagation mechanism have been demonstrated using only a single power line conductor. These systems have shown the potential for symmetric and full duplex communication well in excess of 1 Gb/s in each direction. Multiple Wifi channels as well as simultaneous analog television in the 2.4 and 5.3 GHz unlicensed bands have been demonstrated operating over medium voltage lines. Furthermore, because it can operate anywhere in the 100 MHz - 10 GHz region, this technology can completely avoid the interference issues associated with utilising spectrum shared with other services.

Similar to how we continue to have railroads after the invention of cars and highways, and we continue to have ships after the invention of airlines, all five major wire-line technologies will survive and with the exception of ADSL all the other access technologies are considered truly broadband (with several 100 MB/s bandwidth) and may contribute to the development of 4G networks as they are all IP centric.

In terms of integrating these wire-line networks similar to how an Identity systems policy agents and access manager agents run on web containers on Wifi Access Controllers and WiMAX Base Stations, these software stack can run on network gear such as an ADSL router, a Cable STB, Cable head-end, IPTV Terminal Function, BPL switch/gateway and more.

In terms of the Synergy between an Identity System in all its four layers and all the four perspectives with the 4th Generation Networks one can clearly see the significant roles played by standards and standards initiatives along with the multiple dimensions of convergence that is taking shape in the 4G all Packet Network (Internet Protocol), which is discussed in detail in section 2.3.

2.3 Standards for a Converged 4G Network

This section attempts at Aligning major Industry Standards Initiatives within what is known as the "Communications Media and Entertainment"—CME Industry that enables Open Architectures in a Converged IP Centric World. CME includes all traditional Wireless (T-Mobile, Vodafone, Verizon Wireless, Sprint, etc.), Wire-line Telecommunications companies (Verizon Communications, SBC, BT, etc.), Cable Companies (Cox, Comcast, etc.), Content (Disney, TW, etc.), Media and Entertainment Initiatives around IPTV, VOD, Digital Music, VOIP etc.

Due to the advances in the reach of IP now over different types of Access Networks (ADSL, Cable, FTTH, Satellite, Wifi/WiMAX, GSM/CDMA and more), all Services Over IP has the capability to reach all devices that connect to these Access Networks, such as, a Set Top Box/TV over Cable/DSL, PDA/CellPhone over GSM/CDMA, Laptop/Handheld devices over Wifi/WiMax, a GPS/Display Device over Satellite and more. As the throughput of these Access Networks keeps increasing it's making it possible to deliver all Services - Voice/Video/Data to all these devices across all these access networks. Hence, making it possible to receive a Call over a STB/TV (SIP/Java/OCAP) over and above interactive TV and Internet Access from the TV (as a display device). This scenario is made possible from Laptop/Handheld and PDA's/Cell Phones as well. This development is further augmented with the Circuit Switch and Packet Switch network convergence in the Core based on soft-switch solutions, along with converged services (multi-media applications) that leverage the possibilities of carrying voice, video and data to the same end points. Another key trend is the IT and Network convergence wherein, events in the Networks (sensor networks, as well as service networks) have to correlate and trigger business services and their respective IT services as well. There are composite dimensions to this Convergence, that is leading to an IP centric 4G Network environment, wherein,

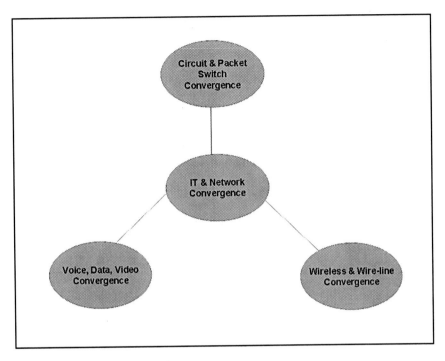

Figure 2:7 Dimensions to Convergence

Interoperability, Integration, Portability (re-place-ability), Security and Contextual Service Delivery are a set of challenges that are currently being addressed, in a manner, wherein, there are not One or a Few dominant players in each space (such as Device Manufacturers, Network Equipment Providers, Service Platform Providers, Service Enablers, Security Framework Providers etc.). Tremendous amounts of effort have been exercised by the Industry to ensure Standards Initiatives that enable Open Architectures—so that the Integrity of the Architecture is maintained across multiple Vendors Implementations. A list of such initiatives that are bringing a sea change for IP Convergence are discussed below. A sea change like this will not be possible without the concerted efforts of all members within the Industry and hence the term A Sea Change. A list of such leading Industry Standards Initiatives within CME include (not an exhaustive list):

Umbrella Bodies
- IETF & ETSI
- W3C & ISO
- TOG and OMG
- ANSI & OSI
- ITU & TMF

Wireless
- OMA and OMTP
- 3GPP (IMS/SIP) and 3GPP2
- WiMAX Forum and Wifi Alliance
- OSA/Parlay/JAIN
- CTIA

Wire-line (+ Cable)
- Ethernet Alliance
- FCIA
- Euro Cable
- Open Cable
- DVB

Media and Entertainment
- Open Media Commons (& ODRL)
- Web3D.Org (Communication with Real-time 3D)
- IMTC (international Multi-media Telecommunications Consortium)
- OSG-i

Identity Related
- Liberty & OASIS
- PayCircle (payment service providers 12+)
- SIM Alliance (SIM cards/Java enabled)
- WLAN Smartcard Consortium (wifi and wimax)
- Open Security Exchange (interoperability of security components)

The Industry Umbrella bodies such as IETF, W3C, ISO/NIST, ANSI, TOG and OMG are Standard bodies that transcend industries and their work is applicable to CME as well as other industries such as the Medical/Healthcare Industry, Automobile Industry, and Transportation Industry, Finance and Banking Industry and more. They have an impact on IT across all Industries through their standards specifications, standards testing and standards adoption. The Industry specific Organisations such as OMA and OpenCable adopt and refer to such specifications and deliverables from these Umbrella Organisations. More information on each of these Organisations can be obtained from there respective web sites (http://www.ietf.org, http://www.w3.org/, http://www.iso.org, http://www.nist.org, http://ansi.org/, http://www.omg.org/ and http://www.opengroup.org/). ITU for International Telecommunications Union and TMF for Telecommunications Management Forum are Industry specific umbrella Organisations that transcend wire-line, wireless, cable, media/entertainment and Identity related organisations. ITU's and TMF's specifications coming out of working groups and standards proposals are very powerful in terms of their direct influence over standards and specifications that come out of other wire-line and wireless specific industry bodies.

Some of the basic Alignment characteristics can be found based on relationships that are viewed by each of these Organisations and by divvying up the space into Client Terminal Level, Application Level, Transport Level, etc. OMA's view of its Alignment (with 3GPP, 3GPP2 and others):

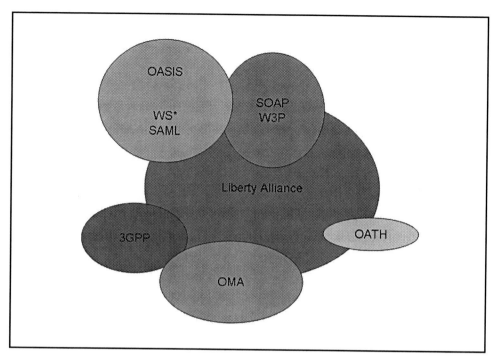

Figure 2:8 OMA Relationships

For example, OMA receives inputs from W3C and IETF and interacts extensively with 3GPP and 3GPP2. OSGi is an interesting initiative from a Java perspective and aligns with specifications coming out of OMA for DM (device management and 3GPP for other initiatives. Similarly OSE (open security exchange) has alliances with Liberty, RSA, SIA (security industry association) and receives inputs from IEEE. Open Media Commons and project DReaM aligns with other industry initiatives around DRM and DAM (rights management and asset management) such as Liberty, CORAL, OMA-DRM, CAL, ODRL and more to ensure interoperability of DRM standards for content-user centric DRM services. Taking all these developments into account if we add another level (to figure 3) above the Application Level and Transport Level - called Client Terminal Level - OMTP specification are geared towards mobile terminals, hence will fall under this category. Similarly OSGi specs for Vehicle's, Home Network and more will also fall under the Client Access layer. Open cable's specifications for the STB again are a good candidate for the Client Access layer. OMA, OCAP, OSA and OSGi gateway services will all be part of the Application Service Layer. Services that are based on a SOA (Service Oriented Architecture) and built out of a common Systems Architecture (such as JEE and related Java technologies) that supports standards such as OCAP, OMA and OSGi, can be accessed from multiple IP end points (embedded server in a vehicle or a home appliance, STB, PDA/Cell phone, etc.), based on the underlying support for Protocols or through gateways. Also WiMAX and Wifi can be placed in the other emerging Transport Level within the mobile domain and standards initiatives such as Open Cable in the Wire line domain within the transport level, as depicted below. This paradigm shift in terms of Standards based Open Architectural Approach allows for Heterogeneous and Non-Integrated environments to more, heterogeneous yet integrated and shared environments. Interoperability, Integration, Portability (re-place ability) —despite heterogeneity with Security and Contextual Service Delivery are addressed when the specifications from these initiatives are aligned. Fortunately, none of these Standards initiatives work in isolation. Similar to OMA and the Liberty Alliance, other organisation's take inputs from TMF, ETSI, ITU and other umbrella bodies and liaison, with other organisations so as to leverage and reuse the work done by others. All of these initiatives are OPEN in nature as there name suggests, OCAP, OSA, OMA, OMTP, OSE, OSGi, and more. that leads not only to an Open end to end Architecture but also towards the notion of IP Convergence, where in Services have "true mobility", accessible from all types of Network-ed Devices. Between now (2006/2007) and by the end of this decade, step changes in the wireless industry will not be characterised by a serial overlay of evolved cellular technologies, such as the move from 2G to 2.5G and now 3G. Instead, it will be marked by the addition of evermore advanced wireless standards to a mixture of local, metro and wide area wireless technologies. These wireless technologies will consist of Wifi and Ultra Wide Band (UWB) in the local area; broadband wireless access technologies like WiMAX, UMTS-TDD and Flash-OFDM in the metro area; and 3G cellular technologies like CDMA 1xEV-DO, W-CDMA and HSDPA in the wide area. This is set to create the "wireless cocktail", a mix of multiple wireless standards combined into a single service platform for the consumer, with software clients that seamlessly and automatically traverse, wireless network types, based on signal strength, accessing Services from Open Service Delivery Platforms. ATIS and IPSF are also two key industry bodies in this space.

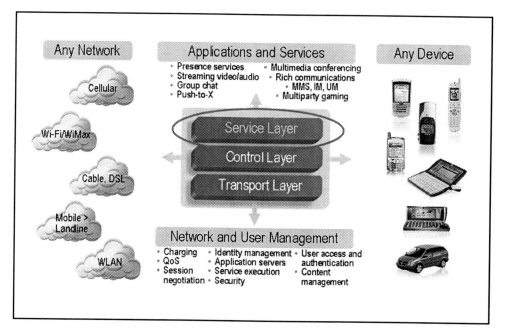

Figure 2:9 Seamless Mobility

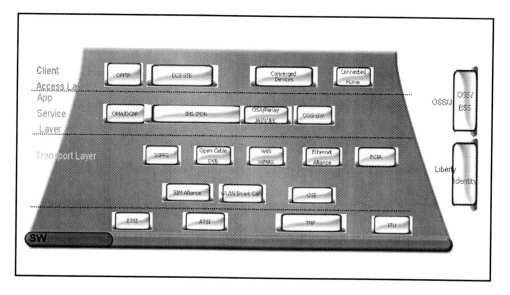

Figure 2:10 Seamless Mobility based on SW Standards

2.3.1 Identity to the Rescue

From an Identity and Security Related Standards perspective, with the alliances (Alliances for Alignment) between Project Liberty and Radicchio, PayCircle (payment service providers), SIM Alliance (SIM cards-3G), WLAN Smartcard Consortium (Wifi and WiMax) and Open Security Exchange (interoperability of security components), its clear that the Architectural Alignment can leverage a Common Security Framework - that is Access Network Agnostic, Client Device Agnostic and Authentication Mechanism Agnostic. Yet it is one that allows for a Distributed (and federated) Session Management, Distributed (and Correlated) Policy Enforcement and a Distributed (and contextual) Profile Sharing Facility. Federation and Identity Systems are reference by the IPSphere Forum as well for the Policy and Control Stratum (Identity Centric Architecture) aligning SOA (Service Signaling Stratum) with the NGN (Packet handling Stratum). These alliances, allow for the Re-USE of Services (all IP Services -Entertainment-IPTV/VOD, Communication (VOIP/SIP) and Business Services) for delivery to more complex client devices, due to the notion of de-coupled presentation logic, provisioning logic and security (policies). Through the use of trans-coding services, display transformation services, a set of rich User Interfaces can be provided for the same service based on the Access Network type and Client device type. Identity Systems and their respective Open API's are leveraged by end user devices such as PDA, STB and more with the use of strong authentication and smart cards, along with embedded devices such as Base Station Controllers, Wifi Access Controllers and more. This ensures that policies can be invoked at the edge to apply the appropriate restrictions. Federated Identity and Policies also ensure that the appropriate context, across service networks and access networks can be shared based on secure profile sharing and Identity Service Integration Service and XML Schema Definitions.

2.4 Conclusion

The proliferation of Wifi and WiMAX networks cannot be stopped. Airline manufacturing companies are looking into embedding Wifi and WiMAX networks in planes and airline carriers are promoting such services in flight. New startup companies in new leased office space do not setup wired LANs anymore; they simply deploy a Wifi LAN in a day. Larger enterprises are deploying Wifi LANs across all their office locations and inter-linking them with VPN or a Wifi Mesh. Wifi Mesh Networks are a common scene in developing countries that are looking to low-cost alternatives. The advances in wire-line access networks such as BPL, DSL, Cable, etc. compliment these Wifi networks rather than compete with them due to performance factors and the requirements around private/secure local networks. Traversal between Wifi LANs and WiMax WANs are made seamless with varying throughput. Wifi and WiMAX networks enhance the usefulness of related technologies such as Infrared and RFID. Identity plays a key role here between all these advances in technologies including RFID. This end scenario eventually offers true ubiquity for end users accessing not just Wifii and WiMax networks but also all other types of networks as envisioned by the 4G network working group. These developments along with standards such as SOAP, SAML, XKMS, XACML, XRI and RFID, also extend the capabilities of Identity Solutions to validate not just web users, but validate identity of web devices (user devices, network devices and RDID devices), web services, web sites and web applications.

One key development that needs to be noted is the potential reach of an IMS network into all these 4G access networks, with the HSS (a network facing Identity System). Majority of the NEP (such as Ericsson and Alcatel) may integrate there WiMAX and Wifi gear with IMS solutions created. Even with heavy market acceptance of IMS in 2007, 2008 and 2009, IMS's reach may not include all the access networks in its entirety (maybe by 2015). In such situations (see Identity enabled IMS chapter), the Federation Manager Layer integration of an IDS with an HSS allows for demarcation between to types of IDS (one that is Network facing and another that is Service and Content facing). Therefore regardless of a user session's PATH (direct to IDS) or via an IMS seamless access to service that the user is entitled to is possible.

The integration of Services, Network elements, Devices and Users data with Network Identity and a pervasive programming paradigm (end-to-end Java) that supports multiple standards, helps set the foundation for context driven/preference based session centric, content/service delivery to all Access networks and Access devices. This implies leveraging an Identity System and other related security tools to validate the identity of not only users and web sites, but also validation of identity of nodes, network elements, devices and services. A sea change brought by all these standards initiatives, leads to convergence, wherein the User gets bombarded and overwhelmed with ubiquitous reach and proliferation of Services. Identity Systems offers Control and ensures that contextual delivery of Services is made possible. so that the User gets whatever he/she wants, when he/she wants it, where ever with non-intrusive behaviours (acting as the policy and control stratum). Convergence in this IP Centered world also includes Sensor networks (not just request response but also sense response) and the Programmability of Service Networks, Core Network elements and programmable client devices. Given this convergence in the Core Network and wide success of sensor Access Networks and dynamic programmable IP services deployed in the Service Networks, for a pervasive virtual personal network to flourish, a heavy emphasis on the User (a user's identity, a user's sessions and a user's context) is mandated and an Identity System that is extended to all layers and types of networks and all programmable IP services within the Service Network becomes highly critical, to address "mobility with security".

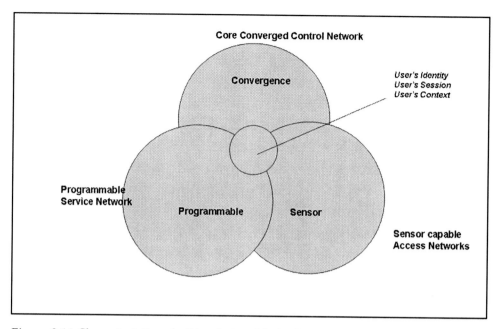

Figure 2:11 Characteristics of a Identity enabled 4G Network

3. Identity enabled Sensor Networks

3.1 Introduction and Overview

In September 2004, a paper titled "Identity enabled Networks- The Core Service Building Block of Service Oriented Architectures" was published *http://www.opengroup.org/events/q405/idesoa.pdf*. It was part of a series on SOA "Service Oriented Architectures" and discussed how an Identity System is the Core Service Building Block (SBB) in a SOA. This five part series included:

- Model Driven Architecture enabling Service Oriented Architectures *http://www.opengroup.org/events/q405/mdasoa.pdf*
- Identity Enabled Networks –The Core Service BB of Service Oriented Architectures *http://www.opengroup.org/events/q405/idesoa.pdf*
- Event Driven Architectures augmenting Oriented Architectures *http://www.opengroup.org/events/q405/edamdasoa.pdf*
- Component based Architectures supplementing Service Oriented Architectures *http://www.opengroup.org/events/q405/cbaedamdasoa.pdf*
- Utility Compute Architectures supporting Service Oriented Architectures *http://www.opengroup.org/events/q405/ucacbaedamdasoa.pdf*

The IDEN paper also highlighted how an Identity System acts as the glue between Services, Data, Users, Devices and Networks within the Context of SOA. The IDEN chapter also explored the possibilities around Telecom Industry initiatives (3GPP's GUP, IETF's ENUM, TMF's ETOM, etc.), and how they are applied to IDEN—such as GUP (generic user profile)—folding into WS-PP, Web Services Personal Profile (as part of the liberty alliance and liberty specifications) and more.

This chapter on identity enabled sensor networks is part of the first six chapters from a network and network services perspective that expands on the notion of "Identity Enabled Networks", that includes:

- Identity enabled 4G Networks
- Identity enabled Sensor Networks
- Identity enabled Programmable Networks
- Identity enabled IMS Network Services
- Identity enabled NG IN Services
- Identity enabled OAM&P Services

Each introduces the Identity System from the respective perspective around sensor, pervasive, programmable and converged Next Generation networks from an Access Network, Core Network, Service Network perspective and the value proposition combined with synergies brought to these networks by an Identity system acting as the Central "user centric" glue.

3.2 Sensor Networks

In chapter 1 we discussed the significance of an Identity System from a Networking perspective and described how an Identity System transcends Service Networks, the Core Network and different Access Networks to offer Services to all types of devices.

Amongst these three tiers of networks discussed here namely; a) Service Networks (a.k.a. Service Delivery Networks—Programmable Networks for IP Service Delivery), b) Core Network (Core Converged Networks—where the Softswitch acts as the OS of the Converged Network) and c) Access Networks (abstracted as Virtual Personal Networks that transcends Wireless and Wire-line broadband access) –sensors play a major role in all three, especially in more highly evolved Service (or Service Delivery—SDN) networks, Core Converged Next Generation Networks and in all types of Access Networks. Service Networks are the Service Delivery Networks that host Services and

Content (see *http://www.sun.com/service/sunps/architect/delivery/sdn-arch-overview.pdf*), and are run by either service providers for enterprises or enterprises within its enterprise network. Services hosted can include traditional business applications, (such as ERP, SCM, etc,), web services, IP communication services, IP entertainment services etc. The Service Delivery Networks typically leverage extensive OS security capabilities such as, Secure Execution, Process/User Rights Management, Service Containers, Cryptographic Frameworks and more in addition to many Network security capabilities.

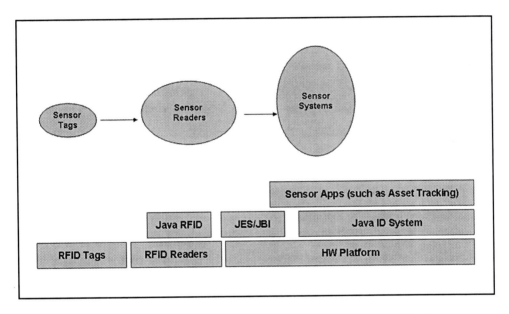

Figure 3:1 Identity enabled Sensor Network for Asset Tracking Application

The Core network is typically run by the Telecom companies/Carriers, with the main purpose of providing connectivity between Service networks and different types of Access Networks with Session Control and a Security Framework. The core network is evolving into a converged network, today, with the implementation of "soft switches" and the likes that integrate both "packet based" core and the "circuit-switch" based core. Within the Core Control layer a set of Services run: typically run by telecom companies, again, such as MM applications (Multi-media), OAM applications, OSS services, routing services and more. However, lately with the implementation of large scale Identity Systems by telecom companies worldwide, such as Telstra in Australia, to Vodafone in Europe to Cingular in the US, an Identity System not only acts as a Core Service Building Block in a "Service Oriented Architecture" but also becomes a Core Service that is hosted within the Core Network and allows for federation of many services from many Service Networks (SDN). There are varying types of Access networks as depicted in the figure, that allow for many types of devices, including cell phones, PDA/handhelds, TV, embedded devices in a CAR (such as ONStar and Navigation systems), and more to access services from the service networks via the core.

Although the role played by wireless sensor technology within the core and service network is significant, this chapter focuses on the strategic role played by sensor technology within access networks and when combined with identity systems the significance it has on many industries including inventory management/supply chain, retail services, health care/hospitals, mobile workforces from an information management, perspectives.

The follow-on chapters also align specific types (programmable, sensor, converged etc.) to specific tiers within the network. For example, programmable networks are more relevant and prevalent in the service network space, convergence (PSTN/IP etc.) are more relevant and prevalent in the core network and more. This is not to say that convergence is not taking shape in the Service network in the form of converged services (applications that use voice (over IP), Video (over IP) and Data services together), or the Access Networks (wire-line/wireless, P2P/personal). Similarly, programmability is critical for active/sensor networks and the core network that has embedded network elements.

3.2.1 What is a Sensor Network?

Wireless sensor networks are potentially one of the most important technologies of this century. Consequently, billions of dollars are being committed to the research and development of sensor networks in order to address the many technical challenges and wide range of immediate applications. Advances in hardware development have made available the prospect of low cost, low power, miniature devices for use in remote sensing applications. The combination of these factors has improved the viability of utilising a sensor network consisting of a large number of intelligent sensors, enabling the collection, processing analysis and dissemination of valuable information gathered in a variety of environments. A sensor network is an array (possibly very large) of sensors of diverse type interconnected by a communications network. Sensor data is shared between the sensors and used as input to a distributed estimation system which aims to extract as much relevant information from the available sensor data. The fundamental objectives for sensor networks are reliability, accuracy, flexibility, cost effectiveness and ease of deployment. A sensor network is made up of individual multifunctional sensor nodes. The sensor node itself may be composed of various elements such as various multi-mode sensing hardware (acoustic, seismic, infrared, magnetic, chemical, imagers, micro radars), embedded processor, memory, power-supply, communications device (wireless and/or wired) and location determination capabilities (through local or global techniques). Sensor networks are predominantly data-centric rather than address-centric. That is, queries are directed to a region containing a cluster of sensors rather than specific sensor addresses. Given the similarity in the data obtained by sensors in a dense cluster, aggregation of the data is performed locally. That is, a summary or analysis of the local data is prepared by an aggregator node within the cluster, thus reducing the communication bandwidth requirements. Aggregation of data increases the level of accuracy and incorporates data redundancy to compensate node failures. A network hierarchy and clustering of sensor nodes allows for network scalability, robustness, efficient resource utilisation and lower power consumption. Dissemination of sensor data in an efficient manner requires the dedicated routing protocols to identify shortest paths. Redundancy must be accounted for to avoid congestion resulting from different nodes sending and receiving the same information. At the same time, redundancy must be exploited to ensure network reliability. Data dissemination may be either query driven or based on continuous updates. A sensor network can be described by services, data and physical layer respectively. Recognising the significance of sensor networks and the associated network protocol requirements, the IEEE has defined a standard for personal area networks, (the IEEE 802.15 standard), specifically for networks with a 5 to 10 m radius. Implicit throughout the operation of a sensor network is a variety of information processing techniques for the manipulation and analysis of sensor data, extraction of significant features, along with the efficient storage and transmission of the important information. *(Defined by http://www. sensornetworks.net.au).*

Professor Jim Kurose of the University of Massachusetts (UMass) defines Sensor networks as "a sensing, computing and communication infrastructure that allows us to instrument, observe and respond to phenomena in the natural environment and in our physical and cyber infrastructure. The sensors themselves can range from small passive micro sensors (e.g., "smart dust") to larger scale, controllable weather-sensing platforms. Their computation and communication infrastructure will be radically different from that found in today's Internet-based systems, reflecting the device- and application-driven nature of these systems".

There are a wide range of benefits of these sensor networks, namely:

Sensing accuracy: The utilisation of a larger number and variety of sensor nodes provides potential for greater accuracy in the information gathered as compared to that obtained from a single sensor. The ability to effectively increase sensing resolution without necessarily increasing network traffic will increase the reliability of the information for the end user application.

Area coverage: A distributed wireless network incorporating sparse network properties will enable the sensor network to span a greater geographical area without adverse impact on the overall network cost.

Fault tolerance: Device redundancy and consequently information redundancy can be utilised to ensure a level of fault tolerance in individual sensors.

Connectivity: Multiple sensor networks may be connected through sink nodes, along with existing wired networks (e.g. Internet). The clustering of networks enables each individual network to focus on specific areas or events and share only relevant information with other networks enhancing the overall knowledge base through distributed sensing and information processing.

Minimal human interaction: The potential for self-organising and self-maintaining networks along with highly adaptive network topology significantly reduce the need for further human interaction with a network other than the receipt of information.

Operability in harsh environments: Robust sensor design, integrated with high levels of fault tolerance and network reliability enable the deployment of sensor networks in dangerous and hostile environments, allowing access to information previously unattainable from such close proximity.

Dynamic sensor scheduling: Dynamic reaction to network conditions and the optimisation of network performance through sensor scheduling. This may be achieved by enabling the sensor nodes to modify communication requirements in response to network conditions and events detected by the network, so that essential information is given the highest priority.

3.2.2 Applications and capabilities of this technology

The application and capabilities of this technology includes:

- Low cost, scalable surveillance solutions using unmanned devices as an integrated sensor network for theft/loss of property in retail, warehouse and home locations.
- Advanced surveillance networks incorporating automated anomaly detection and adaptive reasoning in conjunction with secure protocols for event reporting (when tightly integrated with identity system and logical and physical access control mechanisms are correlated).

- Early disaster monitoring of sensitive environments (in the event of bushfires or flooding for example), employing a large geographically distributed sparse sensor network, utilising inbuilt communication capabilities to potentially save lives as well as minimise associated economic impacts. (As well as protecting products and inventory in retail and warehouse locations).

- Reconfigurable networks able to optimise performance and information collection and dissemination according to varying local conditions and sensor node failure or isolation (in conjunction with identity based services such as location and weather services).

- Manufacturing control utilising a network of intelligent sensors able to collect various information pertaining to local weather, water supply and conditions in such a way as too provide feedback for the efficient distribution of water/electricity (from wind mills), integrated with long and short term forecasts.

- Infrastructure security through a network and variety of sensor types provided early warnings of potential problems threats and reducing false positive alarms through the fusion of information from multiple sensor types.

- Industrial sensing for equipment monitoring and maintenance, as well as efficiency enhancements in process flow.

- Embedded device sensors in cars (automotives), TV/STB, Cell phones, PDA's, RFID equipments, etc.).

- Sensors on humans (for varying uses –such as continuous monitoring of heart/pulse, blood pressure, and more).

3.2.2.1 Sample Use cases of Sensors in conjunction with user's Identity

Biometrics:

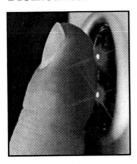

How it works: Customers register their fingerprints with a bank account and, at checkout, scan their fingers to pay for a transaction.
Provider: Pay by Touch, BioPay
Adoption: Pay By Touch has 100 customers in ten states, most of whom are just testing the technology.
Case study: Grocery chain Piggly Wiggly saw a 15% customer adoption.
Pros: Fingers can't be lost or left behind at home.

Large scale commercial deployments of such systems in the retail markets would require features such as federation management, access management and SSO, where the provider pay-by touch and bio pay, align their service with a Circle of Trust (for example a COT formed by Best Buy, Safeway, Home depot, and others). A restaurant chain that is part of this COT might even leverage the ID system (in conjunction with the bio-metric sensors) to offer customised menu's based on preferences and profile of the consumer.

Short-Range Radio Frequency:

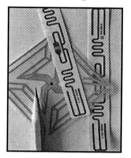

How it works: Credit cards or small gadgets embedded with a micro-chip are waved in front of readers instead of swiped and signed.

Provider: JP Morgan Chase's Visa and MasterCards, MBNA's Master-Card and Exxon Mobil's Speed Pass.

Adoption: ABI Research expects between 35 million and 50 million embedded cards to be accepted at up to 50,000 locations by the end of 2006.

Case Study: JPMorgan Chase, Citibank and MBNA issued 16,000 embedded cards in 2003. Given the option, 20% of consumers opt for this method over cash. Exxon Mobil has over 6 million subscribers.

Pros: Faster than paying by cash or credit.

Large scale commercial deployments of such systems in the gas stations/service stations would require features such as federation management, access management and SSO, where the provider such as speed-pass, align their services with a Circle of Trust (for example a COT formed by Acura Service, Exxon Mobile, and others). A service station (such as an Acura dealership based service) that is part of this COT might even leverage the ID system (in conjunction with the embedded sensors) to offer pro-active maintenance services based on preferences and profile of the owner of the vehicle (where the owner has opted-in for such pro-active service as part of an extended service warranty).

Transponders

How it works: Dashboard transponders automatically deduct payments from prepaid accounts when driving past or under a road reader.

Provider: Various regional companies, such as FasTrack, E-ZPass, SunPass, EZ Tag and FastLane.

Adoption: Traffic Technologies, which helps agencies set up automated tolls, estimates 15 million users nationwide.

Case Study: With its toll-heavy highways, New York's E-ZPass has 6 million subscribers.

Pros: Drivers don't have to dig for change.

A large scale national and global deployment of these systems will require capabilities such as federation, secure framework to share profiles/preferences etc. If each system works independently, users can't use a transponder from one system on another. For a user driving from Virginia to California or renting a Car in Germany (when he/she is from the US) — one single transponder device will allow for global roaming when an Identity system is integrated.

Infrared

How it works: Consumers list their bank accounts, credit card information and merchant loyalty programs in their Palm handhelds and beam the information to the merchant's readers at checkout. After payment is processed, the reader beams back an electronic receipt and coupons to the handheld.

Provider: VeriFone, Ingenico, PalmSource, Visa

Adoption: Because the technology hasn't been rolled out to merchants on a large-scale basis, actual adoption rates are unavailable.

Pros: The software can use coupons and sync electronic receipts with other financial tracking software.

A large scale national and global deployment of these systems will require capabilities such as federation and secure framework to share profiles/preferences etc. If each system works independently, users can't use these services from one system on another. For a user traversing different retail chains (such as Sears, PF Changs and more) being part of a COT and feeding their profile/preferences into the Identity Provider, will allow for seamless traversal and usage of such services.

Mobile Phones

How it works: For vending machines and other automated systems, consumers call a number and radio signals trigger the machine to dispense the product. The charge for the product and the call appears on the phone bill. Consumers can also wave cell phones that are embedded with a chip or Bluetooth-enabled at a receiver to buy product.
Provider: Nokia, NTT DoCoMo, Motorola
Adoption: In South Korea and Japan, there are over 3 million users and 20,000 locations accepting cell phones as payments.
Case Study: The phone payment method works at Coca-Cola vending machines in Europe and parking lots in Amsterdam.
Pros: Fast and convenient, since cell phone usage is ubiquitous throughout Asia.

Again a large scale national and global deployment of these systems will require capabilities such as federation and secure framework to share profiles/preferences etc. If each system works independently, users can't use these services from one system on another. For a user traveling from Japan to Amsterdam to the US and using such different services being part of a COT and feeding their profile/preferences into the Identity Provider, will allow for seamless traversal and usage of such services.

Based on these use cases and based on certain inherent characteristics it is clear the there are a base set of
security requirements that need to be addressed.

3.3 Base set of Security requirements for sensor networks

Authors of Eliana Stayrou and others define sensor network's security requirements as follows;

As mentioned earlier in this chapter, "sensor networks are used in a number of domains that handle sensitive information. Due to this, there are many considerations that should be investigated and are related with protecting sensitive information traveling between nodes (which are either sensor nodes or the base station) from been disclosure to unauthorised third parties. The scope of this section is to analyse basic security concepts before moving into a detailed discussion of the various security issues. It is essential to first understand the security requirements that are raised in a sensor environment; by doing so, we could apply appropriate security techniques to ensure the protection and safety of data and systems involved in a more spherical approach. By knowing what we are trying to protect, we could develop a comprehensive and strong security approach to overcome possible security breaches; after all, in order to protect something you must first know that is in danger. Since sensor networks are still a developing technology, researchers and developers agree that their efforts should be concentrated in developing and integrating security from the initial phases of sensor applications development; by doing so, they hope to provide a stronger and complete protection against illegal activities maintaining at the same time the stability of the system, rather than adding on security functionality after the application is finished. Moving on, the next section analyses the security requirements that constitute fundamental objectives based on which every sensor application should adhere in order to guarantee an appropriate level of security.

Confidentiality

Confidentiality requirement is needed to ensure that sensitive information is well protected and not revealed to unauthorised third parties. The confidentiality objective is required in sensors' environment to protect information traveling between the sensor nodes of the network or between the sensors and the base station from disclosure, since an adversary having the appropriate equipment may eavesdrop on the communication. By eavesdropping, the adversary could overhear critical information such as sensing data and routing information. Based on the sensitivity of the data stolen, an adversary may cause severe damage since he can use the sensing data for many illegal purposes i.e. sabotage blackmail. For example, competitors may use the data to produce a better product i.e. safety monitoring sensor application. Furthermore, by stealing routing information the adversary could introduce his own malicious nodes into the network in an attempt to overhear the entire communication. If we consider eavesdropping to be a network level threat, then a local level threat could be a compromised node that an adversary has in his possession. Compromised nodes are a big threat to confidentiality objective since the adversary could steal critical data stored on nodes such as cryptographic keys that are used to encrypt the communication.

Authentication

As in conventional systems, authentication techniques verify the identity of the participants in a communication, distinguishing in this way legitimate users from intruders. In the case of sensor networks, it is essential for each sensor node and base station to have the ability to verify that the data received was really send by a trusted sender and not by an adversary that tricked legitimate nodes into accepting false data. If such a case happens and false data are supplied into the network, then the behavior of the network could not be predicted and most of times will not outcome as expected. Authentication objective is essential to be achieved when clustering of nodes is performed. I remind you that clustering involves grouping nodes based on some attribute such as their location, sensing data etc. and that each cluster usually has a cluster head that is the node that joins its cluster with the rest of the sensor network (meaning that the communication among different clusters is performed through the cluster heads). In these cases, where clustering is required, there are two authentication situations which should be investigated; first it is critical to ensure that the nodes contained in each cluster will exchange data only with the authorised nodes contained and which are trusted by the specified cluster (based on some authentication protocol). Otherwise, if nodes within a cluster receive data from nodes that are not trusted within the current community of nodes and further process it, then the expected data from that cluster will be based on false data and may cause damage. The second authentication situation involves the communication between the cluster heads of each cluster; communication must be established only with cluster heads that can prove their identity. No malicious node should be able to masquerade as a cluster head and communicate with a legitimate cluster head, sending it false data or either compromising exchanged data.

Integrity

Moving on to the integrity objective, there is the danger that information could be altered when exchanged over insecure networks. Lack of integrity could result in many problems since the consequences of using inaccurate information could be disastrous, for example for the healthcare sector where lives are endangered. Integrity controls must be implemented to ensure that information will not be altered in any unexpected way. Many sensor applications, such as pollution and healthcare monitoring, rely on the integrity of the information to function with accurate outcomes; it is unacceptable to measure the magnitude of the pollution caused by chemicals waste and find out later on that the information provided was improperly altered by the factory that was located near by the monitored lake. Therefore, there is an urgent need to make sure that information is traveling from one end to the other without being intercepted and modified in the process.

Freshness

One of the many attacks launched against sensor networks is the message replay attack where an adversary may capture messages exchanged between nodes and replay them later to cause confusion to the network. Data freshness objective ensures that messages are fresh, meaning that they obey in a message ordering and have not been reused. To achieve freshness, network protocols must be designed in a way to identify duplicate packets and discard them preventing potential mix-up.

Secure Management

Management is required in every system that is constituted from multi components and handles sensitive information. In the case of sensor networks, we need secure management on base station level; since sensor nodes communication ends up at the base station, issues like key distribution to sensor nodes in order to establish encryption and routing information need secure management. Furthermore, clustering requires secure management as well, since each group of nodes may include a large number of nodes that need to be authenticated with each other and exchange data in a secure manner. In addition, clustering in each sensor network can change dynamically and rapidly. Therefore, secure protocols for group management are required for adding and removing members and authenticating data from groups of nodes.

Availability

Availability ensures that services and information can be accessed at the time that they are required. In sensor networks there are many risks that could result in loss of availability such as sensor node capturing and denial of service attacks. Lack of availability may affect the operation of many critical real time applications like those in the healthcare sector that require a 24/7 operation that could even result in the loss of life. Therefore, it is critical to ensure resilience to attacks targeting the availability of the system and find ways to fill in the gap created by the capturing or disablement of a specific node by assigning its duties to some other nodes in the network.

Quality of Service

Quality of Service objective is a big headache to security. And when we are speaking about sensor networks with all the limitations they have (reference the second part of the article to find out more on limitations), quality of service becomes even more constrained. Security mechanisms must be lightweight so that the overhead caused for example by encryption must be minimised and not affect the performance of the network. Performance and quality in sensor networks involve the timely delivery of data to prevent for example propagation of pollution and the accuracy with which the data reported match what is actually occurring in their environment.

The majority of these requirements and others revolving around distributed sessions, a session's context, rules/policies and more can be addressed when an Identity System is fully leveraged.

3.4 Identity enabled Sensor Networks

There are a few key related technologies to Sensor Networks such as RFID (radio frequency identification) technology that has gained popularity due to requirements mandated by firms such as Wal-Mart, and many others. Also due to the nature of RFID and Sensor devices and Sensor networks, embedding Event Containers and Execution Environments within the core and service networks (such as JAIN SLEE —also see references on "Event Driven Architecture augmenting Service Oriented Architectures)", provides the pathway to take the information generated form Sensor Networks and act on them through the execution of Services based on the data. Other related technologies include ECC (elliptic cryptography), Sizzle (a small print http/s server), biometrics, etc. JXTA a P2P system development framework and technology as well as JINI/Java Spaces a robust Technology Framework embedded in contemporary Grid Computing environments also leverage Sensor technology to a great extent. From this context we see clearly the role played by an Identity System—as the glue between "Services", "Networks" and "Data"—generated form Sensors/Sensor Networks, ranging from sensor enabled personal networks, sensor enabled peer-to-peer networks and sensor enabled contemporary grids as well.

Reasons for Identity enabling Sensor Networks:

Based on the discussions so far the key value proposition of an Identity Systems for Sensor Networks (and the Data they generate) includes;

- Appropriate invocation of Notifications—IM, SMS, email or simple electronic messages
- Appropriate invocation of Services—Multi-media (IMS) and web services (any IP service)
- Appropriate correlation of Data and Events to Users (users as an employee, as a consumer etc.)
- Appropriate security Framework around a Sensor Network and the respective data collected
- Applying Rules & Policies based on Sensor device data (programmability)

- Applying Rules & Policies based on Sensor's collected data (water condition/sprinkler system etc.)
- Applying users preference onto Sensor networks (Home Security Alarm and Owner interventions)
- Applying Event Models based on changes (adaptive networks and information centric development)
- Applying Intelligence to Sensor Networks in conjunction with Users (personal network such as Bluetooth, WLAN such as 802.11g and WWAN such as GPRS/UMTS)
- Applying User Centricity to P2P Services based on JXTA technology platform – within Sensor networks
- Applying User Centricity to Grid Services based on JINI technology platform - within Sensor networks

To highlight the last point made it is important to understand the central and integral role played by an identity system today. An identity system acts as the host of several identities of a user, manages the user's sessions across devices and transcending access networks (agnostic to access network) providing access to appropriate application and creating a personal environment for the end-user. Using the popular example of a Sprinkler System in one's million dollar home, imagine the capability to manage the systems schedule and operations from anywhere in the world from your handheld, in response to the sensor's data generated (embedded as part of the sprinkler system). Such management capabilities can be offered to a user to manage any electronic home device (TV, VCR, DVD, Stereo, refrigerator, kitchen appliances, washer dryer, heating/plumbing, bulbs, spa, swimming pool and more). The same is true to a warehouse environment, retail center, office complex etc. This is what Sun's CTO (Dr. Greg Papadopoulos) refers to as the next big wave (an IP heartbeat in everything). Once we achieve this digitisation we need a common security framework that can validate the identities of users, services, devices, networks and things, plus correlate the data associated with a user in relation to devices, services, networks and things. This common security framework can be implemented with an Identity System, along with the appropriate context (such as location and presence coupled with contextual data associated with heat, moisture, erosion, etc.).

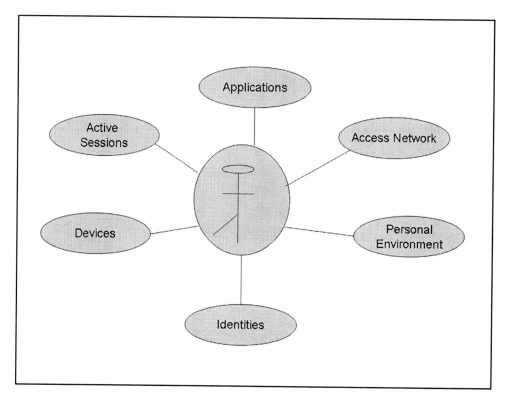

Figure 3:2 Identity linking devices and sensor + personal networks via Generic

Imagine the sensor devices embedded in your SUV detect a failure with your tyre or brakes and interacts with your GPS system to display all available open tyre or brakes stores within a 10 mile radius, with the additional information on the availability of stock for your specific make. This requires an identity system that is integrated with the GPS system in your SUV, integrated with the sensor devices, the inventory software on the retail stores, location based services and more to offer the additional level of convenience to an end user—which could potentially be a market differentiator for a BMW or Lexus. This requires small/miniature footprint http servers running on sensor networks with ECC type security mechanism and an Identity System tightly integrated to the same via Agents similar to an Identity System's integration to web containers (JSE), application containers (JEE) and Event Containers (JAIN SLEE). This extension is made possible through the SDK offered for Identity Systems, similar to Sun Java Identity System. Imagine the convenience to consumers who get notification (based on their presence either via IM, SMS, email, call etc.), from the sensors in the refrigerator that cooling cannot be sustained — in conjunction with a service call placed to a serviceman "by the refrigerator" with appropriate service policy code/number etc. This requires the user feeding their respective GE appliance service profile, call-in number etc., and such a profile being managed by the identity system, along with the identity enabled versions of the notification services. Similarly there are several thousand scenarios and use cases that can be practically possible with the integration of sensor networks to identity systems. Another significance of Identity and Sensors can be viewed from a P2P/Jxta Services perspective. In a personal network enabled with p2p technology is for a user to carry his services, experiences and data (files, photos, videos etc.) across all access networks and devices. That is he/she can consume the services from a display in a Car/SUV, from a workstation at work or from a TV at home. Jxta as a technology lets you abstract the physical network with a Jxta virtual network of peers, which can be accessed from many devices. These personal networks can have embedded sensors playing a key role at the physical layer, yet offering that information to the virtual layer based on the security framework that an Identity system offers.

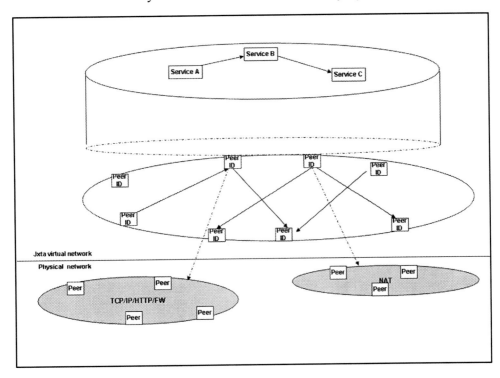

Figure 3:3 Identity enabled Personal Network (with Sensors)

One example of a personal network, that leverages sensors, where an Identity system adds additional security, user centricity and commercialisation (from a Carrier perspective) involves for example a Sprinkler system (either in a commercial complex – such as a Hotel or an Office complex or a residential system). Sensors add value by adjusting the frequency of watering based on changing weather conditions, automatically (such as rain delay). Adding the concepts behind a personal network, what it would give the end user is the capability to manage and administer this sprinkler system from anywhere, on any device as long as the Service management interfaces get exported and access able by multiple peers (i.e., from a device embedded in a SUV while the user is traveling or from a PDA/Cell phone or from the UI embedded in the Garage). Now by identity enabling this environment – one can actually align other services and behaviour of such services from other business entities. Let's say that we have the service contract on these sprinkler systems with a firm named Bio Turf, wherein they service the sprinkler system every six months and fix any problems as part of the annual service agreement (renewable at a pre-determined rate). Typically in a situation like a pipe being cut by the lawn mower – will involve manual turn-off of the water supply and making a call to the service provider (such as Bio Turf), however if you are on vacation for 4 weeks in July – the consumer will find the grass dry and almost dead – by the time he/she places a service call. Instead with federated identity systems, as part of the user profile – one can add a number to call in such circumstances, have the service provider validate such a request/call by the system (with the user) via email, notification, sms etc. and have it fixed the very next day (as part of the service contract). This would involve provisioning such a service (from Bio Turf) for the user and might involve federation (for example between Marriott properties and Bio Turf that belong to different Circles of Trusts), setting up a profile where Marriott opts in for such a pro-active service for a premium etc. This perspective can be applied to any physical product, its supplier and its maintenance service providers for consumers (whether individual residential consumers or business consumers). By offering an Identity System's services as a IDP (Identity Service Provider) – telecom companies have the opportunity to offer such commercial competitively differentiating COT's.

AT&T (former SBC, BellSouth and AT&T) in the US has just launched a remote-home monitoring service that lets users control home lighting and appliances live via Cingular's Wireless phones or their PC's. These are some of the services offered, in conjunction with Nobu and i-Control Networks:

- Smart Sprinklers -turns off when it rains
- Medicine Cabinet doors are detected when opened
- Caller ID displayed on TV (when watching TV)
- Blinds are centrally controlled
- Movie setting dims the lights
- Live video of your pets or nanny is sent to phone
- Motion sensors send a message when windows/doors open
- Garage door can be opened and closed from work
- Pool temperature set on the drive home

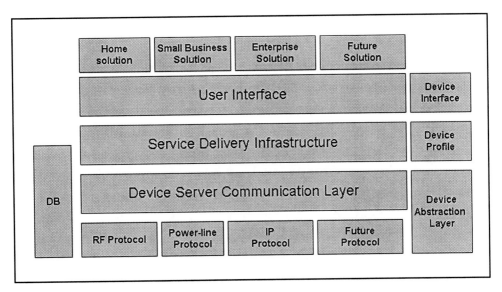

Figure 3:4 RF Protocol invoking Services

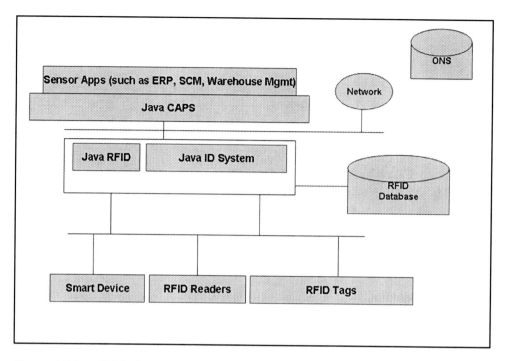

Figure 3:5 Java RFID System Architecture

All these developments in terms of sensor home networks and sensor corporate networks are actually delivering more power in the palm of your hand via mobile devices offered by wireless carriers. We are definitely entering a new era where the possibilities are infinite in terms of network evolution. Imagine the user being in a position to define his/her key important things (such as cars, garage doors etc.) to the network and being in a position to select amongst many expected behaviour of services with regards to those things. This is where the NG Identity Systems will evolve into (the policy and control stratum) areas such as—call me when any of my automobiles are speeding beyond 10miles over the speed limit (regardless of who is driving it).

3.5 Extending Internet Security to Wireless Sensors

Today e-commerce on the Internet would not be possible, if not for TLS (transport level security) and its predecessor SSL (Secure Socket Layer) that ensures privacy and security for online transactions. SSL/TLS is supported on the server (Web Server) and the client side (Web Browser). The use of SSL unfortunately imposes a significant performance penalty on the server side (three to nine times slower than regular web servers) and slower response (cause for major frustration for Ecommerce users). There are five factors that make things even worse;

- More and smaller connected devices (Cell phones, PDA, handheld, home appliances, scientific equipment, on board automotive computers, smart card, medical devices etc.) are networking for data collection and remote functions. Where very large keys are a problem for these resource constrained devices, found in sensor networks as well

Very large keys are a problem for very small devices.

Figure 3:6 Resource consumption of very large keys

- Transaction Volumes are expected to double each year as millions get connected each day
- Demand for increased security based on developments in standards bodies to the resource availability to hackers
- Need to cater for consumers' desire for more appropriate and context-sensitive levels of privacy in their online activities
- Increased number of applications stemming from sensor networks

To highlight the significance of the last point on increased number of sensor applications, we can see, five areas where these applications are exploding.

- Industrial applications –in manufacturing, hundreds of tiny sensors remotely monitor manufacturing equipment for temperature, stress, vibration and other variables, alerting technicians before failures occur.
- Military and Homeland Security applications – in shipping containers wireless sensors alert customs officials if a container was opened in transit.
- Healthcare application – wearable smart devices gather patient biometrics for remote medical professionals.
- Agricultural Applications – wireless sensor devices implanted in farmland monitor moisture levels for irrigation purposes.
- Environmental Applications – wireless sensors implanted in animals track there movement, placed throughout the habitat.

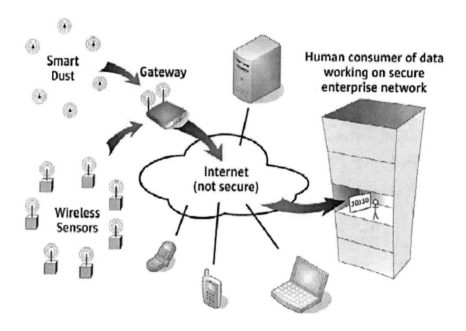

Extending the Internet to wireless sensors and smart dust.

Figure 3:7 Sensor Networks integrated back to the Enterprise Network via the Internet

These limitations on processing power, memory and more make data processing tasks on these devices difficult and time consuming.

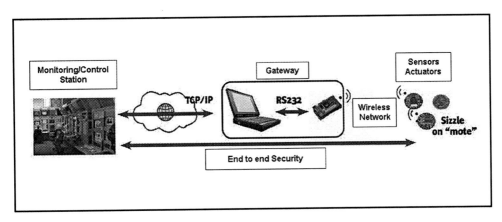

Figure 3:8 Sizzle, ECC and SSL/TLS offering end to end security

This Next Generation Crypto project (also viewed as Identity based Encryption) focuses on three key components:

- implementation of an elliptic curve crypto library and security architectures for various platforms ranging from small sensors to high-performance web servers
- implementation of a common hardware architecture for accelerating ECC as well as RSA
- enabling broad industry adoption of ECC by
    —promoting ECC standardisation within SSL, the dominant security protocol used on the Internet, and
    —contributing ECC technology to OpenSSL and NSS/Mozilla the two most popular open source cryptographic libraries

With multiple Open Source Software initiatives and support, such as;

- The latest version of <u>OpenSSL</u> with Sun's ECC contribution can be found at *ftp://ftp.openssl.org/snapshot/*.
- Netscape Security Services (<u>NSS</u>) version <u>3.8</u> and later include Sun's ECC contribution.
- An ECC-enabled version of the Firefox browser with support for ECC cipher suites in SSL and ECC certificate enrollment is available and can be tested against the new <u>ECC interoperability server</u>.

And, Standardisation initiatives that includes;

- ECC Cipher Suites for TLS, IETF Internet-draft specifying the use of Elliptic Curve Cryptography with SSL. Click here for the latest version and revision history.
- Elliptic Curve Diffie-Hellman Key Exchange for the SSH Transport Level Protocol, IETF Internet-draft draft-stebila-secsh-ecdh-00.txt specifying the use of Elliptic Curve Cryptography with SSH, Nov. 2003

3.6 Identify based Encryption (ECC) for Sensor Networks

Given the background in the light weighted nature of ECC and Sizzle, it is easy to run an Access Manager agent on the same web container that supports ECC as well, to ensure Identity Systems value proposition to Sensor Networks are fully leveraged.

At the 10th annual ECC conference in Toronto Canada, September 2006, Xavier Boyen's presentation on "Practical Aspects of Identity based Encryption" states that IBE (Identity based encryption) is extremely scalable (which is the need of the hour in terms of billions of devices communicating via millions of sensor networks), for the following reasons:

- Easy to scale via load balancing (horizontally and vertically with embedded encryption cores)
- Easy to Administer (backup and disaster recovery)
- "stateless" key servers
- No growing store of certificates
- No growing store of private keys
- No revocation lists

This perspective adds tremendous value proposition in terms of an Identity Centric Architecture aligning SOA to NG Sensor Networks and Personal Networks

3.7 Conclusion

The integration of Services, Network elements, Devices and Users data with Network Identity helps set the foundation for context driven/preference based content/service delivery to all Access networks and Access devices (another objective of an integrated 4G Network).

Also the proliferation of wireless sensor networks cannot be stopped and is a strategic factor for carriers. The advances in Wireless Metropolitan and Wide Area Networks such as WiMAX, EVDO etc. raise very similar issues to those around sensor networks, particularly where privacy/security and federation between enterprises are concerned. As traversal between LANs and Wireless WANs are made seamless with varying throughput from devices, sensors enhance the usefulness of related technologies such as Infrared and RFID, Sizzle and ECC. The end scenario eventually offers true ubiquity for end users accessing not just networks but also Services from all other types of networks.

There are five use-cases that are covered around how machine to machine (m2m - analogous to sensor networks) communications are leveraged to deliver Services based on events taking shape in a Identity enabled Sensor Network.

- Ice cream vending machines communicate their in-stock status daily with the company's logistics control center (Vodafone)
- In the UK, M2M-equipped trains can notify maintenance if they need repairs as they enter rail yards
- M2M for home automation, which would allow residents to control their homes' temperature and lighting via mobile text message (Nokia)
- Wire-less solar-powered parking payment stations developed by Sun Microsystems technology partner of Quebec are making life easier for parking enforcement personnel, drivers, and city officials (8D Technologies)
- A Sensor network enabled parking lot providing automated advising of vacant spots in different displays as one enters the lot

There are several thousand such use cases that exist today in terms of functions performed in areas such as: RFID Industry Solution for Mandate Compliance, RFID Industry Solution for Warehouse Management, RFID Industry Solution for Physical Asset Tracking and RFID Industry Solution for Drug Authentication, having an impact on manufacturing, distribution, retail, healthcare and many more.

With Sun's JavaCAPS RFID project, we can expect to see the convergence between sensor networks (and sensor data) and Web Services and SOA—where the paradigm shifts from request and response to sense-request to controlled-response through a common Identity System (and a Policy Control Stratum) that ties the identities of things/machines to the identities associated with services and the identities of the respective users.

Here is an excellent chapter titled "Convergence Technologies for Sensor Systems for Next Generation Networks", *http://portal.acm.org/citation.cfm?id=1071516&CFID=4565683&CFTOKEN=11585463&ret=1#F* ulltext that talks to the wide spectrum of Java Technologies, such as JME, JEE, JAIN SLEE, RTSJ and more in conjunction with the alignment of developments in sensor networks, NGN, SIP/IMS, SOA/SDP and more.

4. Identity enabled Programmable Network

4.1 Introduction and Overview

This chapter is part of a series that expands on the notion of "Identity Enabled Networks" from a Networking perspective, i.e.:

- Identity enabled Sensor Networks
- Identity enabled 4G Networks
- Identity enabled Programmable Networks
- Identity enabled IMS Networks
- Identity enabled IN Services
- Identity enabled OAM/OSS Services

4.2 Programmable Networks

In chapter 1 we discussed the significance of an Identity System from a Networking perspective and described how an Identity System transcends Service Networks, the Core Network and different Access Networks to offer Services to all types of devices.

Amongst these three tiers of networks discussed:

Namely; a) Service Networks (a.k.a., Service Delivery Networks – Programmable Networks for IP Service Delivery), b) Core Network (Core Converged Networks—where the soft-switch acts as the OS of the Converged Network) and c) Access Networks (abstracted as Virtual Personal Networks that transcends Wireless and Wire-line broadband access) –programmable networks play a major role in all three, especially in more highly evolved Service (or Service Delivery –SDN) networks, Core Converged Next Generation Networks and in all types of Access Networks. Service Networks are the Service Delivery Networks that host Services and Content and are run by either service providers for enterprises or enterprises within its enterprise network. Services hosted can include traditional business applications, (such as ERP, SCM, etc,), web services, IP communication services, IP entertainment services etc. The Service Delivery Networks typically leverage, extensive OS security capabilities, such as, Secure Execution, Process/User Rights Management, Service Containers, Cryptographic Frameworks and more in addition to many Network security capabilities.

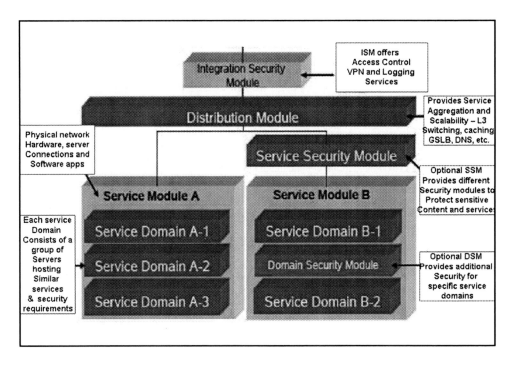

Figure 4:1 Systemic Security in a Service (Delivery) Network — Programmable and Active

The Core network is typically run by the Telecom companies/Carriers, with the main purpose of providing connectivity between Service networks and different types of Access Networks. The core network is evolving into a converged control network today, with the implementation of "soft switches" and the likes, that integrates both "packet based" core and the "circuit-switch" based core. Within the Core a set of Services; typically run by telecom companies again, such as MM applications (multi-media), OAM&P applications, OSS services, routing services and more. However, lately with the implementation of large scale Identity Systems by telecom companies worldwide, such as Telstra in Australia, to Vodafone in Europe to Cingular in the US, an Identity System not only acts as a Core Service Building Block in a "Service Oriented Architecture", but also becomes a Core Service that is hosted within the Core Network (as HSS or an IDS) and allows for federation of many services from many Service Networks (SDN).

There are varying types of Access networks as depicted in chapter 2, that allow for many types of devices, including cell phones, PDA/handhelds, TV, embedded devices in a CAR (such as ON-Star and Navigation systems) and more, to access services from the service networks via the core.

Although the role played by programmable devices within the core and access network is significant, this chapter focuses on the strategic role played by programmability within service networks and when combined with identity systems the significance it has on many industries and there respective services including inventory management/ supply chain, retail services, health care/hospitals, mobile workforces from an information management, perspective.

The follow-on chapters also align specific types (programmable, sensor, converged, etc.) to specific tiers within the network. For example, programmable networks are more relevant and prevalent in the service network space, convergence (PSTN/IP etc.) are more relevant and prevalent in the core network and more. This is not to say that convergence is not taking shape in the Service network in the form of converged services (applications that use voice (over IP), Video (over IP) and Data services together), or the Access Networks (wire-line/wireless, P2P/personal). Similarly programmability is critical for Active/ Programmable/sensor networks and the core network that has embedded network elements.

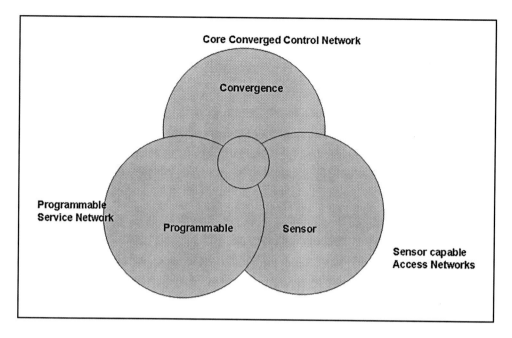

Figure 4:2 Convergence, Programmability and Sensor capabilities for Service, Access and Core Networks

Given this convergence in the Core Network and wide success of sensor Access Networks and dynamic programmable IP services deployed in the Service Networks, for a pervasive virtual personal network to flourish, a heavy emphasis on the User (a user's identity, a user's sessions and a user's context) is mandated and an Identity System that is extended to all layers and types of networks and all programmable IP services within the Service Network becomes highly critical, to address mobility with security.

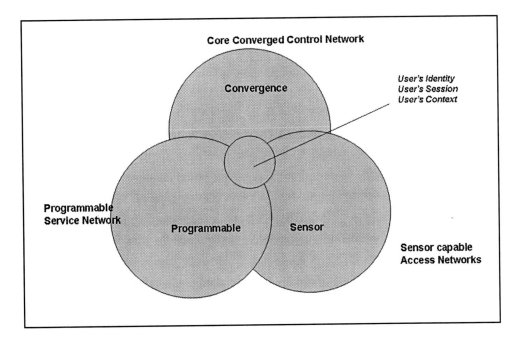

Figure 4:3 Transcending user's identity, session and context.

4.3 What is a Programmable (IP Service) Network?

Today, programmable networks are being viewed as the solution for the fast, flexible and dynamic deployment of new telecommunications network services (also aligning with SOA- Service Oriented Architecture). " Programmable Networks for IP Service deployment" a book authored by Alex Galis, Spyros Dennazis, Celestin Brou and Cornel Klien is a good forward-looking resource that provides detailed review of the state of the art and guidelines for designing managed IP programmable networks. This book explains how end users, operators and service providers can inject service-specific application code into networks to obtain required network support for new services. Programmable Networks for IP Service Deployment covers programmable network architecture, platforms, deployment, management and security, as well as dynamic services provisioning, so one can prepare now for working with the next generation of telecom technology. This book also includes real-world examples of the deployment of cutting-edge network services such as DiffServ and Web TV Distribution. Also, at the vanguard of programmable network research is the Future

Active/Programmable IP Networks (FAIN) project. The authors of this book discuss their research in FAIN, helping us get on the inside track to tomorrow's technology *(http://www.ist-fain.org/overview.html)*.

When we take this advancement into perspective with "web services" and SOA that is driving the Enterprise IT Architectures, programmability need not be contained to telecom services alone and can be very practically applicable to the IT world as well and its respective services. In fact, the core principle behind SOA is the notion of "Service Building Blocks" wherein, a SBB is understood as a reusable and replaceable service that is an enabler for creating user centric applications, such as Location Services, Billing Services, Payment Services, Presence Services and more. The first chapter in this series also defines an Identity System as a Core SBB in a SOA.

Also the series on SOA at: *(http://www.opengroup.org/events/q405/rad-hakrishnan-papers.htm)* talks to agility achieved through code mobility; a similar approach to programmable networks –which in turn implies SOA based Utility Computing Grids are Programmable Networks as well. Taking into account this convergence between IT services and Telecom services as programmable IP services, there are a wide range of benefits of these programmable networks.

FAIN as an organisation provides an overview of Programmable and Active Networks as well as some expected results. Since the early 90s the business world witnessed the rapid development of Internet and IP networks in private and corporate areas. The wide acceptance of IP originated from its unparalleled ability to provide ubiquitous access and low prices regardless of underlying networking technologies. Moreover, based on the existing best-effort IP transport service, new application services can be offered on a global scale by almost everyone, simply by connecting a new web server to the Internet. However developing and deploying new network services, i.e. services which operate on the IP layer, through best practice and standardisation is too slow and cannot match the steps in which requirements of various applications, e.g. multimedia multiparty communication, are growing. Examples of such services are signaling for quality of service (QoS), reliable multicast or Web Proxies/Caches/Switches/Filters (see chapter on Identity enabled Enterprise Networks-section on Identity enabled XML proxies, caches, filters and accelerators, that talks to this reliability). Similar to the intelligent network (IN) architecture in the PSTN world, the current Internet architecture needs to be enhanced in order to allow for a more rapid introduction of such services.

4.3.1 Programmable/Active Networks

Programmable Networks have been proposed as a solution for the fast and flexible deployment of new network services. The basic idea of active networks is to enable third parties (end users, operators, and service providers) to inject application-specific services (in the form of code) into the network. Applications are thus able to utilise these services to obtain required network support in terms of, e.g. performance, that is now becoming network-aware. As such, active networks allow dynamic injection of code as a promising way to realise application-specific service logic, or perform dynamic service provision on demand.

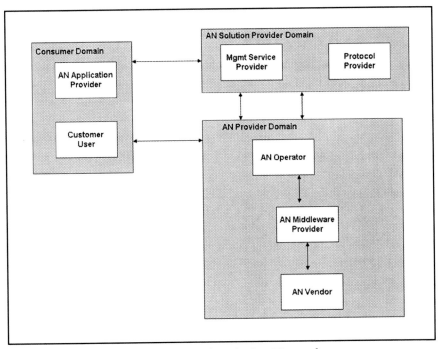

Figure 4:4 Core ID multiple domains of an Active Network

From FAIN's perspective, there are primarily three domains, the Consumer domain, the Solution provider domain and the Network Provider domain.

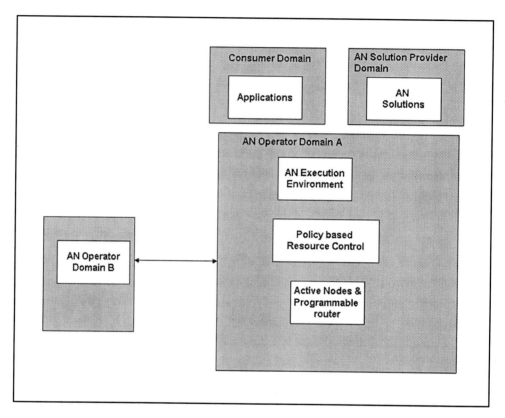

Figure 4:5 Multiple Layers within a Domain of an Active/Programmable Network

There are three layers within the Network provider domain, that abstract service execution to its own layer, with an active node its own layer that includes security management, network management and service provisioning functions and a network elements to its own layer (such as a programmable router). This approach of abstraction makes changes in programs in one layer having less impact to other layers.

From an IT perspective, we have achieved such extensive programmability in the network again through abstraction in the form of firmware/hyper visors and other virtualisation techniques from the hardware (compute and storage) and ample abstraction layers exist for management services, secure execution environments (OS containers), application containers (Java EE and SE, JAIN SLEE etc.) and more.

4.3.3 Applications and capabilities of this technology

- Low cost, scalable solutions using programmable devices that addresses impact free changes in all layers and tiers. This is Strategic Maneuverability in the form of addressing change from all directions – business, Telecom networks, IT, consumers, emerging technologies and more.
- All IP Services hence the basis for rich converged IP Services and IP applications that leverage Voice, Data and Multi-Media.
- A Framework for Resource Management in Active/Programmable Nodes – dynamic allocation of virtualised resources to services that require the same.
- Active/Programmable Virtual Networks Services – introduced by an abstraction layer making dynamic deployment timely in nature.
- Distributed Control of Multicast Internet communications with Variable QoS Constraints and Dynamic Protocol Provisioning in Active/Programmable Networks.
- Efficient Packet Monitoring for Network Management and Packet Filtering for Low-Cost Network Monitoring.
- Acts also as an Enterprise Model for Active/Programmable Networks (Services stemming from Enterprise Service Delivery Networks)..
- Active Service Logic Execution Environment (such as JAIN SLEE) that acts as the glue over a Soft switch fabric.
- Leverages and synergises with the scalable ad-hoc mesh networks and mobile sensor networks- that also leverage programmable embedded devices (at the edges of the network) – using this layer of added information/intelligence..

4.4 Base set of Security requirements for Programmable Networks

As mentioned earlier in this chapter, programmable networks are used in a number of domains that handle sensitive information. Due to this, there are many considerations that should be investigated and are related with protecting sensitive information traveling between nodes (which are either programmable nodes or the programmable network elements) from being disclosed to unauthorised third parties. The scope of this section is to analyse basic security concepts before moving into a detailed discussion of the various security issues. It is essential to first understand the security requirements that are raised in a programmable (and distributed) environment.

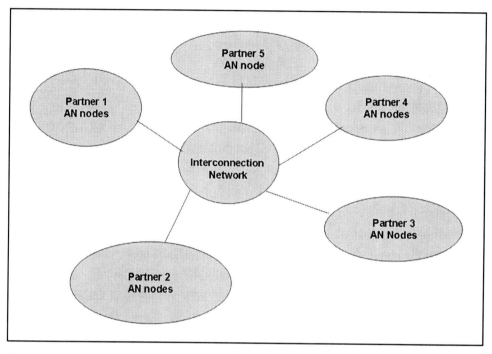

Figure 4:6 Core ID Key foundation requirement for an Active/Programmable Network—Trust Network

A base security framework is required to be agreed upon by Carriers (network owners), Enterprises, and potential business entities that enter into agreements and partnerships. This base security framework has to be adhering to standards for easy additions and removal of business entities into a federated framework. The majority of these, stem from the same requirements, of a Sensor Network.

Confidentiality
Confidentiality requirement is needed to ensure that sensitive information (including mobile code in a programmable/active network) is well protected and not revealed to unauthorised third parties. The confidentiality objective is required in programmable network to protect

code/configuration information/virtual machine traveling between the programmable nodes of the network or between the nodes and the network element from disclosure, since an adversary having the appropriate equipment may eavesdrop on the communication. By eavesdropping, the adversary could overhear critical code/information such as user data and routing information. Based on the sensitivity of the data stolen, an adversary may cause severe damage since he can use the data for many illegal purposes i.e. sabotage blackmail. Furthermore, by stealing routing information the adversary could introduce his own malicious nodes into the network in an attempt to overhear the entire communication. If we consider eavesdropping to be a network level threat, then a local level threat could be a compromised programmable node that an adversary has in his possession. Compromised programmable nodes are a big threat to confidentiality objective since the adversary could steal critical data stored on nodes such as cryptographic keys that are used to encrypt the communication.

Authentication

As in conventional systems, authentication techniques verify the identity of the participants in a communication, distinguishing in this way legitimate users from intruders. In the case of programmable networks, it is essential for each active node and network element to have the ability to verify that the data received was really send by a trusted sender and not by an adversary that tricked legitimate nodes into accepting false data. If such a case happens and false data are supplied into the programmable network, then the behaviour of the network could not be predicted and most of times will not outcome as expected. Authentication objective is essential to be achieved when clustering of nodes is performed. I remind you that clustering involves grouping nodes based on some attribute such as their location, data etc. and that each cluster usually has a cluster head that is the node that joins its cluster with the rest of the programmable network (meaning that the communication among different clusters is performed through the cluster heads). In these cases, where clustering is required, there are two authentication situations which should be investigated; first it is critical to ensure that the nodes contained in each cluster will exchange data only with the authorised nodes contained and which are trusted by the specified cluster (based on some authentication protocol). Otherwise, if nodes within a cluster receive data from nodes that are not trusted within the current community of nodes and further process it, then the expected data from that cluster will be based on false data and may cause damage. The second authentication situation involves the communication between the cluster heads of each cluster; communication must be established only with cluster heads that can prove their identity (identity of nodes). No malicious node should be able to masquerade as a cluster head and communicate with a legitimate cluster head, sending it false data or either compromising exchanged data.

Integrity

Moving on to the integrity objective, there is the danger that information and/or mobile code could be altered when exchanged over domains in programmable networks. Lack of integrity could result in many problems since the consequences of using inaccurate information could be disastrous. Integrity controls must be implemented to ensure that information and mobile code will not be altered in any unexpected way. Many applications, such as billing and network monitoring, rely on the integrity of the information to function with accurate outcomes; it is unacceptable to measure the magnitude of the downtown caused by a faulty component and find out later on that the information provided was improperly altered. Therefore, there is urgent need to make sure that information and mobile code is traveling from one end to the other without being intercepted and modified in the process.

Freshness

One of the many attacks launched against programmable/active networks is the message replay attack where an adversary may capture messages exchanged between nodes and replay them later to cause confusion to the network. Data freshness objective ensures that messages are fresh, meaning that they obey in a message ordering and have not been reused. To achieve freshness, network protocols must be designed in a way to identify duplicate packets and discard them preventing potential mix-up.

Secure Management

Management is required in every system that is constituted from multi components and handles sensitive information. In the case of programmable networks, we need secure management on network element level; since programmable nodes communication ends up at the network element, issues like key distribution to programmable nodes in order to establish encryption and routing information need secure management. Furthermore, clustering requires secure management as well, since each group of nodes may include a large number of nodes that need to be authenticated with each other and exchange data in a secure manner. In addition, clustering in each sensor network can change dynamically and rapidly. Therefore, secure protocols for group management are required for adding and removing members, and authenticating data from groups of nodes.

Availability

Availability ensures that services and information can be accessed at the time that they are required. In programmable/active networks there are many risks that could result in loss of availability such as active node capturing and denial of service attacks. Lack of availability may affect the operation of many critical real time applications like those in the healthcare sector that require a 24/7 operation that could even result in the loss of life. Therefore, it is critical to ensure resilience to attacks targeting the availability of the system and find ways to fill in the gap created by the capturing or disablement of a specific node by assigning its duties to some other nodes in the network.

Quality of Service

Quality of Service objective is a big headache to security. Security mechanisms must be lightweight so that the overhead caused for example by encryption must be minimised and not affect the performance of the active/programmable network. Performance and quality in sensor networks involve the timely delivery of data to prevent for example propagation of pollution and the accuracy with which the data reported match what is actually occurring in their environment.

The majority of these requirements and others revolving around distributed sessions, a session's context, rules/policies, federation and more can be addressed when an Identity System is fully leveraged.

4.5 Identity enabling Programmable Networks

There are a few key related technologies to Programmable Networks such as dynamic GRID technology that have gained popularity due to requirements mandated by SOA, web services, utility computing models, multi-core/multi-threaded systems (a.k.a., throughput computing) and many others. Also due to the nature of programmable/active networks, embedding Event Containers and Execution Environments within the core and service networks (such as JAIN SLEE., provides the pathway to take the information generated from within and outside the Core Networks and act on them through the execution of Services based on the data.

4.5.1 Reasons for Identity enabling Programmable Networks

Based on the discussions so far, the key value proposition of an Identity System for Programmable Networks (and the activeness and dynamism that is inherent) includes:

- Enabling Customer Oriented Service Provisioning by Flexible Code and Resource Management in Active/Programmable and Programmable Networks
- A Policy –Based Management Approaches for Active/Programmable Networks
- A Security Architecture for Active/Programmable IP Networks
- A Service Deployment Architecture for Heterogeneous Active/Programmable Network Nodes
- An Identity System offering IN/AIN like Services to Converged Services (Services created with VOIP, IP Video/IPTV, and Data technologies).
- Active/Programmable Networks Management Approaches
- Authorisation in an Active/Programmable Network Node
- Delegation of Management for QoS Aware Active/Programmable Network
- Provisioning and Security Requirements in Active/Programmable Networks

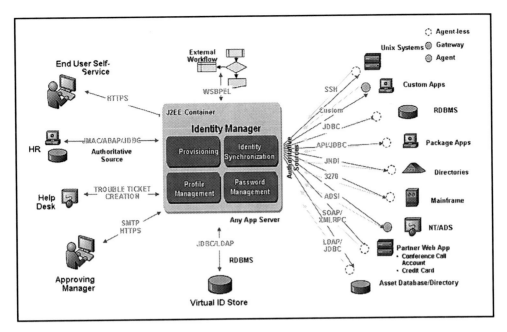

Figure 4:7 Light weight adaptors

Some of the characteristics of these programmable networks in terms of managing virtualised environments include (an example list from Sun's N1 Systems Manager);

- Bare metal provisioning for Operating Systems (such as, Solaris, Linux and Windows)
- Slick, web-based user interface
- Firewall friendly agent interaction protocols
- Role based access control
- Firmware installation
- Server power management and control
- Hardware Monitoring
- In band OS resource utilisation monitoring
- Connected patch management
- Package, application and profile provisioning
- "Make A like B" server comparison and provisioning operations
- Patch-level compliance reporting
- Proxy support for increased scalability and network accessibility
- Checkpoint and restore capabilities
- Knowledge based install verification
- Integrated registration and inventory management

This implies a requirement for a common flexible security framework for this ever-changing network, in terms of nodes provisioned, OS running, patch levels, packages installed and more. These programmable networks are either service delivery platforms to deliver Web Services, Communication Services, IPTV Services and more (all IP Services) and it is important to understand the central and integral role played by an identity system today. An identity system acts as the host of several identities of a user, manages the user's sessions, across devices and transcending access networks (agnostic to access network) providing access to appropriate application and creating a personal environment for the end-user. Once we achieve this digitisation and programmability we need a common security framework that can validate the identities of users, services, devices, networks and things, plus correlate the data associated with a user in relation to devices, services, networks and things. This common security framework can be implemented with an Identity System, along with the appropriate context (such as location and presence coupled with contextual data associated with heat, moisture, erosion etc.).

A lot of this depends on how well an Operating System extended itself to Security requirements and an Identity infrastructure. For example, Solaris 10 11/06 is currently in process for Common Criteria Certification at EAL4+ with Controlled Access, Role-Based Access Control, and Labeled Security Protection Profiles (CAPP, RBAC, LSPP) for SPARC® and x64/x86 servers. Solaris 10 3/05 was awarded Common Criteria Certification at the highest levels for an OS, helping to assure customers that their mission-critical systems are running on a well protected, trustworthy platform. Also, Virtualisation improvements include Logical Domains and enhanced Solaris Containers. Using Logical Domains one can now dynamically provision and run up to 32 OS instances on each UltraSPARC® T1-based systems. Running inside the Logical Domain instances, Solaris Containers allow the isolation of software applications and services, enabling the creation of many private execution environments within a single instance of Solaris. Customers can detach, clone and move containers for greater utilisation of system resources, simplified testing and deployment and improved application security. Solaris(TM) Cluster also supports these virtualisation technologies. Also Open source Xen hypervisor, a para-virtualisation technology that presents a software interface to virtual machines is available today from the OpenSolaris Xen community project at: *http://opensolaris.org/os/community/xen/.*

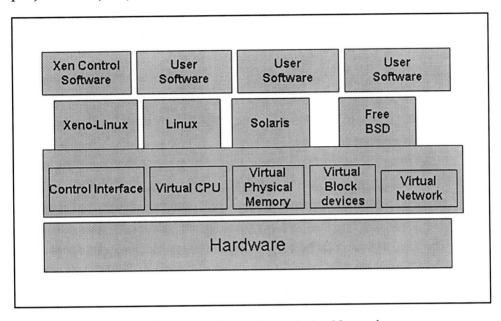

Figure 4:8 Multiple levels of virtualization in an Active Network

This para-virtualisation (Open Solaris XEN) technology (advances in hyper visor technologies) will be a key characteristic of Identity enabled Programmable Networks, primarily to due hardware advances such as 16 core chips and 64 hardware level threaded processors that has the capacity to run these abstraction layers, with dedicated cores that handle security (Identity based encryption –discussed in the chapter on sensor networks). Similar to Identity based Encryption (which addresses AuthN, privacy, integrity and confidentiality), Identity based Systemic Security is equally important when we see dynamic infrastructure in a Programmable Active Network. This implies adhering to the following five principles (Sun's DE: Glenn Brunette);

- Self Preservation—an object must be configured, used and managed in such a way that it protects itself from **unauthorised** external influence (hence identity enabled components within a programmable network so as to ensure interaction only takes place with AuthN and AuthZ objects).

- Defense in Depth—Security must be integrated systemically throughout the architecture at all layers (this is where the Identity Eigenvector comes into play, where in the Identity Systems Anchors all security tools and systems implemented – such as Identity enabled Firewall, Identity enabled Encryption, Identity enabled Compute and Network elements and more).

- Least privilege—Every program and every user of a system must operate using the least set of privileges to compete the job – privileges and rights of users and programs are definitely aligned with an Identity System.

- Compartmentalisation—A very useful approach for keeping separated or isolated unrelated interfaces, services, data sets, systems, networks and user communities—Even with the vertical integration of multiple fragmented Identity System one gets this compartmentalisation across access devices, access networks, core network, services and content " when we treat the entire network as a computer".

- Proportionality—Security controls should be proportionate to the risk level—a good example is the notion of AuthN Levels in an identity system wherein a Service is bound to an AUthN Level —leaving trivial non-security sensitive services with low-end authN level and security sensitive services requiring stringer levels of AuthN—which might lead to stronger levels of Encryption, Session level controls and more.

He further adds five or more patterns that will address these principles;

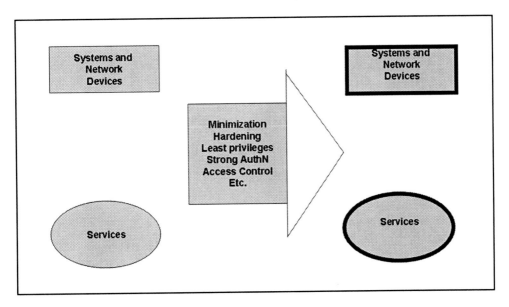

Figure 4:9 Making IT and Network elements into Secure Components in a Pro-

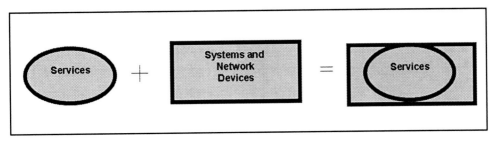

Figure 4:10 Secure Execution environment in a Programmable Network

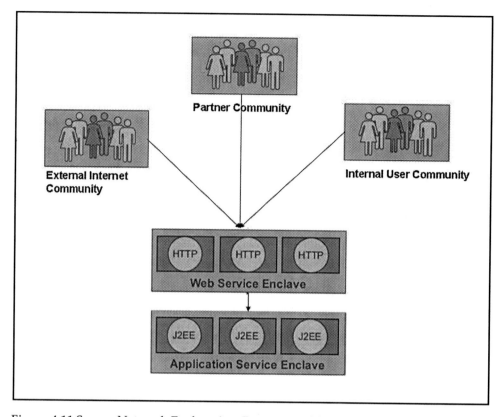

Figure 4:11 Secure Network Enclave in a Programmable Network

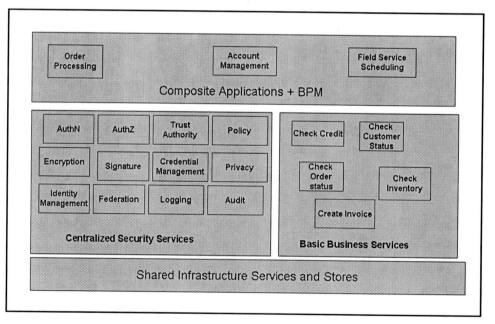

Figure 4:12 Shared Application and Infrastructure Services in a Programmable Network

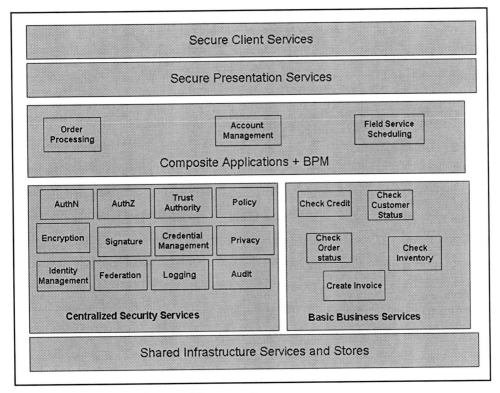

Figure 4:13 Secure Desktop and Presentation

These patterns along with the notion of Identity eigenvector (Identity System forms the foundation for Security functions), are expected to address systemic security in a Programmable Virtualised Network.

4.6 Conclusion

The integration of Services, Network elements, Devices and Users data with Network Identity helps set the foundation for context driven/preference based session centric, content/service delivery to all Access networks and Access devices. This implies leveraging an Identity System and other related security tools to validate the identity of not only users and web sites, but also validation of identity of nodes, network elements, devices, services and more.

5. Identity enabled IMS Network Services

5.1 Introduction and Overview

This chapter explores the possibilities of leveraging Standards based Identity System (Liberty and SAML, based) for a Telecommunication environment, specifically supporting an IMS (3GPP- IP Multi Media Subsystem) Architecture and provides a vision for the future trends in converged communication/web services. Initially we saw the proliferation of Telecom Services to Cell Phones and Mobile Devices over 3G and 2.5 G Networks – where in a Cell Phone/Mobile Device evolved into a more complex device that handles (IP)TV, email, SMS, IM, Games, Pictures, Videos, Video mail and more. This, in conjunction with the deployment of 802.11 (Wifi), 802.16 (WiMax) access networks, and the evolution into 4G networks where seamless traversal between all types of wireless networks is made possible—makes Identity enabled Service Delivery even more appealing. Along the same lines, both Wire-line and Wireless Communication Service Providers (CSPs) are seeking new ways to expand into delivering data services securely with offerings in broadband access networks ranging from DSL to Cable Modem as well.

Telecom Services utilise voice, data and video (multi-media) to deliver more complex and advanced services such as Context sensitive delivery of Entertainment. The goal is to transcend all types of access networks and access devices and deliver User Sensitive (preference, profile and policy based), Location based, Context driven Services with true Service Mobility, going beyond user and terminal mobility. All major Network Equipment Providers (NEP's) have similar vision and strategy, wherein the same set of Services Over IP (SOIP) can be delivered across all types of access networks and access devices that support SIP (Session

Initiation Protocol) and with SIP's support for SAML. Different dialects of XML are used here, including, SAML/SPML, MOML/MSML, CpML, XKMS, VXML and more. The IP Multimedia Subsystem (IMS) is a standardised Next Generation Networking (NGN) architecture for telecom operators that want to provide mobile and fixed multimedia services. It uses a Voice-over-IP (VoIP) implementation based on a 3GPP standardised implementation of SIP, and runs over the standard Internet Protocol (IP). Existing phone systems (both packet-switched and circuit-switched) are supported. The aim of IMS is not only to provide new services but all the services, current and future, that the internet provides. In this way, IMS will give network operators and service providers the ability to control and charge for individual services. In addition, users will be able to execute all their services when roaming as well as from their home networks. To achieve these goals, IMS uses open standard IP protocols, defined by the IETF. So, a multimedia session between two IMS users, between an IMS user and a user on the Internet, and between two users on the Internet is established using exactly the same protocol. Moreover, the interfaces for service developers are also based on IP protocols. Hence the claim that, IMS truly merges the internet with the cellular world; it uses cellular technologies to provide ubiquitous access and internet technologies, to provide appealing services.

5.2 IMS and HSS

Based on standards and specifications proposed by 3GPP, NEP's (Network Equipment Providers) like Alcatel, Nortel, Siemens, Ericsson and others are creating IP Multi Media System (IMS) and Home Subscriber Service (HSS), solutions.

The following links takes you to the respective white papers from these NEP's on their IMS Solution Architecture:
* *http://www.lucent.com/products/solution/0,,CTID+2019-STID+10488-SOID+1284 LOCL+1,00.html*
* *http://www.nortel.com/solutions/cms/collateral/nn110920-021205.pdf*
* *http://communications.siemens.com/repository/737/73795/WP_IMS.pdf*
* *http://www.ericsson.com/products/white_chapters_pdf/ims_ip_multimedia_subsystem.pdf*

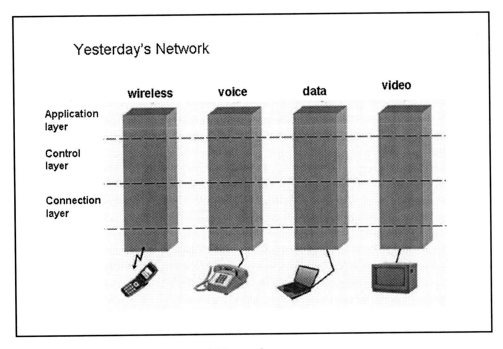

Figure 5:1 Yesterday's Fragmented Network

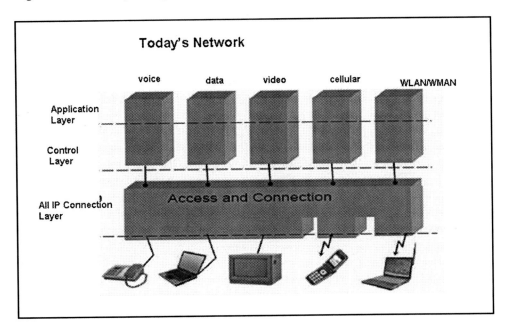

Figure 5:2 Today's Network with a Common IP based Connection Layer

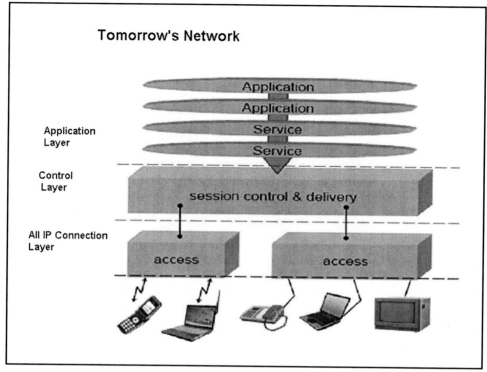

Figure 5:3 IMS based Common Connection and Control Layer

The above three figures show how <u>IMS helps the Network evolve</u>. The common control layer (that enables true convergence) that will be deployed just in time for the NG Networks (4G- a combination of WiMAX, meshWifi, 3.5G/3G, BPL, Cable, FTH, and more), NG Devices (IPbased) and NG Network Services (IPTV, VOD, Video Calls, SOIP, MM-games, music and more)—what will be the foundation for the 21st century network. The majority of the sophisticated use cases depicted in movies such as Paycheck, The Island and the Minority Report, will be possible as more and more telecom companies deploy IMS in 2007, 2008 and 2009. The NEP (network equipment vendors) such as Alcatel, Motorola, Siemens, Ericsson and Nortel have produced all the major components required for IMS and in many cases have worked with Sun to Identity enable IMS. Identity Systems integration with IMS, DRM, Sensor Networks, Web Services, NAC, ILM and more lays the foundation for the implementation of these use cases that will leverage this evolution in the network. IMS is being rolled out globally—imagine making a video call while you are in a trip (business and pleasure) to Agra, India and you want to share the fabulous view of the Taj Mahal at that very same moment from your camera enabled wireless device to your family accessing the network via a STB/TV over a Cable Network, while having a conversation about it, your spouse wanting to save the moment ensures that a copy gets recorded and stored in your personal family video collection (nPVR transmitting to an internet video album web service), with DRM enforcing the rights as you grant them, for sharing on future dates. All these functions (video transmission, voice call, back-end DRM, nPVR. billing, and more) are ID enabled and will work in tandem to fulfill the user's needs. Identity Systems reach from devices, to access networks to the control network to multiple service and content networks will make this possible.

Sun's CTO Dr. Greg Papadopoulos has stated the following with regard's to IMS and Identity Systems "User identity takes on a much greater role in an IMS environment and the HSS is at the center. It's helpful to think of the HSS as the nexus between the IT and the core network worlds. HSS acts as the central repository for user-related information such as security information (who am I?), location information (where am I calling from?), and user profile information (what services am I subscribed to?) to name a few. When you consider the 100s of millions of people with multiple profiles and multiple devices engaging in multimedia sessions with a huge array of interesting services this starts to add a lot of complexity to the system. IMS requires that your IT systems support complex subscriber identity structures, so that subscribers can have multiple "addresses." To do so, operators will need a robust identity management system that provides control and flexibility to take into account the key changes in the way that they manage and use subscriber identities". He further states, "One big piece of IMS is the notion of session. It's a way to provide call control and manage multimedia sessions over IP networks. Today when you make a phone call, a connection is established and torn down the instant you hang-up or attempt to do something else, like send an SMS or take a picture. There's no ability to combine these services together. A few years ago, the Third Generation Partnership Project (3GPP) decided to adopt the IETF-defined Session Initiation Protocol (SIP) as the basis of a new session-control layer for 3G core networks. Choosing SIP was a significant decision that ultimately is going to have manifold implications in the telecom world. With SIP, operators can combine services from the circuit-switched and packet-switched domains in the same session, and for sessions to be dynamically created 'on the fly.' Things like adding a video stream while on a voice call will become commonplace. The beauty of SIP is that it's based on HTTP making it fairly easy to create new services. SIP service developers can use all the service frameworks developed for HTTP, such as CGI and Java servlets".

The common characteristics of all these IMS solution's architecture are:

- A layered approach in the form of
    a) Connectivity Layer (edge)
    b) Control/Session Layer
    c) Services Layer
    d) OAM/OSS Layer

- Access Network Agnostic – wireless (GSM/CDMA/WLAN) and wire line
- Device Agnostic/SIP enabled Devices (Cell Phone/PDA, TV/STB and Laptop/Computer)
- There is an OAM/Vertical layer that addresses operations, administration and management plus, the provisioning, billing and mediation (OSS) – This can be thought of as the OAM+OSS layer.
- All IP Services –Voice (VOIP), Video (IPTV/VOD) and Data Services from the Service Layer are actually Service enablers (what is also defined as a Service Building Block in a Service Oriented Architecture where these Services are reusable and replaceable for multiple converged/traditional applications).
- Services include Presence, Location, Group List Management, PTT (push to talk), IM/Chat, Video conferencing, and more, all running on a SIP application Server, with the goal of User Centric Services (convenience, cohesiveness and profile/preference driven).
- The connectivity layer extends to the edges, access networks and gateway controllers between networks.
- The control layer handled session management/session setup between end points and acts as a policy controller .
- HSS (home subscriber service) within the Control Layer is a highly distributed architecture, that provides support to the call control servers in order to complete the routing/roaming procedures by solving

authentication, authorisation, naming/addressing resolution, location dependencies, etc.

From a high level function architecture of the HSS is depicted below:

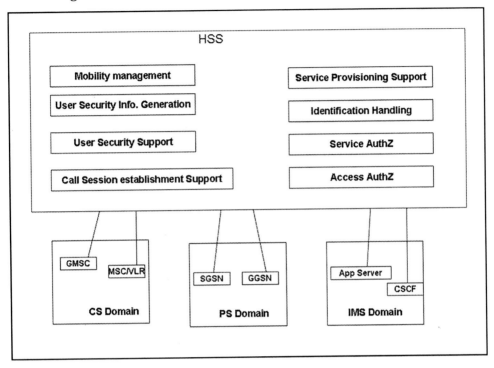

Figure 5:4 Role of HSS

Key characteristics of the HSS include;

- HSS is the master database for a given user
- HSS is the entity containing the subscription-related information to support the network entities actually handling calls/sessions
- A Home Network may contain one or several HSS
- HSS provides support to the call control servers in order to complete the routing/roaming procedures by solving authentication, authorisation, naming/addressing resolution, location dependencies, etc.
- HSS is based on a highly distributable architecture

Where the HSS as a master database holds;

- User Identification, Numbering and addressing information

- User Security information: Network access control information for authentication and authorisation
- User Location information at inter-system level: the HSS supports the user registration, and stores inter-system location information, etc.
- User profile information

HSS also leverages the following;

- HLR (home location registrar)
- GAA (general authentication architecture -proposed)
- GBA (general bootstrap architecture -proposed)

And Key HSS protocols include;

- SIP – Session Initiation Protocol, defined by the IETF for signaling, to initiate/modify/terminate multimedia sessions over IP networks
- Diameter – A protocol designed by the IETF for the transmission of authentication, authorization and accounting information; specified by 3GPP and 3GPP2
- HTTP – The Hypertext Transfer Protocol, used for the transmission of arbitrary data throughout computer networks
- LDAP – The Lightweight Directory Access Protocol, used to provide applications with access to a directory store
- Liberty – An architecture and protocols for exchanging information about identity and authorization

With touch points that includes (but not limited to);

- IMS Services
- GUP (Generic User Profile)
- ENUM
- Liberty compliant Identity System
- & Web Services

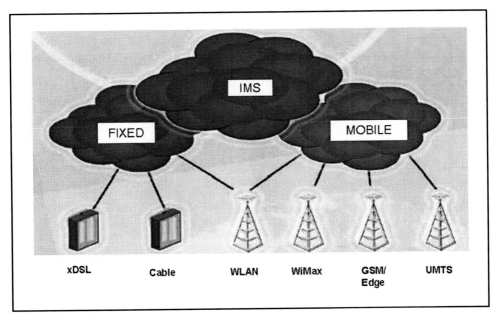

Figure 5:5 IMS's reach to all types of Fixed and Mobile Access Networks

5.3 Identity enabling IMS

From reviewing the overview and capabilities between the two systems (IMS and Identity System), it is clear and obvious that there are major market forces and technical reasons behind the need for loose integration (loosely coupled SOA) and potentially more tight integration at later phases.

The primary market forces that drive these integration requirements are:

- Major wireless and wire line CSP's (Communications Service Providers) across the globe are participating and acting as lead members of the Liberty Alliance and have large scale initiatives within their enterprise implementing Liberty Compliant Identity Systems, in past few years (such as Vodafone in Europe, Cingular in the US, Telstra in Australia and many more).
- Several hundred ISV's (Independent Software vendors) who have developed these Service enablers/Service Building Blocks are basing their service with an Identity System as a Core SBB (such as Location-Net/AutoDesk's Location Based Service that leverages published API's associated with Identity Systems and PayCircle's payment services

181

that leverage a common identity system). These Services are currently being deployed with CSP's networks as the IMS Service layers (which are also Identity enabled/based Services that offer Reduced SignON and Single Sign ON).

- The requirements around the notion of Converged Services that will include IMS Services (multi-media) as well as other external IP based Services (web services) that extends to multiple domains.
- The requirements around reaching seamlessly to Services residing in the Enterprise Service Networks (such as GSA's Employee Services, Banking Services from Citibank, etc.), while accessing IMS services in certain scenario's.
- The requirements for an Integrated end-to-end common Security Framework across multiple applications – that includes profile management and policy management.
- Integrated and Identity enabled OAM and OSS Services.
- The requirements around User Centric Service Delivery – wherein a user carries his/her experiences across services, domains, networks and devices (this includes between IMS implementations and outside its realm).
- IETF's acceptance of SIP extensions to SAML, creating multiple SIP Client Applications that can interact and establish and Identity Session.
- The significant inroads made by Liberty compliant Identity Systems in the Services Layer (in fact an implementation of an Identity System by a Service Provider (IDSP) can also act as one of the external service as part of the Service Layer, similar to Content Delivery Services and Location Services.

Realising these market forces a few major NEP's already offer SSO/ (single-sign on) features between all IMS services and in some cases support Federation (via Liberty/SAML compliance) in there IMS Solutions through a loosely coupled integration Architecture.

5.3.1 Approach A: Loosely Coupled Integration

As stated above, in a loosely coupled integration approach, an Identity Service can interact with an IMS environment as one amongst the many different Services in the Services Layer. Many Identity System's Access Management Layer runs as an application on a JEE container. Therefore this Access Management functionality can reside in one of the application servers in the services layer. This loose integration implies the following;

1. Access and Federation Management: Some type of correlation between the authentication that takes place within the HSS (HLR) environment (the network facing identity system) and the Service facing Identity System (any liberty/saml compliant Identity System). For example – using the MSIDN (mobile subscriber identification number) as a unique identifier for an individual which is part of the 23.008 specifications around HSS, one can correlate, to a user in external Identity System that requires a different type of authentication. This would reduce the number of sign-on that would be required especially when a user is accessing services that are not security sensitive in nature (trivial services such as mapping service, weather services, etc.). *This can be accomplished with SIP/SAML to HTTP/ SAML gateways and bridges between existing Identity Systems and the IMS environment or with SIP Signaling with SAML (see Chapter 14).*

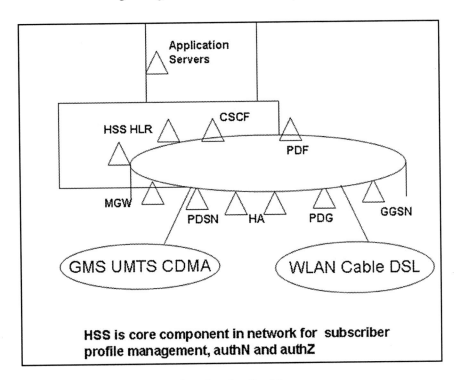

Figure 5:6 Identity Service as another Service Enabler

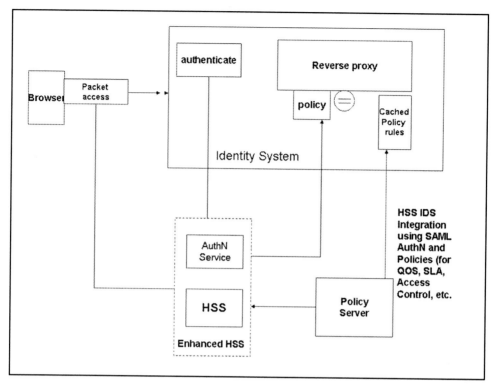

Figure 5:7 Correlated Authentication (Network facing to Service facing)

2. Identity Management: Another perspective that will supplement a loose integration is the workflow, provisioning and synchronisation capabilities offered by the Identity Management layer and leveraging the same to integrate Network facing Identity Systems – such as HSS/ HLR, AAA, RADIUS, GUP, ENUM and more., to ensure the "seamless mobility" of a user between devices/access networks and different services.

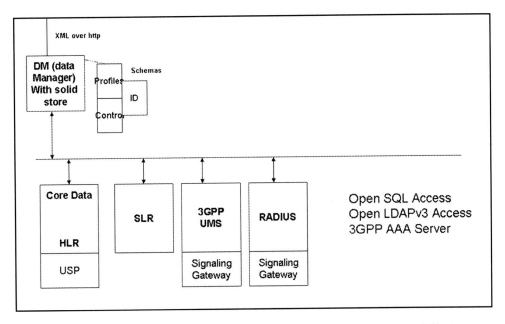

Figure 5:8 Data Mapping/Meta Views and Workflows between Network Facing

Such a system can essentially talk SQL/JDBC, SQL/ODBC, LDAP/ JNDI, XML/SOAP and more, plus support different repositories (including Directory Servers, RDBMS, ODBMS, File Systems, NIS+/NIS and more.

5.3.2 Approach B: Tightly Coupled integration

Beyond what we see taking shape today there are other pressing needs in the market today and in the near future that requires a tighter alignment between Service Centric Identity Systems and Network Facing Identity Systems. There are many aspects to this integration that needs to be taken into account before we delve into the reasons. The notion of authentication levels is a service centric view within Liberty compliant identity systems, wherein, services have different levels of authentication tied to it. Therefore if a user has let's say a weak level of authentication and however requires access to a service that requires a stronger level of authentication, within the session lifecycle managed by an Identity System's Access Management service, the user can be authenticated against stronger levels of authentication and service access can be offered or denied, depending on the success or failure of the authentication. This service centric view of Authentication level is quite strategic when we attempt at integrating the network facing Identity Systems with Service facing Identity systems, purely because of the fact that a user's access to a service is not immediate just because he/she has an authenticated with the Network (say via UE-user equipment, MSIDN, SIM or any other mechanism).

Also Service centric Digital Rights Management makes it possible for users to access services and content managed by a DRM solution, in a device agnostic manner. That is, when, I subscribe and pay for a content I would not want to be limited to use it with a specific device.

Keeping these two service centric perspectives in mind, there are more reasons for tighter integration between Network facing Identity Systems and Service Centric Identity Systems;

1. Extend Communications Network authentication to facilitate web, email, and trivial web service—to ensure seamless access and trusting a weak authentication—seamless access.
2. Range of Identity validation schemes—Device, Biometrics (voice, face, etc.), handset for validating, enhanced device validation (RFID), — essentially offering the capability to authenticate me for a session -over this set of devices and connections.
3. DRM—Can watch any subscribed content anywhere on any network/device, user authentication vs. device resident keys, etc.
4. Device Capabilities—Cache capabilities—profile in network to be accessed.
5. Network offers range of QOS dynamically to content streaming (e.g., transition from WLAN to WWAN).
6. User Porta—User preferences for solution delivery/service delivery. Plus, Service Profile Management—User profile on a per service base.
7. Network perspective of user- User agent when user not connected /reachable.
8. Network Storage—"Never lose your address book".
9. Device Management—Identification, Apps over the air, Diagnostics.

10. Distributed policy framework—Push Access Network specific policies—Push Device specific policies to the edge—Push Service behavior policies—Push user centric policies and Federate Policies/ Profile.

11. Extensions to next generation networks (4G)—Integrated with service/access controllers, Integrated with OAM and OSS, Integrate with other Access Networks such as Cable/STB.

12. Apply additional security logic/restrictions to service access based on network events (can be supported via SEM—security event model + App Server Container development).

13. End to end session persistence (supported by Access Manager running on JEE Container with HA DB) – Sessions associated with Network Connections, Call Session and Service Sessions.

14. Distributed Session Management – Seamless Mobility requires networking between Call Sessions, Network Connection Session, and Identity's User Session (token based), Service Session and other related sessions.

This implies leveraging a Common Liberty/SAML compliant Identity System for both Service focused and Network focused activities. Similar to how a Supply Chain System implemented with JEE as a common system architecture (i2) and CRM system implemented with JEE as a common system architecture (Siebel), can be integrated more seamlessly, these network facing and service facing identity systems with clearly defined functional decomposition can be integrated, via a Common Systems Architecture (a Common Identity System). In a tightly coupled environment Network facing Identity Services (such as HSS/ HLR, AAA, GUP, ENUM, etc.) are implemented with a Common Identity System Architecture that is distributable in nature.

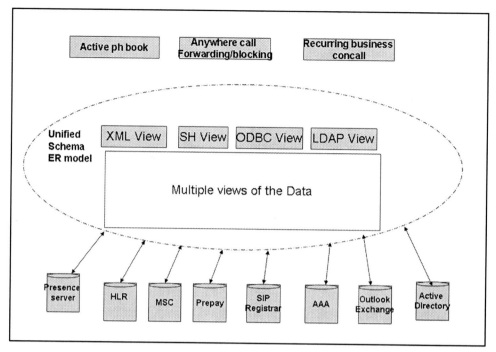

Figure 5:9 Tight coupling between Network Facing IDS and Service Centric IDS

This layer is repository agnostic and Authentication Mechanism agnostic (i.e., can support an exhaustive list of authentication types) and has a common set of published API's that service and networks can reuse. This implies an Access Management Layer that supports direct SIP/Diameter interfaces, without a gateway or bridge, to do any translations. Also the Access Management layer that is Authentication mechanism agnostic, will work in conjunction with meta-views (including GUP as a mapping mechanism) to reach other sources of data.

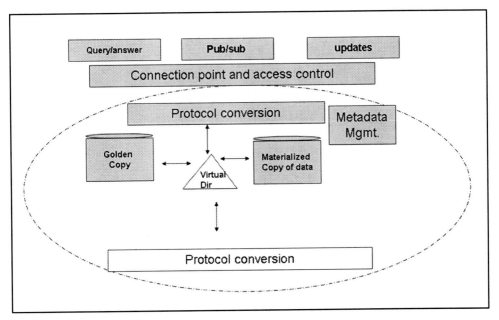

Figure 5:10 Tight coupling between Network Facing IDS and Service Centric IDS

We are seeing momentum in this direction with majority of Liberty compliant Identity Systems supporting, AAA, RADIUS etc. OAM/OSS vendors are implementing their service based on these common APIs and NEPs are building their Next generation network facing Identity Systems with these factors in mind. This approach to tight coupling eliminates redundancy and leverages the notion of reuse around SOA (not reinventing the wheel again), such that tightly aligned identity based service, such as billing, payment, rights management etc., are service enablers, that can be leveraged by many applications and combination of applications (via Service Brokering).

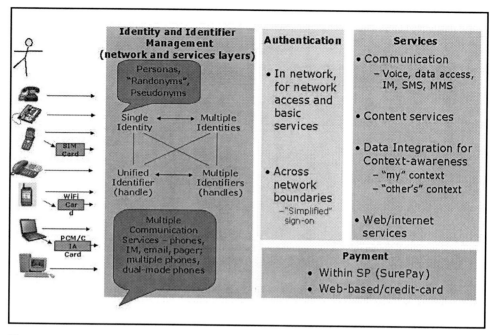

Figure 5:11 Tight coupling between Network Facing IDS and Service Centric IDS

A common systems architecture that supports distributed authentications, distributed session management and distributed services and an environment that ties together, communications services, content services, context aware services and web services.

5.5 Conclusion

The integration of Services, Network elements, Devices and Users data with Network Identity helps set the foundation for context driven/preference based content/service delivery to all Access networks and Access devices, with seamless traversal between them. Over time between 2006 and 2015, with the evolution of 4G networks and IMS, network facing Identity Systems will consolidate around HSS (HLR, AAA, RADIUS etc.,) and integrate using Federation with Service Centric Identity Systems.

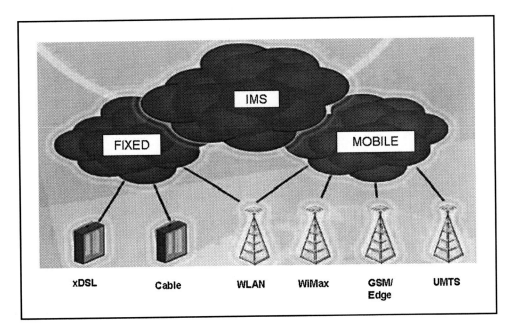

Figure 5:12 IMS evolving the Network and transforming Service Delivery

IMS has to be viewed from two contexts; a) it helps the Network evolve in terms of converged common control layer for all IP networks and b) creating possibilities to transform and deliver traditional fragmented services (data for the internet, voice for PSTN and video over cable, etc.) into a cohesive set of converged contextual services.

6. Identity enabled NG IN Services

6.1 Introduction and Overview

This chapter is part of a series that expands on the notion of "Identity Enabled Networks" from a Networking perspective, i.e.:

- Identity enabled Sensor Networks
- Identity enabled 4G Networks
- Identity enabled Programmable Networks
- Identity enabled NG IN Services
- Identity enabled IMS Networks
- Identity enabled OAM/OSS Services

6.2 NG IN Services

In the introduction chapter we discussed the significance of an Identity System from a Services perspective and described how an Identity System transcends Service Networks, the Core Network and different Access Networks to offer all types of Services to all types of devices. Amongst these three types of services discussed here; namely; OSS (Operations Support Services), NGIN Services (integrating traditional IN, WIN and AIN services with IN services for IP communications) and Converged Services (Services that leverage Voice, Video (or Multimedia) and Data) -play a major role in more highly evolved Service (or Service Delivery -SDN) networks and the Core Converged Next Generation Network.

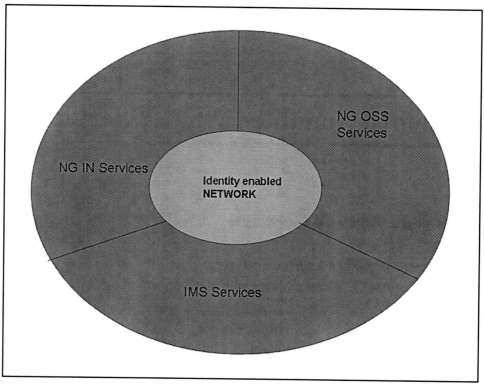

Figure 6:1 Identity enabled IN, OSS and IMS Services

Service Networks are the Service Delivery Networks that host Services and Content (see *http://www.sun.com/service/sunps/architect/delivery/sdn-arch-overview.pdf*), and are run by either service providers (telecom companies in many cases) for enterprises or enterprises within its own enterprise network. Services hosted can include traditional business applications, (such as ERP, SCM, etc,), web services (granular business services), IP communication services, IP entertainment services etc. The figure below here depicts how an IMS network, in conjunction with OSS/BSS systems deliver services to both Enterprise and end Consumers. The Service Networks connects to this Converged Core through a Carriers IP network. An Identity enabled IMS, OSS, IN services and converged services deliver such user centric solutions across access networks.

Examples of IN Services include;

- **N11 access service** — with this service, a unique code is used to access a service gateway to information service providers (ISPs), such as newspapers or libraries. The subscriber may either pre select an ISP for automatic routing or request block calls to ISPs.

- **basic routing**—basic routing function allows the subscriber to route calls to a single destination as defined in the system.
- **single number service**— Routing by single number service allows calls to have different call treatments based on the originating geographic area and the calling party identification.
- **routing by day of week**—The routing by day-of-week function allows the service subscriber to apply variable call routings based on the day of the week that the call is placed.
- **routing by time of day**—The routing by time-of-day function allows service subscribers to apply variable call routings based on the time of the day that the call is made.
- **selective routing**—This service is tied to the call-forwarding feature generally offered as a switch-based feature. With the AIN, when a call to a selective routing customer is forwarded, the SCP determines where to route the forwarded call based on the caller's number.
- **call allocator**—The call allocator service feature allows the service subscriber to specify the percentage of calls to be distributed randomly up to five alternate call handling treatments.
- **alternate destination on busy (ADOB)**—The ADOB service feature allows the service subscriber to specify a sequence of destinations to which calls will be routed if the first destination is busy.
- **command routing**—A service subscriber predefines a set of alternate call treatments to handle traffic in cases of emergency, unanticipated or anticipated demand peaks, or for any other reason that warrants an alternate call treatment.
- **call gate**—This is a versatile out-going call screening service. Call gate supports a personal identification number (PIN) and screening based on time of day and day of week.
- **personal access**—Personal access is a type of "follow me" service. A virtual telephone number is assigned to the personal access service subscriber. When a caller dials this number, the software determines how to route the call.
- **calling party pays**—Calling party pays is a service offered to cel-

lular customers. It notifies the calling party that they are trying to reach a cellular number. If they choose to complete the call, they will incur the connect charge of the called party. If they elect not to incur the cost, the call may either be terminated or routed to called party's voice mail.

- **remote access to call forwarding (Ultraforward)**—The Ultraforward service allows remote access to call forwarding. Callers may, from any location in the world, call in remotely and activate and/or change their call forwarding number.

- **portable number service (PNS)**—PNS features enhanced call forwarding for large business subscribers. It provides subscribers with the ability to maintain a personal itinerary which includes time-of-day, day-of-week (TOD/DOW) schedules, call searching schedules, and call routing information. PNS subscribers also have the ability to override their schedules with default routing instructions. This service is intended for companies with employees who are in highly mobile environments requiring immediate availability.

- **enhanced 800 service (Freephone)**—A customer's call to an 800-service subscriber can be routed to different destinations, instances of routing include the geographic location of the caller, the time and day the call is made and the caller responses to prompts. The subscriber sets alternate routing parameters for the call if the destination is busy or unavailable, thereby redirecting and allowing for completion of the call.

- **mass calling service (MCS)**—MCS is a polling and information service that permits simultaneous calling by a large number of callers to one or more telephone numbers. MCS provides a variety of announcement-related services that connect a large number of callers (who dial an advertised number) to recorded announcement devices. Two types of offerings are mass announcements, such as time and weather and tele-voting, which allows callers to register their opinions on a topic of general interest.

- **automatic route selection/least cost routing**—With this service, subscribers design a priority route for every telephone number dialed. The system either directs calls or blocks calls to restricted privilege users.

- **work-at-home**—This service allows an individual to be reached at home by dialing an office number, as well as allowing the employee to dial an access code from home, make long-distance calls, and have them billed and tracked to a business telephone number.

- **inmate service**—This service routes prisoners' calls, tracks the call information, and offers call control features such as prompts for personal identification numbers, blocking certain called numbers and time or day restrictions.

- **holding room**—Transportation companies' passengers use this service to inform families or business associates of transportation delays or cancellations.

- **call prompter**—The call prompter service feature allows a service subscriber to provide an announcement that requests the caller to enter a digit or series of digits via a dual tone multi-frequency (DTMF) telephone. These digits provide information that is used to direct routing or as a security check during call processing.

- **call counter**—The call counter service feature increases a counter in the tele-voting (TV) counting application when a call is made to a TV number. The counts are managed in the SCP, which can accumulate and send the results during a specific time period.

- **500 access service**—This routing service allows personal communications service (PCS) providers the ability to route calls to subscribers who use a virtual 500 number.

- **PBX extend service**—This service provides a simple way for users to gain access to the Internet network.

- **advertising effectiveness service**—This service collects information on incoming calls (for example, ANI, time, and date). This information is useful to advertisers to determine the demographics of their customers.

- **virtual foreign exchange service**—Uses the public switched network to provide the same service as wired foreign exchange service.

- **automated customer name and address (ACNA)**—ACNA enables customers to block their lines from being accessed by the service.

- **AIN for the case teams (ACT)**—ACT allows technicians to dial from a customer premise location anywhere in the service region and connect to a service representative supported by an ACD. Through voice prompts, the technician is guided to the specific representative within a case team pool within seconds, with no toll charges to the customer.

- **regional intercept**—Regional intercept instructs callers of new telephone numbers and locations of regional customers. This service also forwards calls to the new telephone number of the subscriber. Various levels of the service can be offered, based upon the customer's selection.

- **work-at-home billing**—A person who is working at home dials a 4-digit feature access code, which prompts the system to track and record the billing information for the calls. Calls tracked in this manner are billed directly to the company rather than to the individual.

- **inbound call restriction**—This service allows a customer to restrict certain calls from coming into the subscriber's location. This service is flexible enough to restrict calls either by area code, NNX, or particular telephone numbers. Restrictions may even be specified by day of week or time of day.

- **outbound call restriction**— This service allows a customer to restrict certain calls from being completed from the subscriber's location. This service is flexible enough to restrict calls by either area code, NNX or particular telephone numbers. Restrictions may even be specific to day of week or time of day.

- **flexible hot line**—This service allows a customer to pick up a telephone handset and automatically connect to a merchant without dialing any digits. An example of this is a rent-a-car phone in an airport, which allows a customer to notify the rent-a-car company to pick them up at the terminal.

What needs to be noted is that the majority of the AIN applications are Call Processing and Call Control centric, however with the evolution in the Network into one with a Common Control Communication layer and high bandwidth Access Networks, for all IP Services (IP Multi Media, IP TV and IP Calls), the NG IN Services is actually offering intelligence not purely for a Call control, Call processing and Call routing but is evolving into one that handles Multi-Media (Data, Voice and Video) Services and hence is actually handling:

- Service control (Identity based – QOS and SLA – see next chapter),

- Service processing (execution in SLEE and JEE) and
- Service routing (orchestration and choreography of multi-media services),
- Policy based Control of all IP Devices and IP Access Networks,
- Identity enabled Location,
- Presence,
- Payment,
- Contact Book
- and more (see Appendix for Liberty Service Interface Specification).

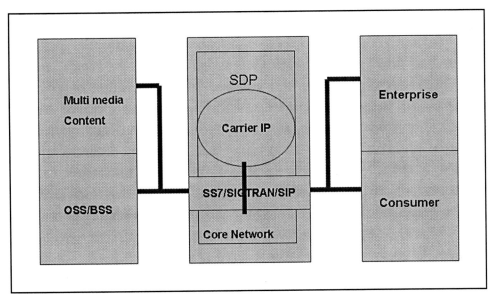

Figure 6:2 Identity pervading MM, OSS/BSS, SDP, Core Network and Enterprise Network

The Service Delivery Networks typically leverage extensive OS and network security capabilities. This includes Secure Execution, Process/ User Rights Management, Service Containers, Cryptographic Frameworks, IP-Sec and more. Within the Core Converged Network, telecommunications Companies have the challenge of evolving their OSS Services and new revenue generating Converged Services. The Core network is typically run by the Telecom companies/Carriers, with the main purpose of providing connectivity between Service networks and different types of Access Networks. The core network is evolving into a converged network today, with the implementation of "soft switches" and the likes, that integrates both "packet based" core control layer and the "circuit-switch" based core. Within the Core a set of Services run; typically run by telecom companies, again, such as OAM applications, OSS services, IN services, routing services and more. However, lately with the implementation of large scale Identity Systems by telecom companies worldwide, such as Telstra in Australia, to Vodafone in Europe to Cingular in the US, an Identity System not only acts as a Core Service Building Block in a "Service Oriented Architecture", but also becomes a Core Service that is hosted within the Core Network and allows for federation of many services from many Service Networks (SDN). If the telecommunications infrastructure is at the heart of the business of an operator, then: Intelligence in the Network is key for User Centric Services - IN for traditional PSTN networks and AIN for Cellular and PSTN networks has to evolve into the Next Generation IN Services that takes into account the proliferation of Voice in the IP world, to bridge the world of PSTN, Wireless/Cellular and IP based communication services. The Next Generation Intelligent Network (NGIN) platform needs to bring traditional Intelligent Network features to the IP telephone networks of today and tomorrow, to provide new features, increased flexibility, and powerful service creation tools to meet new customer demands with USER definable data. The NGIN platform should come with a pre-packaged applications like Intelligent Routing (static and dynamic) and also provides the building blocks for service providers and their customers to build their own services.

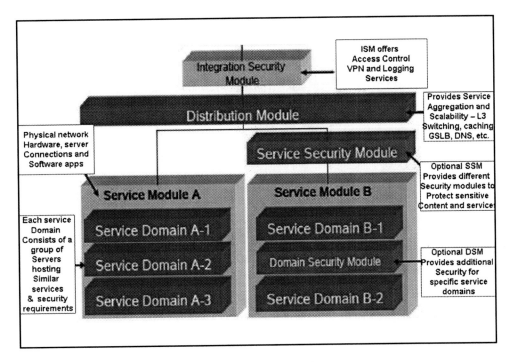

Figure 6:3 Identity enabled SDN that hosts IN Services

The NGIN platform must support drag-and-drop graphical service creation environment for the design and deployment of call flows consistent with the unified nature of calls today and one that defines the complete caller experience including IVR, intelligent routing, and external database integration, all without costly multi-vendor platform integration.

Routing rules and other application logic may be entirely contained within the NGIN platform, or may be dependent on data that resides within an enterprise outside of the service provider's network. The interface to enterprise data is based on XML, providing a simple, standard, and secure way for customers to utilise and control network resources to deliver their own data-driven applications

Bridging IN to Internet with Services, such as PINT, SPIRIT and WEB-IN. In addition integrating the Network facing Identity systems, such as AAA servers, RADIUS servers, HLR/HSS Servers, ENUM servers and GUP servers with a common GLUE—a distributable policy engine - to carry the user's experience from a TV/STB over Cable to a Handheld over Cellular to a Laptop over Wifi. Johan Zuidweg, the author of the "Next Generation Intelligent Networks" states that the NGIN services and applications managing a telecommunications infrastructure are responsible for (in terms of support) for the following:

- SIBs and SBBs
- H.323
- SIP
- MGCP and Soft-switching
- PINT, SPIRITS and Web-IN
- Service Mgmt and Config over the Internet (similar to SPML)
- GSM, GPRS and CAMEL
- WAP, iMODE, MexE, SIM
- SMS, Location and Payment
- 3GPP, UMTS and OSA

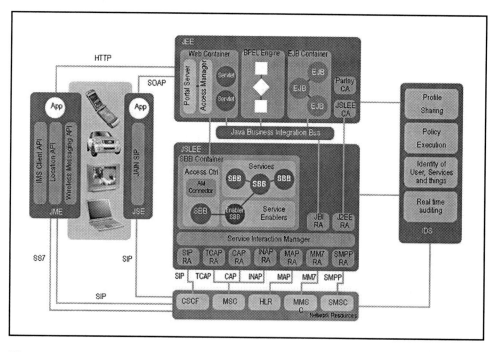

Figure 6:4 Legacy and NG IN Services on a SLEE

The above diagram depicts some of the key NG IN Services that can run on a JAIN SLEE environment as a SBB. Similarly the diagram also depicts a scenario where services from the JEE and JSLEE environments interact from a user perspective. Both the JEE and SLEE environments leverage the Identity System for profile, preferences and policy services.

6.3 Identity enabling IN Services

For NG IN Services, while all the required gateways, bridges, adaptors and translators are offered via a JAIN SLEE container to ensure a seamless (IP) service access from all types of Networks, an Identity System can be the system that offers not just Access Control and Access Policies, but it can very well offer the additional level of user centric intelligence (in the form of information), when services are accessed and consumed by users. There are many generic security requirements of an IN system from an Identity System standpoint and there are a few unique requirements of an IN system from sharing intelligence with services—in a secure manner within trusted environments, between operators, with a global reach. Also there are extensive integration efforts already in place between JAIN SLEE containers and JEE Containers with pre-developed adaptors and with the JBI (java Business Integration) Bus—so Services in Carrier environment can invoke and interact with Services in the Enterprise Business space; e.g. a Support Service call placed by a stranded consumer on a road in a desert in Arizona to a AAA service can continue to invoke business services that include - data about the user's location (to dispatch support), payment services to know whether the service is part of bundle or one that requires additional payment etc. Intelligence here however is not artificial, it's intelligence gained through information more around contextual information. Adding context to the Services that get invoked based on an event with the appropriate intelligence. However in conjunction with this invocation and interaction between telecom services and business services—appropriate user profile has to be shared near real time between these services—adding the layer of intelligence (Next Generation) for more complex interactive Calls and User session (user's interactions with the Network). This calls for Identity enabling both JEE based business services and JAIN SLEE based communication services to offer a common security framework as well as contextual information in a federated manner—so service can respond according to the situation at hand.

6.3.1 Reasons for Identity enabling NG IN Services:

Based on the discussions so far the key value proposition of an Identity System for NG IN System includes;

- Enabling Customer Oriented Service invocation based on Events
- Enabling Customer Oriented Service invocation based on Context
- A Policy-Based Management Approach for both JAIN SLEE and JEE environments
- Distributed Policies that address Policies for Users, for NE and for Events/Components etc.
- Support for Policy hierarchy based on IN Service hierarchy
- Support for Distributed Session Management
- Support for Session and Token based Policies
- A Security Architecture for a number of Security needs including the validation of identity of users, services (code), system, network components, network elements, devices and more
- A Service Provisioning capability across Carriers and Domains (federated provisioning)
- An Identity System offering IN/AIN like Services for OSS/BSS Services
- Session based Policy/Rules
- Integration with legacy AAA, RADIUS, HLR's, GUP and more
- Delegation of Management for QoS
- Provisioning of Security Requirements in Active/Programmable Networks
- SSO for OSS
- Auditing and Active Security Event Modeling
- Auditing and Active Security Event Modeling
- Policy based OSS deployments
- Heterogeneous Network Equipment's Access Control Integration of Access Management with Key Management

A common system that could potentially integrate multiple communication profiles of users (ENUM, GUP, HSS and more) with other Service specific profiles - providing the information that extends as intelligence. GUP (stands for Generic User Profile) is a 3GPP standard that proposes an approach to consolidate/map disparate identity systems; within an umbrella solutions so that a user can have active sessions based on his identity data and access multiple applications (IP Services) from multiple devices over differing access networks. The same is applicable for an NG IN environment. The NGIN Services also leverage GUP and ENUM like profile services.

Also, given the programmability of the network (service network), the sensor capabilities of the access Networks and the convergence in the core network (towards an Packet network) - where all Services are delivered over IP (SOIP) - combining and packaging services with new pricing models and assuring quality of experience over defined boundaries etc., requires the next generation of OSS systems (and IPSF based SLA/QOS Systems or Policy Control Systems) that can address the needs associated with these Next Generation networks. To ensure interoperability and common understanding/expectations of the behaviours of these OSS systems across carriers, it needs to adhere to basic standards. At the same time "web services" and services developed based on SOA leverage Identity Systems, so does IMS services (rich IP based multi media communication services) and so does converged services (that leverage Voice, Video and Data) such as a web based CRM system that allows for end-users to interface with customer service representatives online using Voice and Video over IP.

Given this background and the number one requirement for enabling Customer Oriented Service Provisioning with Flexible Code and Resource Management in a Network, the Identity enabled IP Services have to interface with an OSS system that also understands the user's identity, preferences, sessions and context. Added to this requirement is the understanding of the requirements around Service Provisioning capability across Carriers and Domains (federated provisioning), which will again drive the requirements around standardisation of provisioning languages, provisioning approaches and workflows, agreed by the key stakeholders (service providers, telecom companies, and more). SPML (for Service Provisioning Markup Language) is one mechanism built into identity system to address this specific requirement.

Currently this is addressed via technique through the wisdom of proprietary agents, adaptors and Connectors; however SPML is an open standards-based variation of XML. Members of OASIS (Organisation for the Advancement of Structured Information Standards) have demonstrated the interoperability of service provisioning using its latest specification: Service Provisioning Markup Language (SPML). The technology was designed to work with the World Wide Web Consortium's SOAP (define), the OASIS Standard SAML (define), the OASIS WS-Security specification, and other open standards.

Requirements revolving around Policy support and a Policy -Based Management Approach are another key area that can be addressed by an Identity System for OSS and OAM solutions. From an OAM perspective distributed Policies that address Policies for Users, Policies for NE, and Policies for Components (Hard ware and software) etc., are very critical and this is already highlighted in table 1.

The deployment of such policies and the distribution of the same requires policy hierarchy and grouping capabilities, such as Session and token based policies. An Identity System offers a Security Architecture for a number of Security needs including the validation of identity of users, services (code), system, network components, network elements, devices and more, especially with the combination of biometric tools, key management systems, code validation, and more. Both in OSS and OAM environments extensive auditing capabilities and security event modeling becomes critical. For example, correlating logical and physical access control can trigger events based on anomalies. This requires secure shipping of logs and trails from different layers - access management layer, identity management layer, repository layer, network element layer, and more consolidated and mined for analysis- real-time to address potential security breaches. These and many other factors have ensured that NEP's (network equipment manufacturers) such as Nokia, Nortel, Lucent, Motorola, Ericsson, Alcatel and others, have leveraged industry standards (Liberty/Oasis) based Identity Systems and their respective API's while building the NG IN & OAM products.

6.4 Conclusion

The integration of Services, Network elements, Devices and Users data with Network Identity helps set the foundation for context driven/ preference based session centric, content/service delivery to all Access networks and Access devices. This implies leveraging an Identity System and other related security tools to validate the identity of not only users and web sites, but also validation of identity of nodes, network elements, devices and services. Identity enabled NG IN Services will allow for the Intelligence information about Call Processing and Service Processing to be shared across these devices and networks in a secure and federated manner.

7. Identity enabled OAM&P Services

7.1 Introduction and Overview

This chapter is part of a series that expands on the notion of "Identity Enabled Networks" from a Networking perspective, i.e.:

- Identity enabled Sensor Networks
- Identity enabled Pervasive Networks
- Identity enabled Programmable Networks
- Identity enabled Converged NG Networks
- Identity enabled OAM&P Services
- Identity enabled IN Services

Each chapter introduces the Identity System and the respective concepts behind sensor, pervasive, programmable and converged Next Generation networks from an Access Network, Core Network, Service Network perspective and the value proposition combined with synergies brought to these networks by an Identity system acting as the Central "user centric" glue. This series is expected to be complete between August 2005 and January 2006.

7.2 OAM & OSS Services

In section IV we discussed the significance of an Identity System from a Services perspective and described how an Identity System transcend Service Networks, the Core Network and different Access Networks to offer all types of Services to all types of devices.

Amongst these four types of services discussed here; namely; a) IMS Services (a.k.a. IP Multi-media Subsystem Services), b) OSS (Operations Support Services) and c) Web Services (any Business Service offered on the Web and built based on SOA) and d) Converged Services (Services that leverage Voice, Video (or Multi-media) and Data) – play a major role in more highly evolved Service (or Service Delivery –SDN) networks and the Core Converged Next Generation Network. Service Networks are the Service Delivery Networks that host Services and Content (see *http://www.sun.com/service/sunps/architect/delivery/sdn-arch-overview.pdf*), and are run by either service providers (telecom companies in many cases) for enterprises or enterprises within its own enterprise network. Services hosted can include traditional business applications, (such as ERP, SCM, etc,), web services (granular business services), IP communication services, IP entertainment services etc. The figure below depicts how an IMS network, in conjunction with OSS/BSS systems deliver services to both Enterprise and end Consumers. The Service Networks connects to this Converged Core through a Carriers IP network. An Identity enabled IMS, OSS, web services and converged services deliver such user centric solutions across access networks.

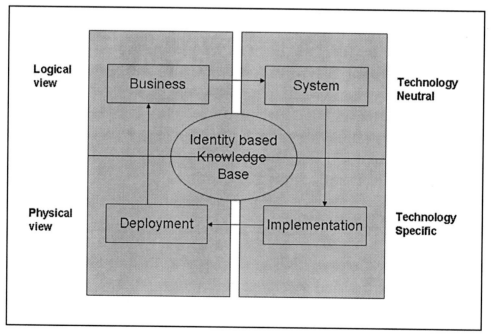

Figure 7:1 NGOSS environment in conjunction with a SP view

The Service Delivery Networks typically leverage,extensive OS and network security capabilities, such as, Secure Execution, Process/User Rights Management, Service Containers, Cryptographic Frameworks, IPSec and more. Within the Core Converged Network, telecommunications Companies have the challenge of evolving, their OSS Services and new revenue generating Converged Services.

The Core network is typically run by the Telecom companies/Carriers, with the main purpose of providing connectivity between Service networks and different types of Access Networks. The core network is evolving into a converged network today, with the implementation of "soft switches" and the likes, that integrates both "packet based" core and the "circuit-switch" based core. Within the Core a set of Services run; typically run by telecom companies, again, such as OAM applications, OSS services, routing services, and more. However, lately with the implementation of large scale Identity Systems by telecom companies worldwide, such as Telstra in Australia, to Vodafone in Europe to Cingular in the US, an Identity System not only acts as a Core Service Building Block in a "Service Oriented Architecture", but also becomes a Core Service that is hosted within the Core Network and allows for federation of many services from many Service Networks (SDN).

If the telecommunications infrastructure is at the heart of the business of an operator, and:

- The features of the infrastructure are used to build the services available to consumers (voice, SMS, e-mail, web access, GPRS, and more)
- Technical quality of the service is the base of the quality of service perceived by the consumers
- It generally implements the latest technologies in domains such as optimization algorithms, data transfer protocols and processors
- It integrates multiple technical layers from different vendors and different time periods
- It has to cover geographically in which each and every citizen is an actual or potential customer
- Then the OSS systems and applications managing a telecommuni-

cations infrastructure are responsible for maintaining it at its optimum state. They cover the functions of configuration, supervision and provisioning for the equipment, networks and services plus, they must face the triple challenge of the QoS, complexity and size of the infrastructure – for all the IP based Next Generation Services they offer. To address this concern around addressing OSS needs for the NG Converged IP service, the OSS/J initiative was embraced several years back and has evolved into a leading solution in this space that offers (from ossj.org):

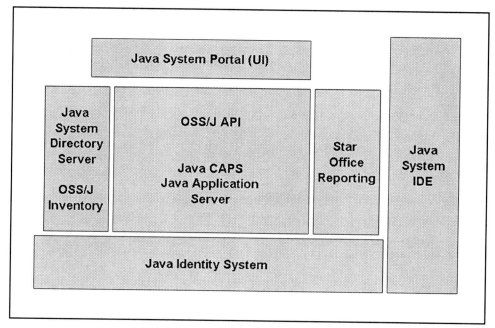

Figure 7:2 Identity enabled OSS/J

- OSS Service Activation API
- OSS QOS API
- OSS Trouble Ticket API
- OSS Billing Mediation API
- OSS Inventory API
- OSS Common API
- OSS Service Quality Management API
- OSS Pricing API
- OSS Discovery API
- OSS Fault Management API

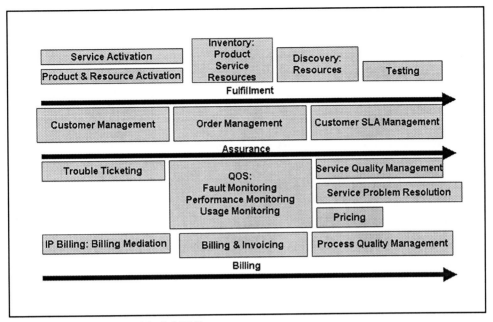

Figure 7:3 Identity enabled OSS/J

OSS Order Management AP This initiative is also highly aligned with TMF (Telecom Management Forum's) NGOSS (Next Generation OSS) initiative and framework (http://www.tmforum.org). NGOSS is a comprehensive, integrated framework for developing, procuring and deploying operational and business support systems and software. It is available as a toolkit of industry-agreed specifications and guidelines that cover key business and technical areas including:

- Business Process Automation delivered in the enhanced Telecom Operations Map (eTOM™)
- Systems Analysis & Design delivered in the Shared Information/ Data Model (SID)
- Solution Design & Integration delivered in the Contract Interface Conformance Testing
- Procurement & Implementation delivered in ROI Model, RFI Template, & Implementation Guide documents

This approach enables all players in the OSS/BSS supply chain to use the elements appropriate for their business but with the confidence that they all fit together with a reduced level of "integration tax."

NGOSS-based solutions use mainstream IT concepts and technologies to deliver a more productive development environment and efficient management infrastructure. NGOSS is prescriptive for only those few 'cardinal points' where interoperability is key while enabling ease of customisation across a wide range of functionality. This allows NGOSS-based systems to be tailored to provide a competitive advantage while also working with legacy systems. See OSS through Java an implementation of NGOSS at *http://www.tmforum.org/browse. asp?catID=1923&linkID=29240.*

OA&M (operations, administration, and management) is a general term used to describe the costs, tasks involved, or other aspects of operating, administering and managing something such as a computer network. It gains more significance as these Networks evolve in programmable/active and converged networks. There are OA&M API that provide guidelines for building system management and event notification applications. Such applications include, but are not limited to, CT bus clocking daemons, board configuration query routines, clocking fault notification, control/signal processor failure event notification, network alarm event notification. These guides include information on OA&M API fundamentals, Event and error handling procedures, Application development guidelines and Information on building applications (header files, library files etc.). Both OSS applications and OAM application (more at the hardware node and network equipment level) have unique sets of requirements around access management and security. Defining the access to OSS systems and controlling it centrally is key to reducing operational risks related to user accesses to OSS systems. It is generally the role of a central operational security team which has to deal with several organisations and systems to secure access. Operational departments must give the basic information that makes it possible to build the security policy document. This document defines the user profiles and their associated applications and systems rights. They must give up-to-date employee status (hiring, changing department, leaving, etc.) so that application accounts can be kept in tune with reality. The user accounts on target systems and applications must be created and modified according to security policy and users' current status. The strong authentication of connecting users is another important system that must be provisioned by the central operational team according to the company security policy: An Identity System here must help the central team to maintain up-to-date user identity information, provision user accounts on OSS applications and strong authentication system. For the OAM applications there are a given set of requirements around security that also involves addressing security concerns around OS, network elements, nodes, cards, interfaces and other such components that go into network elements and servers.

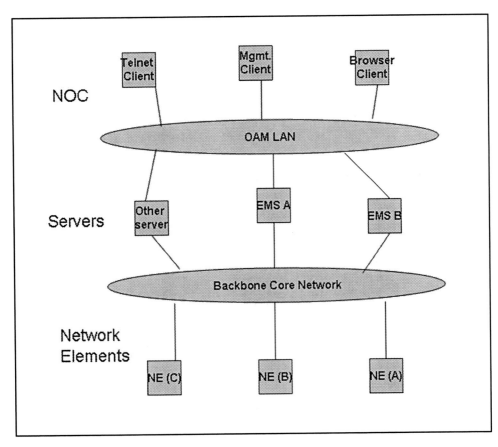

Figure 7:4 OAM systems for Network Equipment in the Core

7.3 Security Requirements for OAM&P environments

SAMPLE OAM AND OSS Security Requirements

Access Management and AAA interfaces	
Authentication—Pluggable Authentication Modules	PAM (Pluggable Authentication Modules) is a suite of shared libraries that enable the local system administrator to choose how applications authenticate users.
Authorisation Interfaces	Once a client is authenticated, applications will need the client's profile and group information to determine the policy for this particular client. The user profile and group information is stored in either Identity/Access Manager. Written in Java and SAML, these modules runs both on the client and server machine to provide password and group database access. These modules can connect to the Identity/Access Manager using SAML protocol.
Authorisation/Authentication -Radius	RADIUS Security Plugins are to be used, the plugins will handle the incoming request by validating the user credentials against the Identity System.
Strong Password Plug-In	
Referential Integrity Plug-In	
External AAA RADIUS	
Web/Http Policy Agent	
Application Server Policy Agent	
Logging appender's/pipes	

Restricted use tokens	In some condition token are pass to application on unsecured channel— If hacker get hold of the token—he will not be able to use that token to sign to another application or generate another token. Specific authentication request returns a special token (SU) • SU can only be used to authenticate once • SU cannot be used to generate another token • SU is not available to administrative users
UNIX Single Sign-on	
Advanced access control capabilities	**Resource based authorization and subtask** 1. Inventory systems provide resource information to the Identity/Access Manager 2. Identity/Access Manager administrators partition resources into groups (this may also be done automatically by the inventory systems) 3. Users or Roles are assigned permissions based on resources, resource types, or groups of resources 4. Access control requests are based on this provisioned information and the current known resource inventory and partitioning
Single Sign-on session state as persistent data	
Session management in Access Manager	Security Services shall provide a mechanism to track all user application session in the solution. This information shall be used to display

all application session in the system. This information shall be persistent across restart / fail-over. It shall possible to maintain all login/logout detailed histories of application session

SPML

Cryptographic key management

ABAC

Last Successful Login

When the user correctly enters their user ID and password, they shall be granted access to. If they are accessing the desktop, they will be presented with a window which shows the date, time and client IP address of the last successful login, and the number of unsuccessful login attempts since that login. This information shall also be available to other Authentication I/F - It will be up to the application (RADIUS/ PAM) to display this information to end user.

System Account Management

This feature allows system account passwords to be managed and be changed on regular basis either manually or automatically. This feature also allows for the automatic creation of system accounts during the installation of an application. This feature addresses the management of system accounts password located on different systems that need to be synchronized with system accounts located on the centralized Identity/ Access Manager. System accounts are invisible to network operator.

Display conf of Warning Banner

It shall be possible for the administrator to optionally configure a warning banner which will be

	Displayed to all users when they log in. It shall be possible to configure whether the warning banner is displayed before or after the user is asked to enter their userid and password.
Graced Login	Graced login means that a user may still login, with a warning, for a certain number of days after their password has expired. Administrator shall be able to change the graced login period, graced login period is in days and default shall be set to 0.
Dormant Account	Dormant account or inactive user. The user account will be disabled if the user have not login for a predetermined period of time.
Limit number of concurrent session	Each NE/EMS shall prevent or limit the simultaneous active usage of the same user id. The number of active sessions shall be configurable on user basis. For NE the default shall be 6 and for EMS default shall 1.
Secure ID	
X509 (Authentication)	
Time of day authorisation	The administrator shall be able to enter a time of day range against each user group, defining the times when the access control permissions of that group are active (default is always active). At all other times, users who are a member of that group shall gain no access control permissions from that group. The time of day range shall, like all other datetimestamps, be entered on the GUI in the user's chosen local time zone but stored internally in GMT.

Delegation policy	Allows you to share administrative responsibilities amongst one or more authorised administrators. The policy sets amongst one or more authorised administrators. The policy sets the control to which entitlements are granted: for example, full vs. partial. Currently solution only provides one level of administration privilege.
Network policy report tools	Shall provide a tool that will allow administrator to find any conflicting policy. Without this functionality it could difficult for administrator to asses why user may not be able to access a specific resource.
Partial NE	This is a refinement of the requirement for advance access control and similar to Resource Based Authorisation but finer grain—instead of being at the NE level, it should be implemented at the component/card/port level. In some deployment, the equipment is shared among different end customers. This is useful when allowing customers to only view/monitor the equipment (card/ports) that they lease.
Pre-provisioning	Allow administrator to pre-provision policies and restricts any change from taking effect until that policy get enabled. This will allow administrator to create rule in advance, assess any conflict with existing rule and to disable policy rule without to actually deleting the rule.
Provision UNIX attribute user profile	Administrator shall be allowed to create new UNIX user attribute associated to a user.

Support of internationalisation	Supports Unicode, enabling companies and their users to present information according to their native language (e.g., Chinese, Japanese). Includes localised message support for log-in, registration, passwords, authentication and authorisation.
Inactivity timeout	1st Level - The administrator shall optionally have the facility to set an inactivity period (default 10 mins). After a predetermined amount of time any UI session will be locked until the user re-enters its credential. (session is not terminated). 2nd Level - The administrator shall optionally have the facility to set an auto logout period (default 30 mins) such that if a logged-in user does not carry out any activity via the GUI for that period (period greater then inactivity timer), then they will be logged out automatically and their user session terminated. The administrator shall be able to override the inactivity or auto logout period on a per-user basis (to set a different value or to disable). Thirty seconds prior to the automatic logout, the user shall be informed via a dialogue box that their session is about to be closed, giving them the option to abort the logout and retain the session.
Strong password enhancement (AM	
Password degree of difference	
Regular expression	

221

Security Alarm	The Audit / logging service shall be able to raise an alarm to whenever indicate that an intrusion was attempted. This alarm shall be manually clearable. You can filter messages based on their level of severity.
Secure log transfer client and server	Remote C++ application shall be able to transfer any security log over a secure channel. Currently the channel is unsecured. (C++ remote application pass security log on the clear).
Support CLI / script	Provide some that will allow script to use the SS audit log. Some security parameter is modified at installation/upgrade time. Any changes need to be logged in centralised manner.
Syslog-ng Support	More reliable / secure way of transferring log.
Support AES encryption	

Table 1: OAM Security Requirements

7.4 Identity enabling OSS/OAM Services

There are many generic security requirements of an OAM and OSS system from an Identity System standpoint and there are a few unique requirements of an OAM/OSS system from Network Equipment, granular management of components within Network Equipments and Session life cycle that need to be addressed. Fortunately all the 11 OSS/J API and other new Java APIs developed by the JCP via JSR and implemented by dozens of OSS vendors, are typically implemented on a JEE (or Java EE) platform. These application Platforms already support Identity Systems and specifically Access Management.

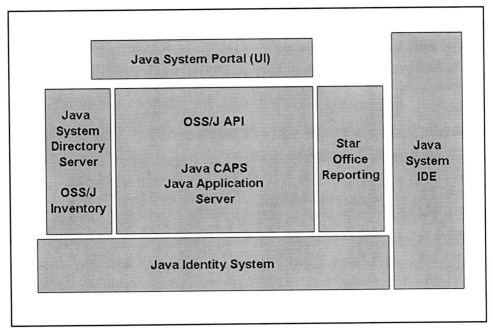

Figure 7:5 OSS for Java implemented in Java EE Containers

7.4.1   Reasons for Identity enabling OSS/OAM Services:

Based on the discussions so far the key value proposition of an Identity System for OSS/OAM System includes;
* Enabling Customer Oriented Service Provisioning by Flexible Code and Resource Management in a Network
* A Policy –Based Management Approach

- Distributed Policies that address Policies for Users, Policies for NE, Policies for Components etc.
- Support Policy Hierarchy
- Support for Distributed Session Management
- Support for Session and Token based Policies
- A Security Architecture for a number of Security needs including the validation of identity of users, services (code), system, network components, network elements, devices and more.
- A Service Provisioning capability across Carriers and Domains (federated provisioning)
- An Identity System offering IN/AIN like Services for OSS/BSS Services
- Session based Policy/Rules
- Integration with legacy AAA, RADIUS, HLR's, GUP and more
- Delegation of Management for QoS
- Provisioning of Security Requirements in Active/Programmable Networks
- SSO for OSS
- Auditing and Active Security Event Modeling
- Policy based OSS deployments
- Heterogeneous Network Equipment's Access Control
- Integration of Access Management with Key Management
- And more.

GUP (stands for Generic User Profile) is an ITU standard that proposes an approach to consolidate/map disparate identity systems; within an umbrella solutions so that a user can have active sessions based on his identity data and access multiple applications (IP Services) from multiple devices over differing access networks. The same is applicable for an OSS & OAM environment.

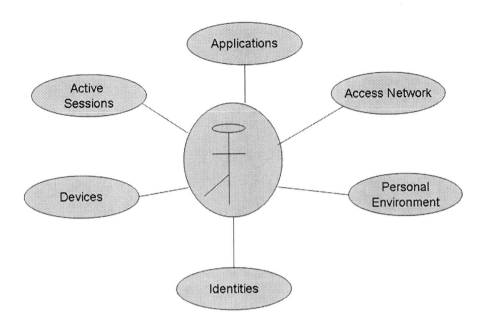

Figure 7:6 GUP for OSS and OAM

One major obvious reason for leveraging an Identity System (with WS-PP and GUP as a Telecom Service –Profile), can be understood when we take the OSS/J TT Service API as an example. If a carrier is spread across countries and continents and has multiple subsidiaries (which is typically the case) and multiple business relationships circles of trust), in order to handle fault management and trouble ticketing across domains, networks, carriers/ subsidiaries and multiple COT, a federated model is a must for the administrative/operations staff/users (via a TT Hub).

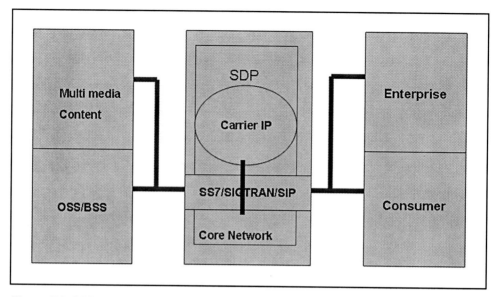

Figure 7:7 OSS Services as Identity enabled Web Services

Also, given the programmability of the network (service network), the sensor capabilities of the access networks and the convergence in the core network (towards a Packet network) –where all Services are delivered over IP (SOIP) – combining and packaging services with new pricing models and assuring quality of experience over defined boundaries etc., requires the next generation of OSS systems that can address the needs associated with these Next Generation networks. To ensure interoperability and common understanding/expectations of the behaviors of these OSS systems across carriers, it needs to adhere to basic standards. At the same time "web services" and services developed based on SOA leverage Identity Systems, so does IMS services (rich IP based multi media communication services) and so converged services (that leverage Voice, Video and Data) such as a web based CRM system that allows for end-users to interface with customer service representatives online using Voice and Video over IP.

Given this background and the number one requirement for enabling Customer Oriented Service Provisioning with Flexible Code and Resource Management in a Network, the Identity enabled IP Service have to interface with an OSS system that also understands the user's identity, preferences, sessions and context. Added to this requirement is the understanding of the requirements around Service Provisioning capability across Carriers and Domains (federated provisioning), which will again drive the requirements around standardisation of provisioning languages, provisioning approaches and workflows, agreed by the key stakeholders (service providers, telecom companies, and more). SPML (for Service Provisioning Markup Language) is one mechanism built into identity system to address this specific requirement. Currently this is addressed via techniques through the wisdom of proprietary agents, adaptors and connectors; however SPML is an open standards-based variation of XML. Members of OASIS (Organization for the Advancement of Structured Information Standards) have demonstrated the interoperability of service provisioning using its latest specification: Service Provisioning Markup Language (SPML). The technology was designed to work with the World Wide Web Consortium's SOAP (define), the OASIS Standard SAML (define), the OASIS WS-Security specification and other open standards.

Requirements revolving around Policy support and a Policy –Based Management Approach are another key area that can be addressed by an Identity System for OSS and OAM solutions. From an OAM perspective distributed Policies that address Policies for Users, Policies for NE, and Policies for Components (Hardware and software) etc. are very critical and are already highlighted in table 1.

The deployment of such policies and the distribution of the same requires policy hierarchy and grouping capabilities, such as Session and token based policies. AN Identity Systems offers a Security Architecture for a number of Security needs including the validation of identity of users, services (code), system, network components, network elements, devices and more, especially with the combination of biometric tools, key management systems, code validation and more. Both in OSS and OAM environments extensive auditing capabilities and security event modeling becomes critical. For example correlating logical and physical access control can trigger events based on anomalies. This requires secure shipping of logs and trails from different layers – access management layer, identity management layer, repository layer, network element layer, and more consolidated and mined for analysis- real-time to address potential security breaches. These and many other factors have ensured that NEP's (network equipment manufacturers) such as Nokia, Nortel, Lucent, Motorola, Ericsson, Alcatel and others, have leveraged industry standards (Liberty/Oasis) based Identity Systems and their respective API's while building the OSS/OAM products.

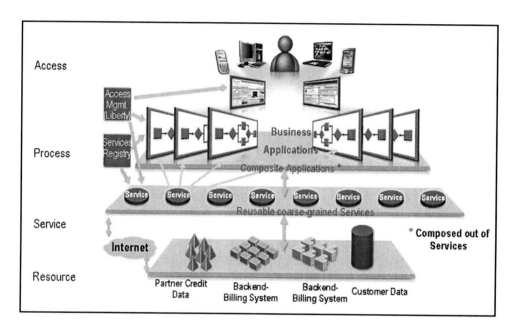

Figure 7:8 Identity enabled OSS for NGN

7.5 Policy based SLA and QOS for IMS and IP Services

Another fantastic development in the Telecom industry recently (Since 2006) is the IPSphere Forum formed by Network Equipment manufacturing companies such as Alcatel, Juniper, Cisco, Ericsson, Nortel and others with the goal of developing a Policy and Control Stratum's Specifications (around SLA and QOS), that takes into account the advances in SOA and Web Services as the Service Signaling Layer and the Next Generation Networks and the Packet Handling Layer. "IPsphere Forum architects the protocol interfaces and framework to enable commercial relationships to have the exceptional application flexibility – the same flexibility that the evolution of the Internet encouraged. IPsphere ensure that every stakeholder can obtain a share of the money flow to encourage active investment, according to what the market values. The result is broader and more market-stimulating sets of business relationships. Simply put: it's about Cooperative IP Services."

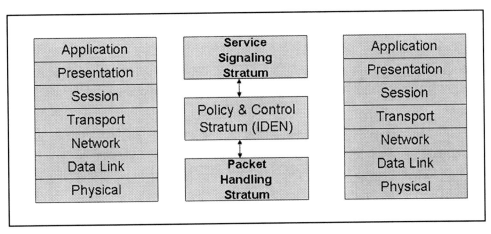

Figure 7:9 Policy Control Stratum aligning SOA with NGN

ISV (Independent software vendors) such as True Base Line, who specialise in this Identity based Policy and Control Layer are also members of this form developing solutions that will allow for QOS And SLA to be managed across Enterprise and Carrier Networks and Applications. These policy based routing engines take into account IPSF and ITSM as well, as depicted below.

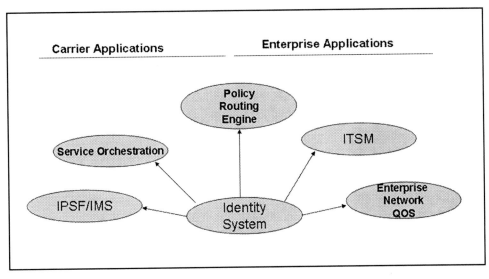

Figure 7:10 Policy Control Stratum aligning IPSF/IMS and ITSM

This Service Management Layer is expected to support all of the modern directions in carrier networking, including IMS, FMC, IPsphere, NGN, TMF, convergence, IPTV and more. Best of all, it should tie all of these diverse goals into a single business framework.

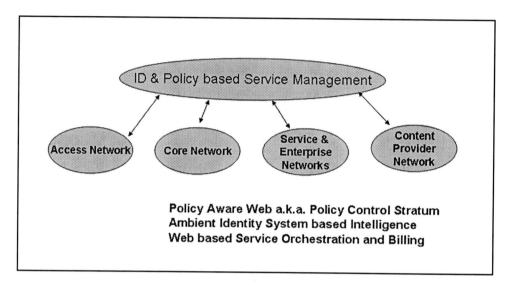

Figure 7:11 Policy based SM transcending all Networks

This Policy and Control Stratum is Identity enabled and works in alignment with Identity enabled ESB and Service Registry, OA&M and OSS Services.

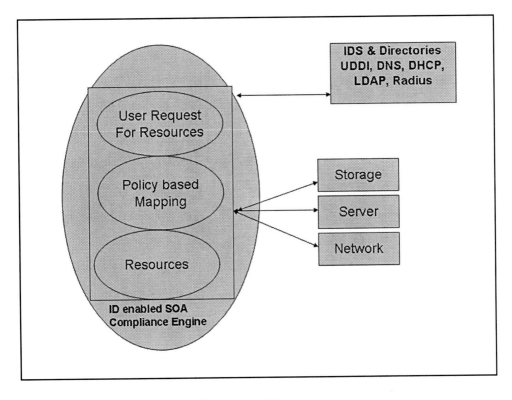

Figure 7:12 Identity enabled Policy Control Stratum

7.6 Conclusion

The integration of Services, Network elements, Devices and Users data with Network Identity helps set the foundation for context driven/ preference based session centric, content/service delivery to all Access networks and Access devices. This implies leveraging an Identity System and other related security tools to validate the identity of not only users and web sites, but also validation of identity of nodes, network elements, devices and services. The latest developments in IPSF and the notion of Identity enabled end to end Service Management for QOS and SLA adds true meaning to Identity Centric Architecture Aligning SOA with NGN – in IPSF speak – the Policy and Control Stratum aligning the Service Signaling Stratum with the Packet Handling Stratum. This is the main message conveyed in the book as well with six chapters dedicated to Identity and Networks and six chapters dedicated to Identity and Services.

8. Identity enabled Web Services

8.1 Introduction

The W3C defines a Web service as a software system designed to support interoperable machine-to-machine interaction over a network. Web services are frequently just application programming interfaces (API) that can be accessed over a network, such as the Internet, and executed on a remote system hosting the requested services. The W3C Web service definition encompasses many different systems, but in common usage the term refers to those services that use SOAP-formatted XML envelopes and have their interfaces described by WSDL. For example, WS-I only recognizes Web services in the context of these specifications.

The Internet and application development technologies such as JEE and .NET, has made numerous consumer (Amazon, eBay, Google etc.) and business applications (ERP, CRM, SCM and more) available online to the general public, from banking to investment to shopping to paying bills to playing music. You name the task and a Web application is at your service. The single most important security safeguard for those tasks is the authentication of the user's identity. That is, the service provider must ensure that the person who's performing those tasks is the authorised user, not an imposter. That's where user IDs and passwords come into play as credentials to prove identity and as a prerequisite for authorised access to applications Within an enterprise, Single Sign-On (SSO) for all its applications in one login pass makes logistical and economic sense. Better yet, you can go a step further: implement federated identity and extend SSO across enterprises, thus reaping even more convenience and time savings for both organizations and users alike.

The majority of the material covered in this chapter is referenced from the paper or article on "Building Identity enabled Web Services" authored by my colleagues at Sun Microsystems in 2005.

Rajeev Angal,

Srividhya (Vidhya) Narayanan,

Pat Patterson, Pirasenna Velandai Thiyagarajan,

& Marina Sum.

8.2 How does SSO work?

8.2.1 Persistent Logins across Applications

Consider this scenario: You want to find a co-worker's phone number in the corporate white pages on the Web and then call him. Your IT department has determined that the white pages contain sensitive information and has implemented access control there. Therefore, before you can look up that phone number, you must first log in to the white pages with your user ID and password. After calling your co-worker, you'd like to access a widget supplier's site from a link on your corporate portal, both access control--protected. Not only must you log in to the portal, you must also do so at the supplier site. In the course of a day, you might find yourself logging in to a dozen different applications. More cumbersome yet, you might have to define and remember a different set of credentials for each application because credential requirements vary, for example, how many characters minimum must be in a password, whether they must be a mixture of alpha-numeric, and so forth. Now consider an alternative: You log in to the white pages. From there, you can browse the corporate portal and then order widgets on the supplier's site throughout the day--all without more logins. Moreover, each application recognises you and grants you access according to your role within the organisation. Your supplier's portal can even tell your location so that you need not type in a shipping address for your widget order.

Sounds like magic? Not really, just access control, SSO, and federation at work:

- Access control ensures that only authorised users can access the protected resources.
- SSO minimises the number of user logins.
- Federation extends access control and SSO across organisational boundaries.

8.2.2 Basics of Web-Based Access Control and SSO

How does Access Manager provide access control and SSO to applications? FIGURE 1 illustrates the workflow.

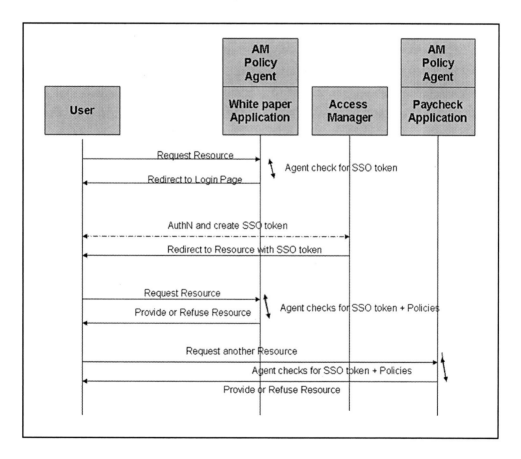

Figure 8:1 Workflow for SSO

Here's a summary of the process:

1. The user attempts to access a protected application on a web browser.

2. A policy agent installed on the Web server or application server intercepts the access and checks for a valid SSO token, which is typically presented as a cookie. You can deploy policy agents to a range of Web servers, application servers, and even enterprise applications from vendors such as Lotus, SAP, and Siebel.

3. The policy agent redirects the user's browser to a login page and earmarks the URL originally requested by the user as a parameter.

4. The user authenticates to Access Manager, typically by typing in a user ID and an associated password. A browser certificate, a smart card, and other similar devices are alternative means of authentication; the user might access an application through one of those devices instead of through a password. Afterwards, Access Manager creates a session with a specific lifetime. For the duration of that session, the user is signed on according to the policies that are in place.

5. Access Manager sends the user's browser a cookie that contains an SSO token and redirects the browser to the originally requested URL. Afterwards, the user's browser repeats the request in step 1, this time with the token-included cookie.

6. The policy agent finds the cookie, extracts the SSO token, and validates it with Access Manager.

If Access Manager's policies have granted the user access to the requested application, the user can proceed. Otherwise, the policy agent denies the request with either an HTTP error or a redirect to a page with an "access denied" message. Subsequent requests for other protected applications will include the SSO token. Again, the Policy Agent validates the SSO token and the user's authorisation and then allows or denies the request, as in step 6. This sequence of events can repeat until the user's session expires or until the user explicitly logs out.

8.2.3   Federated Identity

The SSO mechanism functions well within the enterprise. However, a crucial disadvantage is its dependency on browser cookies, which are limited by design to a single Internet domain only. Federated identity accords access control and SSO across departmental and enterprise boundaries. The advantages are many:

- Establishment of trusted partnerships, that is, tighter, more satisfying customer and employee relationships
- Extended and new revenue opportunities Generation of new, efficient, and productive business models
- A critical component for the implementation of federated identity is the Security Assertion Markup Language (SAML), an XML framework for exchanging data. SAML is managed by the Security Services Technical Committee of the Organisation for the Advancement of Structured Information Standards (OASIS). The Liberty Alliance Project builds on SAML to deliver more extensive federated identity.

8.2.3.1 SAML

The current version of SAML 2.0, SAML enables cross-domain SSO by defining the following:

A set of XML elements that represent identity information (attributes that describe the user), with the assertion being the key element. A pair of profiles (protocols)--the Browser Artifact and the Browser-POST--that use Simple Object Access Protocol (SOAP) and HTTP to exchange identity information.

The two profiles allow an asserting party (also called a SAML producer) to send identity information to a relying party (also called a SAML consumer) so that the latter can provide service. In the scenario described in "Persistent Logins Across Applications," the asserting party is your employer and the relying party, the widget supplier. Your employer sends along your identity information, including your shipping address, so that you can order widgets without having to authenticate at the supplier's site.

The two profiles are similar in nature. The major difference is that, instead of using a "back-channel" SOAP-HTTP request to transmit assertions between parties, the Browser-POST profile does so with a form post. For details on the profiles, visit the OASIS site.

8.2.3.2 SSO Workflow

FIGURE 2 illustrates the SSO workflow for the Browser-Artifact profile.

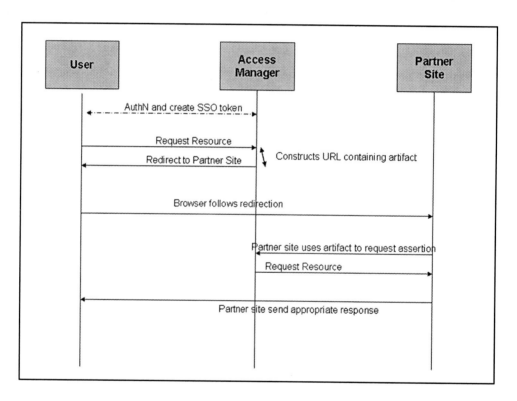

Figure 8:2 SSO Workflow for the Browser-Artifact Profile

Here's a summary of the process:

1. At the start of the day, the user authenticates at the asserting party's site—a protected intranet—in the normal way.
2. Some time later, the user clicks a link on the intranet to access the

relying party's site.

3. The link actually directs the user's browser to a service on the asserting party's site. This service creates and associates an artifact and an assertion so that it can retrieve the assertion later. The artifact comprises a 20-byte source identifier and a 20-byte random handle. The service then constructs a target URL that contains the artifact.

4. Access Manager redirects the user's browser to the relying party's site, from which the user's browser then requests the target URL. This URL contains the SAML artifact as an HTTP parameter.

5. The relying party sends the artifact to the asserting party in a SAML SOAP request over HTTP.

6. The asserting party looks up the assertion (created in step 3) with the artifact and sends the assertion to the relying party.

The relying party now has the assertion, which contains the user's identity, and can then serve content slated for the user.

A key benefit of this federated approach is that since it trusts the accuracy of the identity information from the asserting party, the relying party simply acts on that data and need not maintain a separate identity repository. You can deploy Access Manager as the SAML producer at an asserting party. Relying parties can use Access Manager's Software Development Kit (SDK) to easily implement a SAML relying party.

Let's examine a couple of code samples in the next section and learn how a Java servlet uses the Access Manager SDK to retrieve user identity data through the SAML Browser-Artifact profile.

8.2.1.1 APIs and Code Samples

Here's a recap of the two roles in SAML interactions:

SAML asserting party—This is the identity provider (IDP) with the authority to make assertion statements about users. Users authenticate according to the manner mandated by the IDP.

SAML relying party -- This is the application that provides service to users and that relies on the IDP for authentication assertions.

FIGURE 3 below illustrates the SAML roles and interactions. SAML assertions are generated in site A and consumed in site B.

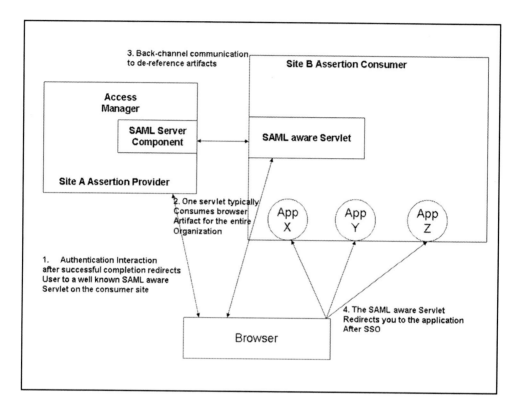

Figure 8:3 SAML Roles and Interactions

Like the roles, the SAML APIs are divided into two categories:

SAML Assertion Producer APIs—You must use these APIs along with a session management and authentication framework. That framework must be present for a SAML asserting party to validate identities, express constraints, and issue valid assertions. Access Manager's SAML Producer API implementation manages its artifact and assertion information relevant to its sessions. That way, you can use the Access Manager SAML Server APIs to create services deployed on the same servlet container as Access Manager.

CODE EXAMPLE 1 demonstrates how you can use SAML Assertion Producer APIs.

```
import javax.servlet.*;
import javax.servlet.http.*;
import com.sun.identity.saml.SAMLClient;
import com.sun.identity.saml.common.SAMLException;
import com.sun.identity.saml.assertion.Assertion;


/**
 * Your service class that will run on the same servlet container
 * instance as Access Manager.
 *
 * Before accessing this servlet, the user must have authenticated with
 * Access Manager.
 *
 * In a real development scenario, the servlet must check for and validate
 * the cookie. If cookie is absent or invalid, the servlet must send
 * failure status.
 */
public class TestSAMLSerice extends HttpServlet {
    public static final String ARTIFACT_ATTRIBUTE = "artifact";
    public static final String ARTIFACT_TARGET =
    "http://col.snowborn.com/SAMLReceiver";

    public void doGet(HttpServletRequest req,
            HttpServletResponse resp) throws ServletException {
    try {
       /**
        * This API will get the user's session token and the session
        * properties from Identity Session cache, then generate an
        * artifact for the target.
        */
       assertion = SAMLClient.doWebArtifact(req, resp,
                ARTIFACT_TARGET);
    } catch(Exception samlEx) {
       throw new ServletException("Error while generating artifact.",
                samlEx);
    }
   }
 }
```

CODE EXAMPLE 1: An Example of How to Use SAML Assertion Producer APIs

SAML Assertion Consumer APIs—In a SAML SSO, site A must know site B's URL, to which it can send Browser-POST and Browser-Artifact profiles, mostly through a secure channel. For each site, only a few public URLs are available to handle SAML interactions. Applications are loosely coupled and depend on those edge components to help with SAML interactions, offering scalability as the number of applications increases. Certain deployment scenarios may warrant tighter integration with the SAML API, however. The two code examples in this section are for use in such scenarios.

```
/**
 * Copyright 2004 Sun Microsystems Inc. All rights Reserved.
 */

import javax.servlet.*;
import javax.servlet.http.*;
import com.sun.identity.saml.SAMLClient;
import com.sun.identity.saml.common.SAMLException;
import com.sun.identity.saml.assertion.Assertion;

/**
 * A simple Java servlet that dereferences artifacts passed as query
 * parameter.
 */
public class TestSAMLServlet extends HttpServlet {
    public static final String ARTIFACT_ATTRIBUTE = "artifact";
    public TestSAMLServlet() {
    }

    public void doGet(HttpServletRequest req,
            HttpServletResponse resp) throws ServletException {
        String[] values = req.getParameterValues(ARTIFCAT_ATTRIBUTE);
        if(values == null) {
            throw new ServletException("Artifact not found in query parameter.")
;
        }
        Assertion assertion = null;
        try {
            /**
             * Given the artifact string, this line communicates with
             * the SAML Assertion Provider, retrieves assertions, and
             * converts them to Assertion objects.
             */
            assertion = SAMLClient.getAssertionByArtifact(values[0]);
        } catch(Exception samlEx) {
            throw new ServletException("Error while dereferencing artifact.",
                    samlEx);
        }
            try {
            PrintWriter out = resp.getWriter();
            out.println(assertion.toString());
        } catch(IOException ioex) {
            throw new ServletException("I/O error while writing assertion.",
                    ioex);
        }
```

CODE EXAMPLE 2: Sample Servlet: Consumption of Artifacts and Dereferences of Assertions

8.2.3.4 Liberty Alliance Project

The Liberty Alliance Project, a consortium of over 150 companies and nonprofit and government organisations, is a collaborative effort that promotes an open standard for federated identity.

Phase 1

Phase 1 of the project took advantage of existing open Web standards, such as SOAP, SAML elements, and Web services security to define an open standard for federated identity. Here are the main features:

Opt-in account linking—Users can link accounts and maintain privacy. For example, you can link your airline mileage account to your car rental account without the airline being aware of your car rental account ID, and vice versa.

SSO—Users can seamlessly switch between provider sites.

Single logout—Logging out from one site logs you out from all the sites you have accessed.

Pseudonym-ity—You can pass assertions from one provider to another without identifying the subject.

Phases 2 and 3

Note—Liberty Alliance uses slightly different terminology from that in SAML for roles: "identity provider" instead of "asserting party" and "service provider" instead of "relying party".

Phase 2 of the project delivers identity-based Web services by means of three components:

Federation Framework for identity federation (ID-FF)—An evolution of phase 1 that supports anonymity, that is, an IDP can anonymously assert to a service provider that the subject can access a service.

Web Services Framework (ID-WSF)—Permission-based attribute sharing, profile discovery and user-interaction service. With this combination, developers can design and deploy dynamic identity-based Web services. See an example in the next section.

Service Interface Specification (ID-SIS) — Predefined sets of attributes for common situations, such as an organisation making assertions that relate to its employees.

Phase 3, which is in process, will offer specifications for a contact book, geographical locations, and presence.

An Example of ID-WSF

Here's an example of how three organisations--a cell-phone provider, a ring-tone vendor, and a bank--can cooperate by means of the Liberty Alliance standard to deliver a satisfying customer experience:
With his cell phone, a user accesses a ring-tone vendor's site. Because of SSO, the ring-tone vendor recognises the user from the cell-phone provider's authentication and allows the user to purchase ring tones from its site, ultimately interacting with the user's bank for payment.

FIGURE 4 illustrates the architectural scheme of the example.

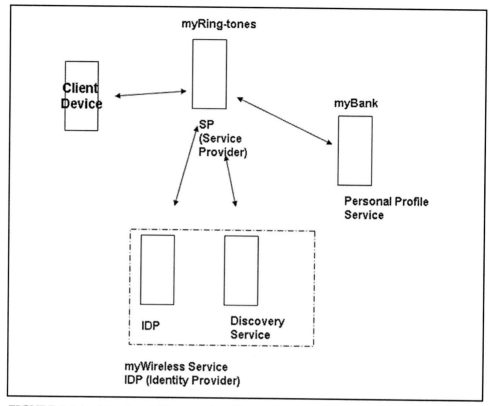

FIGURE 8.4 Architectural Scheme of an Example of ID-WSF

FIGURE 5 below shows the sharing flow of the Liberty Alliance attributes.

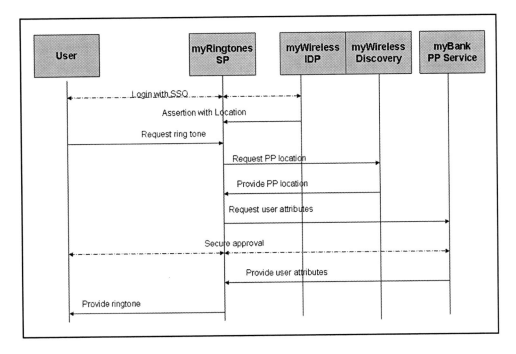

FIGURE 8.5: An Example of Sharing Flow of Liberty Alliance Attributes

The process runs as follows. These steps are a summary of those in FIGURE 5:

- Similarly to the SAML example, SSO is established between the cell-phone provider and the ring-tone vendor. Since the user's cell phone number is unique, he need not provide any credentials. As part of the SSO process, the ring-tone vendor receives an assertion that contains the location of the user's discovery service.
- The user requests a ring tone from the ring-tone vendor.
- The ring-tone vendor requests and receives the user's personal profile location from the discovery service.
- The ring-tone vendor requests and receives from the bank the user's attributes, with which the vendor can use to request payment later on. Optionally, the bank can ask the user for approval of the release of the attributes. For convenience, the user could have opted to allow a number of low-value payments per day without approval.
- The ring-tone vendor provides the service purchased by the user and requests payment from the bank through existing channels.

By implementing the Liberty Alliance protocols, Access Manager enables the deployment of federated identity services. A future technical article will explore Liberty Alliance in more detail and show you how to capitalise on the standards to achieve federated identity in Web applications.

This part of the chapter introduced identity federation as it relates to single sign-on (SSO) and demonstrated how Security Assertion Markup Language (SAML) and the Liberty Identity Federation Framework (ID-FF) offer standard mechanisms for cross-domain SSO. For example, employees can log in to the employer's portal and subsequently access resources at a supplier site without logging in to the latter. That article also briefly described the Liberty Alliance Project's Identity Web Service Framework (ID-WSF) and its capabilities for identity-enabling Web services.

This section introduces ID-WSF and the new developments in the Java Community Process and in Sun's products that enables one to efficiently build identity-enabled Web services. Specifically, we'll learn the following:

- How Liberty ID-WSF identity-enables Web services
- How components that are based on the Java 2 Platform, Enterprise Edition (J2EE platform), such as Java Specification Request (JSR) 196, insulate you from the mechanics of ID-WSF
- How Sun Java Studio Enterprise (henceforth, Java Studio Enterprise) will automate the creation of identity-enabled Web services

8.3 Problem and Solution

8.3.1 The Problem

Many enterprises have heterogeneous, complex IT environments that cause numerous logistical and support issues. To complicate matters, those same enterprises are now exposing and deploying Web services outside the firewall to customers and partners. Transport security protocols, such as Secure Sockets Layer (SSL) and Transport Level Security (TLS), help secure the communication among nodes, but that's not always enough. Even with client-authenticated TLS, the ultimate Web-service provider only knows the identity of its immediate consumer — the intermediary — with no secure records of the ultimate consumer. See Figure 6.

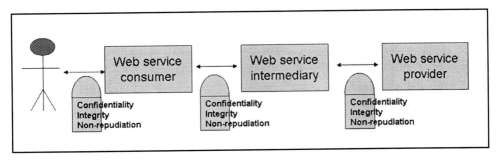

FIGURE 8.6: Web Service Provider unaware of Consumer Identity

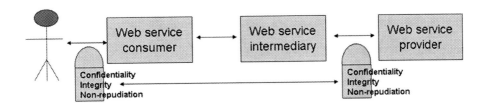

FIGURE 8.7: Web Service Provider unaware of Consumer Identity

End-to-end security is ensured, in part, by the WS-Security standard, which defines how a Web-service consumer signs and, optionally, encrypts messages so that the consumer's identity is transparent to Web-service providers along the processing chain. However, WS-Security stops short of identity-enabling Web services.

Consider this scenario —
An enterprise plans to add a calendar channel to its employee portal with the following capabilities:

- Employees can browse their appointments and subscribe to co-workers' calendars.

- Employees can create their own private appointments that are invisible to others, that is, employees can view those appointments; their co-workers cannot.

The enterprise lacks a single calendar service. An employee's calendar service depends on that individual's location and work group, and no simple mapping exists from an employee's location and work group to the calendar server. That's because calendar migration may lag an employee's move by days or even weeks.

The enterprise now embarks on a plan to collaborate with several partners to enable a subset of employees to subscribe to partner employees' calendars. These questions immediately surface:

- How does the Web-service consumer (the employee portal) prove to the provider that it is acting on behalf of a particular employee?
- How should the Web-service provider (the calendar service) manage trust relationships with a large population of employees?
- How does the enterprise resolve identities across organisational boundaries?
- How does the Web-service consumer locate the correct Web-service provider for a particular employee?
- How does the enterprise accord employee access to partner sites without giving the partners a roster of the employees?
- How does the enterprise extend solutions to its partners without imposing its vendor choices on the partners' own infrastructure?

8.3.2 The Solution

Enter Liberty's ID-WSF. Built on existing industry standards, such as WS-Security, SAML, XML Signature and XML Encryption, ID-WSF extends those standards to resolve the problems of identity-enabling Web services. See Figure 8.

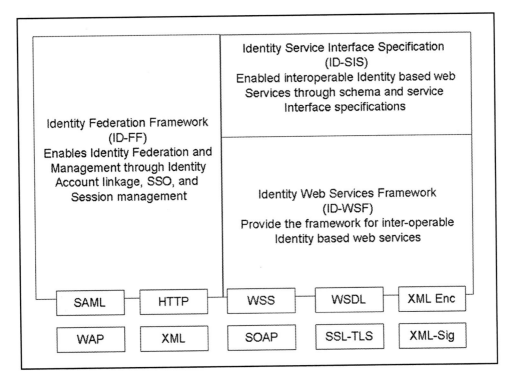

Figure 8.8: Relationship among ID-FF, ID-SIS, IDWSF and others.

ID-WSF comprises the following:

- Mechanisms for leveraging browser-based authentication of end users or, alternatively, for enabling Web services to authenticate users through credentials
- A trusted authority that can issue assertions of user identities, attributes and roles
- A capability that locates an identity-based service, with which Web-service consumers can find the correct Web-service providers for specific users
- A built-in privacy component—so that users can access systems by revealing only that they are authorised to do so
- A mandatory conformance program to promote interoperability

In addition, Liberty's Identity Service Interface Specifications (ID-SIS) build on ID-WSF to deliver service definitions for numerous situations, such as the following:

- **Personal Profile Service**, which specifies the principals' basic profile, such as names and contact details
- **Employee Profile Service**, which stores the employees' basic profile, such as names and contact details
- **Contact Book Service,** with which principals can manage contacts: for friends and family; for business; and even for themselves
- **Geolocation Service,** which presents geographical data associated with principals
- **Presence Service,** which contains presence information associated with principals, that is, their availability for communications over a network, such as instant messaging

In brief, ID-WSF identity-enables Web services by extending the notion of security for Web services to include end users. See Figure 9.

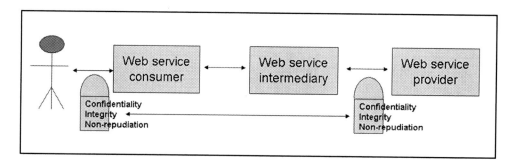

Figure 8.9: Security of Web Services extended to end Users

8.4 Basic Interaction Model for ID-WSF

Let's take a look at a simple ID-WSF interaction, in which a Web-service consumer authenticates an end user and invokes a Web service on the user's behalf. See Figure 10.

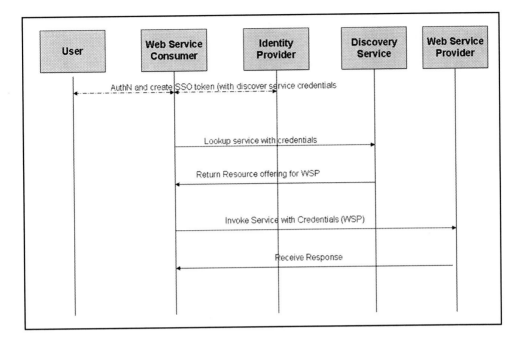

Figure 8.10: A simple ID-WSF interaction

The authentication process proceeds as follows. These steps correspond to those in Figure 10:

- You authenticate end users either by bootstrapping from ID-FF SSO or by presenting the user's credentials to the ID-WSF Authentication Service. Either way, the Web-service consumer obtains a resource offering for the Discovery Service. What does that offering do? Two things—

  —It references a Web service in the context of a particular end user.

  —It holds an endpoint for that service—essentially a URL—and a credential with which the Web-service consumer can access the service at that endpoint on behalf of the end user. The credential is an SAML assertion, that is, a signed XML token that contains a combination of the user's identity, attributes and roles.

- The Web-service consumer locates the target Web-service provider by querying the Discovery Service. That is, the Web-service consumer creates a Discovery Service query with the resource offering, including the credential in a Simple Object Access Protocol (SOAP) header and sends that query to the indicated endpoint.

- The Discovery Service returns a resource offering—another endpoint and credential—for the target Web-service provider. This credential, shown in Figure 5 as "credential (WSP)," differs from the credential that accesses the Discovery Service, shown in Figure 5 as "credential (DS)."
- The Web-service consumer invokes the target Web service with the resource offering, again including the latter in a SOAP header and sending the message to the endpoint specified in the resource offering.
- The Web-service provider responds as appropriate.

8.4.1 JSR 196: Java Authentication Service Provider Interface for Containers

For all its capability in enabling Web-service consumers to locate and invoke Web services on behalf of end users, ID-WSF imposes a certain amount of "boilerplate" on those consumers. See the code example WebservicesConsumerWithoutJSR196.java.

Java System Access Manager (henceforth, Access Manager) contain libraries that simplify interaction with the Authentication and Discovery Services. Still, it's tedious to repeat the same pattern of interaction in each and every Web-service consumer. Here's the saviour: JSR 196 (Java Authentication Service Provider Interface for Containers), with an objective of defining a standard service-provider interface by which you can integrate authentication mechanism providers with containers.

You deploy a JSR 196 provider into a J2EE container (for example, Sun Java System Application Server) to handle authentication. In the context of Liberty ID-WSF, the process entails two requests:

Outgoing request, which adds security tokens, signs messages and interacts with Discovery Service to locate target Web-service providers. Incoming request, which verifies message tokens or signatures and then extracts principal data or assertions before adding them to the client security context.

Consequently, the Web-service consumer and provider can function without much of the boilerplate ID-WSF code. In fact, with the JSR 196 abstraction, the same consumer and provider can operate largely unchanged under different authentication mechanisms. What tremendous time and bandwidth savings!

An Example Scenario

Here's an example of how JSR 196 simplifies development in a scenario of enterprises partnering through Web services.

ABC Circuits, a manufacturer of circuit boards, would like its employees to be able to order parts directly from CMT Chips. Both companies have their own independent identity-management systems. In its system, ABC has accorded a subset of its employees the purchaser role with a purchasing limit attribute that limits their per-transaction dollars. Let's assume that ABC and CMT have already exchanged a base level of metadata, that is, they have each other's Public-Key Infrastructure (PKI) certificates and endpoints and they have defined the role and purchasing limit attributes. ABC would like to—

- Authorise the employees with the purchaser role to purchase chips up to the limit specified in purchasing limit.
- Retain the privacy of the identities of those employees. ABC has learned a tough lesson: When a previous partnership ended in acrimony, the ex-partner used the ABC employee roster to recruit ABC's employees.

8.4.2 Architecture

See Figure 11 for the architecture of the implementation.

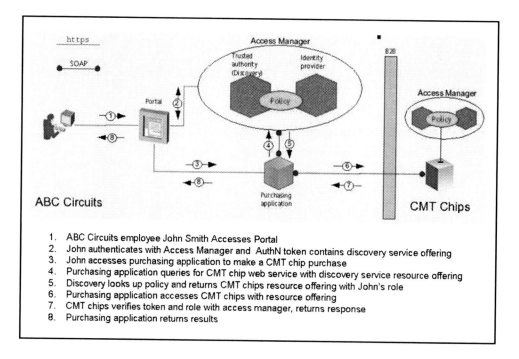

1. ABC Circuits employee John Smith Accesses Portal
2. John authenticates with Access Manager and AuthN token contains discovery service offering
3. John accesses purchasing application to make a CMT chip purchase
4. Purchasing application queries for CMT chip web service with discovery service resource offering
5. Discovery looks up policy and returns CMT chips resource offering with John's role
6. Purchasing application accesses CMT chips with resource offering
7. CMT chips verifies token and role with access manager, returns response
8. Purchasing application returns results

Figure 8.11: Architecture of example scenario

8.4.3 Process

Here is how the scenario plays out in ID-WSF:

1. John Smith, an ABC Circuits employee, accesses the ABC Portal from his browser.
2. The portal authenticates John with Access Manager, which in turn returns an authentication token that contains a resource offering for the Discovery Service.
3. John accesses the Purchasing Application portal to acquire CMT chips.
4. With the resource offering, Purchasing Application queries Access Manager's Discovery Service implementation for the CMT Chips Web service.
5. Discovery Service looks up the policy, verifies that John has the purchaser role, returns the CMT Chips resource offering, including a token that contains John's role and purchasing limit.
6. Purchasing Application accesses CMT Chips with the resource offering.
7. CMT Chips verifies the token and the role with its instance of Ac-

cess Manager, executes the relevant business logic, including a check of the order total against the purchasing limit and returns a response message.

8. Portal Purchasing Application returns the results.

See WebservicesConsumerWithJSR196.java, the source code for the Web-service consumer.

In this scenario, after successful authentication of the user, the Web-service consumer simply assembles the message and hands it off to the JSR 196 provider—trouble free!

See WebservicesProviderWithJSR196.java, which pertains to the Web-service provider.

The provider needs no Liberty-specific code; it simply executes business logic against the incoming request and then responds. The JSR 196 provider verifies the incoming request and high-level access control (that is, it confirms that John has the purchaser role) before signing the outgoing response.

8.5 Policies and Entities for Services

Unlike most of the other chapters there is no section on identifying the value proposition and synergies to integrate an Identity System with Web Services. It is the very foundation why Service Centric Identity System exists today and an Identity System is the Core Service Building Block in Service Oriented Architecture. William Bathurst & Robin Martherus, in their article titled, Extending Identity Management into SOA, (excerpts in the next few pages) introduce a solution for managing and applying policies and controls to Service Oriented Architectures. The ability to create, manage, and apply policies across both technologies (web applications and web services) requires advanced identity management.

Policies
Policy means different things to different people. Here are some com-

mon definitions:

- Rules of practice and procedure
- An established course of action that must be followed
- The set of rules that govern the interaction between a subject and an object
- A written principle or rule to guide decision-making
- A governing principle pertaining to goals, objectives, and/or activities

For purposes of this article, let's consider a policy to be a set of rules that govern the interactions between entities. An entity could be a person, device, service and so on. Policy management can be considered as the act of creating, modifying, monitoring, and enforcing policies. Policies have been in use for some time in the Web server single sign-on world for protecting specific URLs by letting an administrator determine who can access them and under what conditions. Policies of this type, usually called authorisation policies, are tightly integrated into identity management architectures in the Web server single-sign-on context. Authorisation policies have made identity management one of the essential components of any IT infrastructure. Policies are also used as integral parts of Web Service management. In this context, they're used to describe the flow of information between a Web Service client and a service. They dictate the format of a request and a response, how they are to be signed and encrypted, and so on. Authorisation policies can also be included in Web Services policies. At a higher level, an organisation can have a set of business policies. These kinds of policies generally apply across organisations and describe technically abstract rules. For example, an organisation's IT department might dictate that all passwords must be encrypted on the network. Such a policy doesn't describe how the passwords are to be encrypted or even where they're used. It's a very general statement of a rule.

Generalised Entity Management

Using policies to govern the interaction between entities has to take into account that each entity type often has its own policy management. For example, there are a slew of Web Service management products, with their own specialised set of ways for managing entities. They include quality-of-service monitoring to verify adherence to service-level agreements. For example, a Web Service may have a policy stating that if response times are greater than agreed on, some clients may be redirected to an alternative Web Service. Web-based applications also have their own set of policies that control their interactions with users. Efforts underway to combine the features of different types of entity management products into generalised entity management products would bring provisioning and delegated administration to Web Service management. There's no reason to have multiple products that manage different types of entities. Any good identity management system can be used to manage entities other than people, but the products aren't designed to manage anything else. It's not hard to imagine that an application can have its own identity when it attempts to interact with a Web Service. An application's identity is very similar to a person's. An application can authenticate itself, and it has attributes such as its location and whether it's a batch process or interacts with users. However, many standard identity attributes, such as "manager," "phone number," and "e-mail address," are specific to people and inapplicable to applications.

Generalised Policy Management

Just as the management of entities is in the process of being generalised, there's a need to generalise the underlying policy management technology to allow standardised management of existing policy types as well as future ones. At the same time, an infrastructure is necessary that can meet the specific vertical needs of each policy type. Building an infrastructure that can administer and enforce various policy types is complex. Different policy types are usually administered and enforced by different organisations in an enterprise, managing them has required different applications, and different standards have evolved that focus exclusively on one policy type. Policies used to be associated with a specific entity. Take, for example, an authorisation policy for a Web site or a specific resource (the entity being acted on) on that site. Any person using a browser (the entity doing the acting) to access those resources had to be authorised in accordance with the authorisation policy before gaining access. That authorisation policy was designed specifically for those resources on that web site. More advanced authorisation engines allowed the same policy to be used for a larger set of resources on multiple web servers.

Another example might be a process policy assigned to a specific Web Service (the entity being acted on) designating a set of steps required before and after a SOAP request coming from a SOAP client (the acting entity) can be handled. The ideal way of managing policies would be to enable policies to be managed the same way entities are managed. Policy management will be able to take advantage of the same rich feature sets that identity management has enjoyed for some time now. Policies will be able to go through approval-based workflows, for example, imagine that you're modifying a policy that specifies which entities can access a Web Service containing sensitive information and that your corporate security office needs to review the modified policy before it can go live. When you make the change in the policy management system and save it, it will automatically create a ticket for the security office for review and approval. The change doesn't go live until after it's approved. This is similar to the approval process built into many identity management products. Policies can then be treated independently of specific entities, meaning that they can be used and reused for different entity types. For example, you might create a policy stating that some entities can access some resources between 8:00 a.m. and 5:00 p.m. from machines outside the firewall. Then you can associate groups of users and groups of resources with that policy at any time.

Associating Policies with Entities

An association of policies with entities can be based on the entities' attributes and capabilities.

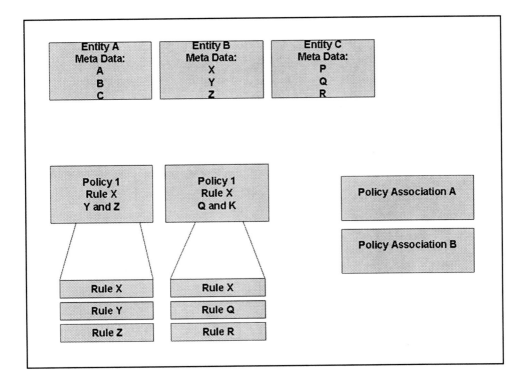

Figure 8.12: Policy, Rule and Entity relationship

Each of the boxes in the figure represents a managed object. The entities can be users, services, devices and the like. Policies can be created
to govern the interactions between these entities. Policies are made
up of a set of rules, which are independent of the policies and can be
assigned to be part of many policies. Policies are then associated with
entities, or groups of entities, based on the entities' metadata.

Policy Association A associates Policy 1 with any entity with Metadata
C or D when it interacts with any entity with Metadata Y or P. The
benefit of the combination of the dynamic nature of association and
delegated administration is that corporate policies can be defined and
associated at the highest level and also require adherence at a lower
level. For example, a corporation might have a corporate policy that
says, "All passwords must be sent over SSL." A policy defining this requirement can be created, along with a dynamic association, to force all
passwords to be sent over SSL. This association wouldn't be reversible
by delegated administrators. Another concept to borrow from identity
management is that of advanced groups. For example, identity man-

agement leverages the power of dynamic and nested groups. Expanding the use of traditional identity management groups beyond groups of users to include collections of policies, rules, and even associations can easily lead to an expansion of traditional "roles." Traditional roles are generally associated with authorisation policies (as defined in role-based access control [RBAC]), but generalised policy management can also mean generalised roles. All types of entities can act in a role, not just for authorisation policies but also to determine which steps to take as part of a process or a company policy.

So what should an expanded policy management system look like?

Architecture for Policy Management

Policy frameworks have three main components as shown in figure below:

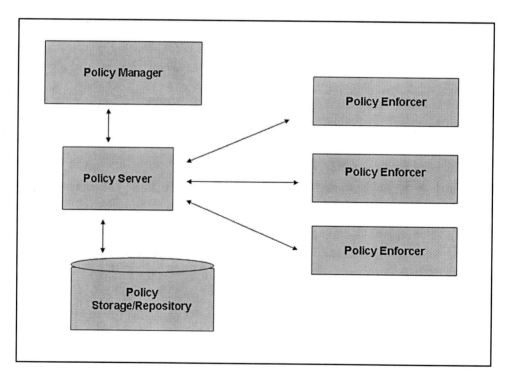

Figure 8.13 Policy, Rule and Entity relationship

- *A policy server:* the central authoritative policy distributor
- *A policy manager:* the GUI application that allows the management (creation, validation, monitoring) of policies
- And a *policy enforcer:* the distributed policy enforcement points, such as gateways and agents. Before an entity can interact with another entity, it must first know what policies govern the interaction. Policy enforcers are part of each entity. For example, Web Services run in an application server, which should have a policy enforcement agent running as part of its process. This policy enforcement agent, which is the policy enforcer, gets policies for the Web Services it controls.

There are two ways an enforcement point can get its relevant policies:
- *Pull:* The policy enforcement agent queries the policy server for the policy expressions that govern interactions associated with the entity it's assigned to, and the policy server returns a policy document containing the policy expressions associated with a specific interaction.
- *Push:* The policy server pushes a policy document containing all the policies that are associated with an entity to the policy enforcer for that entity.

Because of different requirements for different policy enforcers, a generalised policy server must support both the push and pull models of distributing policy documents. In fact, a single interaction between two entities may require both pushing and pulling policy information. For example, Entity A wants to interact with Entity B. The policy server may have pushed Entity B's policies ahead of time. Before Entity A can interact with Entity B, Entity A may need to know some aspects of the policies governing the interaction. Entity A may query Entity B for the relevant policies, or it may query or pull the policy information from the policy server. No current standard is sufficient to provide the flexibility necessary to express all types of policies. WS-Policy is widely used to describe Web Services policies. Authorisation policies are often described by another standard called XACML. WS-Policy by itself can't describe authorisation policies nor can XACML describe Web Services policies. It's unclear if it will be necessary to develop a so-called "Über" policy language capable of describing general policies. The policy server, combined with an entity management server, can be used as an authoritative registry for entities, their capabilities, and their policies. It's essentially a Universal Description, Discovery, and Integration (UDDI) server on steroids. Because policies can be very complex and may be created at different levels by different people, a policy server has to be able to resolve conflicting policies. Rules of precedence should be part of the policy manager application.

8.6 Conclusion

Given the contents in this chapter and the article, two major areas where an Identity System plays a significant role from a Service and SOA, perspective are:

- ID-WSF specifies protocols to implement end-to-end, identity-enabled Web services and JSR 196 defines a mechanism for extending containers to implement authentication schemes, such as ID-WSF. Java Studio Enterprise and Access Manager seamlessly enable the IDWSF and JSR 196 in application development (also see Appendix on this topic).
- The Policy engine of the Identity System can act as the glue between Entities (users, services, devices or any resource including content and files) and Polices, with the Roles-Rules-Resource combination. An Identity System can both push and pull policy documents depending on the context.

This mechanism of leveraging and Identity system for policies and pushing and pulling the same is critical for extending an Identity System to different access networks, devices and equipments (both CPE and NE). This approach is key, not only to establish a secure trusted framework for Services (that includes Web Services, Web applications, OAM&P Services, NG IN Services and more), but is also the linchpin to integrate with entities (users, devices, content, and more). The last chapter on "conclusion and futures" discusses more in Identity enabled IDE (integrated development environment). Identity enabled ESB and Service Registry are directly related to this chapter as well.

9. Identity enabled ESB

9.1 Introduction

This chapter explores the different perspectives from which Architectural Integration takes place, in today's Service Oriented Architectures (SOA) and Network- Service Delivery Platforms (SDP), based on advances in Identity Systems and Enterprise Service Bus (ESB) and Telecom Service Brokers (SB). This chapter proposes the reasons why a tight alignment between ESB and Identity Systems are required and recommends certain approaches to achieve the same. Both an ESB (a.k.a. Service Broker) and an Identity System (a.k.a. Identity Broker) are central and core infrastructure software for SOA (enterprise) and SDP (telecom).

Telecom Services based on SDP utilise voice, data and video (multimedia) to deliver more complex and advanced services such as context sensitive delivery of entertainment, unified communication services and event based sensor enabled responsive integration with traditional business services and business processes. The goal is to transcend all types of access networks and access devices and deliver User Sensitive (preference, profile and policy based), Location based, Context driven Services with true Service Mobility, going beyond, user and terminal mobility. All major Network Equipment Providers (NEPs) have similar vision and strategy, wherein the same set of Services Over IP (SOIP) can be delivered across all types of access networks and access devices that support SIP (Session Initiation Protocol) and with SIP's support for SIMPLE, SAML, HTTP and others. Different dialects of XML are used here, including, SAML/SPML, MOML/MSML, CpML, XKMS, VXML and more from the Network Services in conjunction with XML dialects for business services such as ebXML and others. Lately many Integration software vendors have addressed the need for an Integrated Security framework that addresses Security requirements with extension of their solutions to Network Identity Systems (such as Java Enterprise Identity System).

9.2 ESB and Telecom Service Brokers

The Enterprise Service Bus provides a solution for developing a Web Services-based integration platform in a heterogeneous environment. The system is based on open standards and is comprised of core functionality— of enterprise integration platforms for building service-oriented architectures (SOA) and composite applications. It is the solution for companies wanting to get started with SOA-based business integration. This system provides the foundation for application-to-application integration and automates, manages, optimises business processes and workflows across systems, people, and partners. The ESB also provides real-time exception alerting and management reporting and it basically accelerates integration through Web services enabled JBI-based connectivity (Java Business Integration).

Generic definition of an enterprise service bus (ESB) refers to a software architecture construct, implemented by technologies found in a category of middleware infrastructure products usually based on standards, that provides foundational services for more complex architectures via an event-driven and standards-based messaging engine (the bus).

An ESB generally provides an abstraction layer on top of an implementation of an enterprise messaging system which allows integration architects to exploit the value of messaging without writing code. Contrary to the more classical enterprise application integration (EAI) approach of a monolithic stack in a hub and spoke architecture, the foundation of an enterprise service bus is built of base functions broken up into their constituent parts, with distributed deployment where needed, working in harmony as necessary. ESB does not implement a service-oriented architecture (SOA) but provides the features with which one may be implemented. Although a common belief, ESB is not necessarily web-services based. ESB should be standards-based and flexible, supporting many transport mediums. Based on EAI rather than SOA patterns, it tries to remove the coupling between the service called and the transport medium. Most ESB providers now build ESBs to incorporate SOA principles and increase their sales, e.g. Business Process Execution Language (BPEL).

The majority of the ESB, work in conjunction with a Service Registry. The ability to register, discover and govern Web services is an essential requirement for any Service Oriented Architecture (SOA) implementation. This need may not be fully appreciated in the early stages of an SOA roll-out when dealing with a small number of services. However, large organisations will typically need to support a large number of Web services and as the number of services deployed grows to dozens or hundreds, centralised facilities for access and control of service metadata and artifacts becomes critical. A service registry provides these capabilities and is a key infrastructural component and cornerstone for SOA deployments.

A telecom Service Broker enables operators to deliver unique, revenue-generating services, without requiring expensive, time-consuming modifications to existing operations. The Service Broker service introduction methodology empowers operators to maximise the functionality of their existing network, seamlessly deliver new applications and ensure the utmost in service flexibility. In the Telecom industry the SCIM (Service Control Interaction Manager) is the Service Broker and the HSS is the Service Registry, essentially adopting an SOA approach for IMS –multi-media services.

9.3 Identity based ESB

The generic industry definition of an ESB: "Enterprise Service Bus is a Universal integration backbone. An ESB acts as a shared messaging layer for connecting applications and other services throughout an enterprise computing infrastructure. It supplements its core asynchronous messaging backbone with intelligent transformation and routing to ensure messages are passed reliably. Services participate in the ESB using either web services messaging standards or the Java Business Integration (JBI). ESB is increasingly seen as a core component in a service-oriented infrastructure".

Although the exact definition of an ESB varies, most agree that the following are characteristics of an ESB:

- it requires the clear separation of message headers and message body (and could support Service Interface Identifiers from an Identity System)
- it is usually operating system and language independent; it should work between Java and .Net applications, for example,
- it (often) uses XML and Web services to transport messages
- it includes adapter standards (such as J2C/JCA/JBI) for incorporating existing applications into the bus
- it includes support for asynchronous processing
- it includes intelligent, content-based routing services (and support for Identity based DRM)
- it includes a standardised security model to authorise, authenticate and audit use of the ESB (tight alignment with an Identity System)
- it includes transformation services (such as XSLT) between the format of the sending application and the receiving application, including the transformation of data formats
- it includes validation against schemas for sending and receiving messages (including XSD defined in an Identity System).
- it can uniformly apply business rules, enrichment of the message from other sources, splitting and combining of multiple messages, and the handling of exceptions
- it can conditionally route or transform messages based on a central policy (policies that could be derived from an Identity System)
- it is monitored for message latency and other characteristics described in a Service Level Agreement
- it (often) facilitates "service classes," responding appropriately to higher and lower priority users

- it supports queuing, holding messages if applications are temporarily unavailable
- it handles a "publish and subscribe" messaging model, including event handling
- it is comprised of selectively deployed application adapters in a (geographically) distributed environment.

To a certain extent, an ESB is considered to be a Universal Integration backbone, that also is a highly evolved integration engine that converges functionality performed by traditional EAI systems, ETL systems, B2B integration systems, message oriented middleware and event network to service integration (SDP to SOA) with components that bind on a need basis and with support for near real time integration.

Both an ESB and an Identity System are viewed as Core Infrastructure Software for Service Oriented Architectures, which has key characteristics that includes; Layered Services, Modular and Autonomous, Service Reuse as a SBB, Interoperable, Coarse-Grained and more.

The majority of these characteristics are complimented and supported by an ESB and an Identity System as well.

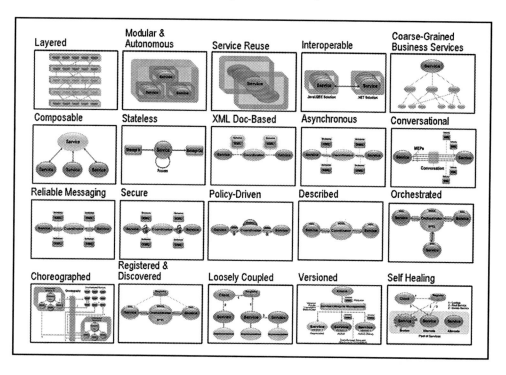

Figure 9:1 Characteristics of SOA

Given these characteristics of Services based on SOA, the tight alignment of Identity Systems with an ESB helps extend the reach of Services and access to Services from, environments such as Sensor Networks (RFID and EPC enabled Business Processes), Programmable/Embedded networks, IMS environment (multi-media communication services), Event Containers (network events) etc. The requirements to align with these emerging trends have already resulted in integration efforts between the ESB environment and an Identity environment. One perspective from which we can view this integration is through a Service Registry (& the Registry Repository) which both an ESB and an Identity System leverage.

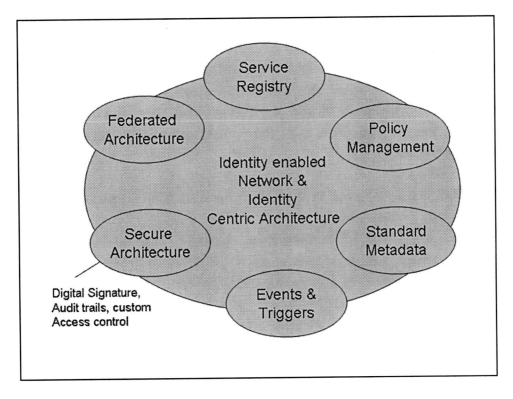

Figure 9:2 Service Registry and Registry Repository

This Service Registry Repository is expected to support majority of the standards in this space including;

- ebXML Registry 3.0
- UDDI 3.0
- XACML 1.0 for Role Based Access Control Policies
- SOAP 1.1 with Attachments
- WSDL 1.1
- XML Signature 1.0
- XSLT 1.0
- Web Services Security: SOAP Message Security 1.0
- Web Services Security: SOAP Message with Attachments (SwA) Profile 1.0
- WS-I: Basic Security Profile 1.0
- WS-I: Basic Profile 1.1
- SAML 2.0

An Identity System is tightly intertwined with this Service Registry for Federation, Security architecture, securely retrieving and sharing XML artifacts, digital signatures and audit trails. Similarly an ESB and SOA leverage this repository for Service Registration, Service Discovery, extensible Information Model, version control, meta-data and many more. Over time the Service Registry, may potentially merge with an Identity System.

9.3.1 Rationale (& Value Proposition) for ESB/IDS Alignment

- Common Security Framework and Security Alignment
- User centric preference based intelligent Service Brokering
- Alignment of Event Execution with Service Invocation (JBI-SLEE-JEE-role based routing)
- Moving from request response to sense response (RFID/ID/ESB)
- Network to Service Alignment (QOS, IMS, access network type, etc.)

9.3.1.1 Common Security Framework for Security Alignment

There are multiple perspectives from which to view the Security Alignment needs between an ESB and an Identity System, that includes the Service Registry perspective, Security for service co-ordination, policy based services coordination, federated orchestration a.k.a. choreography plus, aligning physical to logical-non-conflicting-security needs, validating service identity, coordinating prep-provisioned services and more.

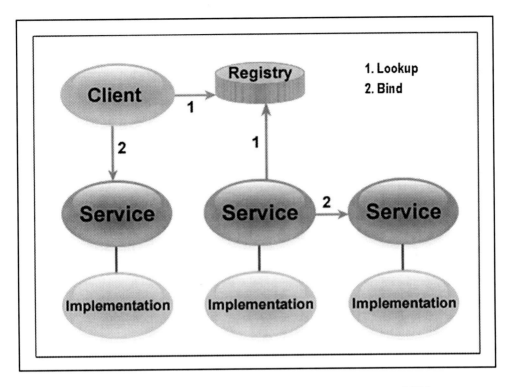

Figure 9:3 Service Registry as a common touch point for an ESB and IDS

The Service Registry is a key component that is touched by the ESB and an Identity System. Integrated Service registry-repositories allow organization and different enterprises to share and link information in a secure manner. Here federation allows for multiple registry repositories to access each other and appear as a single virtual registry repository that allows for convergence. These registry repositories could include those for web services (UDDI based), enterprise private registries, specialised registries such as a HSS for IMS services and subscriber registry/entitlement servers for IPTV and more. Similar to the clients looking up a registry, an ESB can also access a registry on behalf of an authenticated user when multiple services are brokered, orchestrated and choreographed.

Beyond this, there are requirements around federated policy management, federated identity management, federated service discovery and reuse that actually highlight the significance of an identity system as a Service registry.

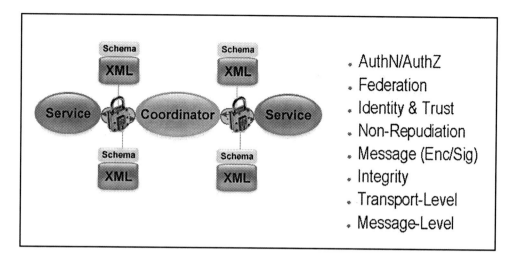

Figure 9:4 Service XML/security schema from IDS

An ESB has to understand and work in conjunction with an Identity broker when orchestrating and coordinating multiple services for an authentication perspective. For example, an Identity system supports service centric authentication levels, and an ESB needs to take these authentication levels into account. In certain cases the ESB validates the identity associated with the service interface (service interface id) for non-repudiation, integrity, etc.

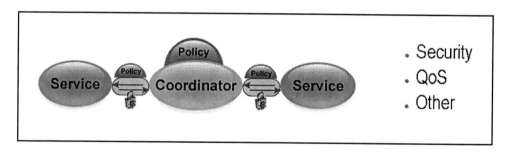

Figure 9:5 Service Policy based coordination

In many scenarios, the ESB has to obtain QOS attributes about a provisioned Service from an Identity System, where such Service profiles are maintained. In conjunction with these profiles appropriate policies are invoked from an Identity System to ensure SLA, OLA, type requirements for Services for specific users and roles are addressed. AN SEB could prioritize the execution of specific services based on QOS policies.

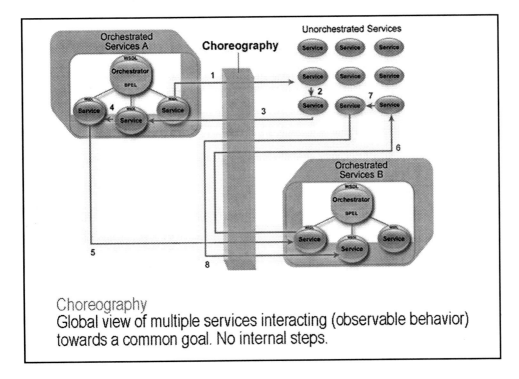

Figure 9:6 Federated Orchestration = Choreography

Beyond orchestration of service within the control of an ESB in many scenarios choreography maybe required when multiple ESB environments are taken into account. Choreography is defined as a Global view of multiple services interacting (observable behaviour) towards a common goal. In such scenarios federated choreography needs to be supported by federated context, federated policies and more.

Service Registry perspective, Security for service co-ordination, policy based services coordination, federated choreography plus, aligning physical to logical-non-conflicting-security needs, validating service identity, coordinating prep-provisioned services and more, not only forms the basis for SOA (enterprise facing business services), but also as the foundation for Telco-SDP (network facing communication services, media/entertainment services and converged services).

9.3.1.2 User centric preference driven Secure Service Brokering

While an ESB's primary functions include orchestration, choreography, integration and brokering of multiple services, within a business process context (including communication services such as IM, email and voicemail), its does not capture any user centric profile, preference and contextual data (such as location, presence, payment/balance, etc.). An Identity System, within an enterprise, within a circle of trust (as an IDP) and between circles of trust (federated IDP), however is instrumental in capturing a User's:

- Profile (such as medical history/medical profile, driving record, credit record, airline club profile, frequent buyer program profiles, user device profile, etc.)
- Preferences (prefer aisle seat. vegetarian meals, non-smoking room, communication via email, notification when limit is reached, and notification when alarm goes off to specific number, etc.)
- Context (location, rental car is broken, physically present within a premises, virtual presence, on vacation at Hawaii etc.)
- Intelligent Service Brokering (communication services and business services)

XML document or XSD (xml schema definition) files.

This profile, preference and context shared by a user in a distributed environment (that includes Access network provider, service provider, content providers, etc.) have to be shared securely in a federated fashion with multiple Services via a Service Broker. Therefore a Service Broker or an ESB has to be Identity based so that there is alignment with requirements such as – profile specific authentication level, profile specific policies, federated sharing of profile and preferences, user notification around context and preference changes, user interventions around context changes and more. The ESB in many cases can act as the conduit that access these XML docs from and identity system and shares the same data with Services that require such data. This is even more important with the Network Convergence that is taking shape around IP (IP based access networks –IPMPLS, IP based Services –VOIP/IPTV/SOIP, and more) allowing for the reach of convergent services (voice, video and data) across all types of access networks and access devices.

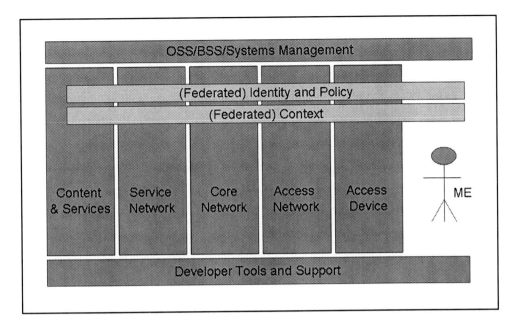

Figure 9:7 Choreography of Services with an ESB that leverages Federated Context

There could be potential convergence between network facing Service Bus or Service Brokers that primarily interact (xml based) with multimedia services (such as Leaps-tone CCE) and Enterprise specific, ESB that primarily interact with Business Services (such as Sun/See-beyond) as both are distributed and leverage a common identity system for profile, preference and context sharing.

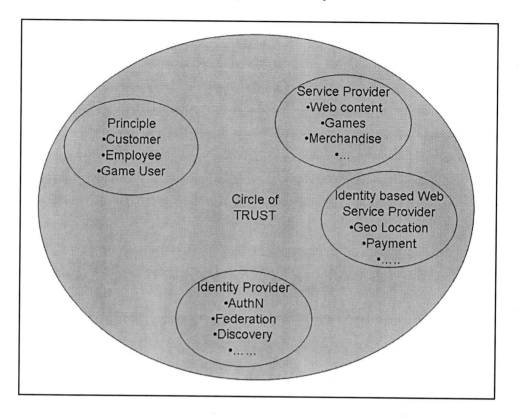

Figure 9:8 Orchestration and Choreography of Services in a distributed environment requires tight alignment

9.3.1.3 Alignment of Event Execution with Service Invocation (JBI-SLEE-JEE-role based routing)

Multiple Industry pundits are calling for EDA (event driven architecture) Alignment with SOA, including Gartner and IDC that support several chapters and conferences in this space. JBI (Java Business Integration) based on JSR 208 is a set of specifications around Java based integration. JBI proposes a Java based ESB that allows for integration between, multiple vendor specific implementations of JEE Containers (such as Sun and BEA), JSLEE containers (such as Open Cloud and JNetx), RTSJ (real time application servers), .NET Services, Java-RFID and more.

There are several thousand use case scenarios today in the Telecom Industry (wire-line & wireless) Retail Industry, Distribution & Logistics

Industry, Travel & Leisure Industry, Manufacturing & Supply Chain, etc., that handles changes in the respective event networks and correlates the same to a Service (based on SOA) for a specific User or Role. This takes the request response paradigm to event based request response.

For example, event changes in the network around a user's presence, location etc., would involve invoking and/or terminating a session with the services that were started. An event change in the form of exceeding a giving call time may invoke a notification service and billing service. These types of Scenarios that align EDA with SOA require tight alignment between the ESB and an Identity System. A location change from Los Angeles to San Francisco triggers events that invokes the appropriate location based weather service for a specific user based on his/her profile, preference and context.

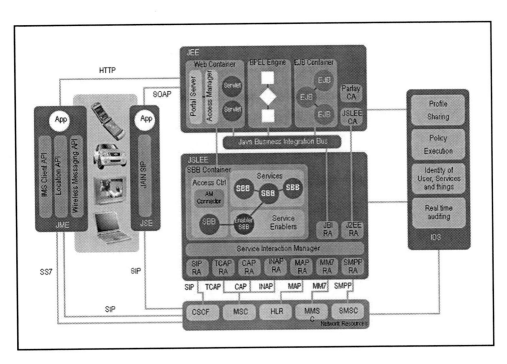

Figure 9:9 JEE and SLEE environments are both Identity enabled and ESB/JBI based.

9.3.1.4 Moving from request response to sense response (RFID/ID/ESB)

Similar to the EDA perspective there are several thousand use case scenarios today in the Telecom Industry (wire-line & wireless) Retail Industry, Distribution & Logistics Industry, Travel & Leisure Industry, Manufacturing & Supply Chain etc., that handle changes in the respective sensor networks and correlate the same to a Service (based on SOA) for a specific User or Role. This takes the request response paradigm to event based request response to sense- invoke event – to request response. For example, a user driving an Acura might be guided to a nearby Acura dealer (GPS network) based on sensor detection of a potential component failure in the vehicle, at the same time aligned with a Maintenance Scheduling Service that offers the available time slots to the owner/driver of the vehicle. This involves an event triggered in Honda/Acura's network based on data captured from the vehicle invoking services from the dealership (inventory tracking service, scheduling service etc.).

In these situations, Product authentication based on EPC, validating the Identity of Things and devices, etc., and the corresponding function of invoking Warehouse management systems, supply chain management systems and ERP systems as Services for specific users, roles, identities etc. becomes relevant.

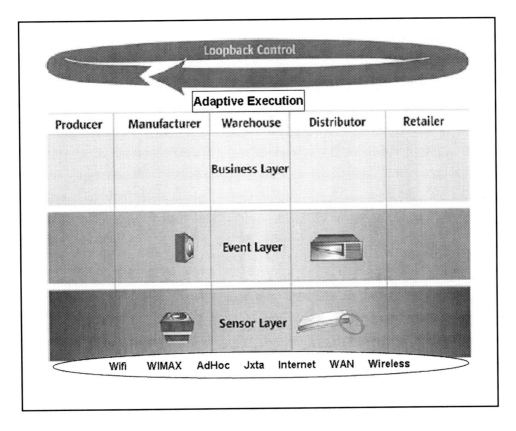

Figure 9.10: IDS and ESB in there respective layers.

An Identity System integrates with all these layers, sensor layer, event layer and business layer, whereas and ESB mostly aligns the event layer to the Service layer, as described earlier, in conjunction with an IDS.

9.3.1.5 Converged Network to IP Service Alignment (QOS, IMS, OAM/OSSJ, access network type)

The most interesting development since 2005 is the notion of access device agnostic and access network agnostic service delivery. This implies true "service mobility" wherein the services that were traditionally accessed from a "silo access network" such as a voice call from PSTN networks, TV services from cable networks and Internet Services (traditional data services) from Wifi LANs etc. can now be accessed from any type of access network. A cable operator can offer all three (voice, data and video) and so can a wire-line operator that brings fiber to the home and so can wireless operators with WiMax 802.16 and 802.20. This also paves the way for multiple end points to participate on a call or conference at the same time – for example, a Cell Phone PDA, a STB/TV and a Laptop/Computer with a Soft phone on the same multimedia-conference. This requires a breakaway thinking in terms of how services get delivered to end users. IP-MPLS as the transport layer that reaches all access networks, IMS as the control layer that handles session control (network facing) and subscriber centric data and a services layer that includes all types of service (service over IP) offered by service providers. This paradigm shift realigns the emphasis from network facing functions to service centric functions – primarily performed by ESB and IDS.

This is probably one of the primary reasons why Telecom companies are investing heavily in Identity initiatives as well as Service broker initiatives all around the globe – for federated identity management, federated DRM and federated orchestration (a.k.a. choreography).

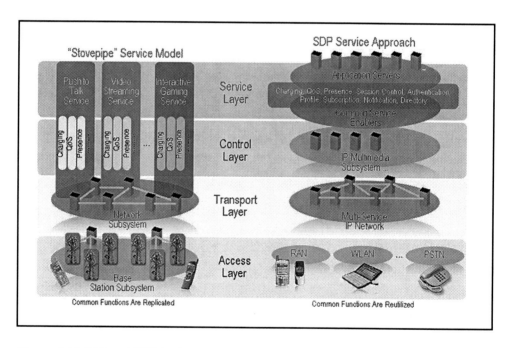

Figure 9.11: IDS and ESB in there respective layers.

Common functions are reused (an SOA principle) in Telecom Service Delivery Platforms where Interoperability between a Service Broker in a SDP (that supports standards such as SCIM –service control interaction manager, an IMS spec) and an ESB (that supports BPEL= business process execution language) is a given here.

9.4 Conclusion

While an Identity Broker manages the full life cycle associated with identities (user, identity of things, service identifiers, profile etc.), an ESB manages parts of the full life cycle associated with Services.

However both are tightly aligned as they are the core middleware infrastructure solutions that sit between Services and Users – in a device and network agnostic manner. Both are infrastructure service building blocks that typically act as the "Glue Code" between Service, Networks, Devices and Users. Services include business services, communication services, media/entertainment services, converged services, and, networks include core IP network, access networks, service networks and content grids.

- Convergence of telecommunications Service Brokers with ESB (intelligent brokering)
- Converged Services that leverage a virtual consolidated registry (federated)
- Contextual and user defined preference, profile and policy based service delivery
- Telecom SDP leverages SOA principles (XML, Identity based Integration)
- Converged IP Networks makes Services device and access networks agnostic (breaking network silo's) and allows for e2e near real-time auditing.

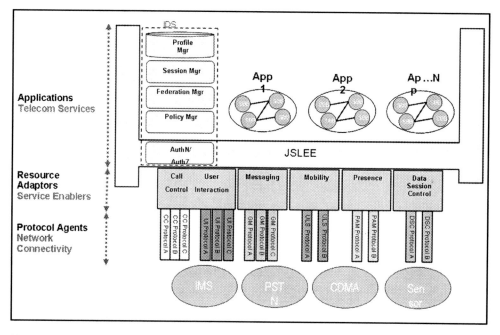

Figure 9.12 IDS and ESB – pervasive across all services.

Both an ESB and an Identity System are distributed across Services, Data and Networks, allowing for a converged NG services;

- A KM Service can be invoked from within a VOIP Call between a customer and a customer support person
- A Patient can allow access to his medical record with recent hospitalisation for a Specialist Doctor over the network while completing a virtual visit/checkup
- An IM, email or voice mail notification can be sent based on presence, when a meeting is cancelled in a Calendar Service
- A team of procurement personnel can view the entire supply chain inventory cycle while on a video conference
- A husband can send live video feed of a scenic location in Europe while on vacation with a video call and share the moment with his spouse and children (between a handheld in his hand and a STB/TV at home)

All these require Identity based Intelligent Service Brokering.

10. Identity enabled DRM

10.1 Introduction

This chapter explores the different perspectives from which Architectural Integration and Functional Alignment takes place, in today's Service Oriented Architectures (SOA) and Network- Service Delivery Platforms (SDP), based on advances in Identity Systems and Open Digital Rights Management Services. This chapter proposes the reasons why a tight alignment between DRM and Identity Systems are required and recommends certain approaches to achieve the same. Both a DRM System and an Identity System are central and core infrastructure software for digital content delivery (multimedia services, entertainment services, document, books, records etc.) within a SOA (enterprise) and SDP (telecom), context.

Telecom Services based on SDP utilise voice, data and video (multimedia) to deliver more complex and advanced services such as context sensitive delivery of entertainment, unified communication services and event based sensor enabled responsive integration with traditional business services and business processes (that shares XML based documents as well). The goal is to transcend all types of access networks and access devices and deliver User Sensitive (preference, profile and policy based), Location based, Context driven Services & Content, with true Service Mobility, going beyond, user and terminal mobility. All major Network Equipment Providers (NEPs) have similar vision and strategy, wherein the same set of Services Over IP (SOIP) can be delivered across all types of access networks and access devices that support SIP (Session Initiation Protocol), over a Core IP based IMS network (IP Multimedia Subsystem). Lately many Integration software vendors have addressed the need for an Integrated Security framework that addresses Security requirements with extension of their solutions to Network Identity Systems (such as Java Enterprise Identity System).

10.2 Identity enabled DRM

The generic industry definition of DRM system "Digital Rights Management (also called Digital
Restrictions Management and often abbreviated to DRM) is the umbrella term referring to any of several technologies used to enforce predefined policies for controlling access to digital data (such as software, music, movies). In more technical terms, DRM handles the description, layering, analysis, valuation, trading, monitoring and enforcement of usage restrictions that accompany a specific instance of a digital work. In the widest possible sense, the term refers to any such management. The term is often confused with copy protection and technical protection measures (TPM). These two terms refer to technologies that control or restrict the use and access of digital media content on electronic devices with such technologies installed.

Majority of today's DRM standards have the following characteristics:

- DRM Silos - content specific to wireless, tied to devices, etc. (they are not network/device agnostic user specific DRM)
- Not Federated and Interoperable DRM (delivery of content from multiple content providing entities that belong to federated COT with interoperable DRM standards)
- Not User Centric DRM (user's intervention to allow access on demand, delegation of rights, transfer of rights, etc. are problematic)
- DRM for Content created by users is not addressed (medical records, books, academic content, legal documents, etc.)
- Tied to specific Service to Content interaction (content is not agnostic to service)

However with convergence we are seeing in many dimensions:

- Device Convergence—a STB/TV, Handheld/Cell-phone, and computing devices (laptop, PC, work-stations, NC, etc.) can accept calls, stream TV/Media and access the Internet
- Access Network Convergence—CDMA, GSM/GPRS, Wifi/WiMax, Cable, DSL, Fibre2home, etc., all leverage IP transport
- Core Control Layer Network—IMS based Core Control Layer that glues all the Access Networks to
- Service networks
- Content/Service Convergence—VOIP, IPTV, Dig-Music, e-Books, VOD, XML docs, etc., leading to the digitisation of all content.
- IT Network Convergence—Developers embedding and instrumenting QOS into code/content, IT acting as a Service Provider of Network Services, etc.

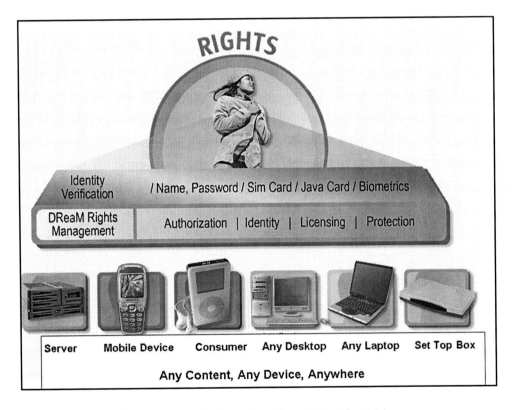

Figure 10.1: Any Content, Any Device, Anywhere (User Centric)

All the five major issues around current generation DRM have to be addressed and tied back to the foundation framework offered by an Identity System, from a user perspective, federation perspective, distributed policy perspective and a session perspective. The rest of this chapter talks as to how this is addressed with an Identity based DRM solution such as OMC (open media commons) project DReaM.

Central to the DReaM solution are four key concepts:

Approaching DRM and CAS from a network identity perspective rather than the traditional device-centric approach. The DReaM architecture supports the separation of rights management system components, which is the systematic de-coupling of authentication, licensing, rights management and protection technologies. This makes it possible to select and choose among these technologies—independently of each other—without compromising the integrity of the solution. For example, usage rights are defined in a separate license management system that is facilitated by DReaM, allowing consumers to use players and DRM clients already installed on their devices without inheriting their limitations. Equally important, identity and authentication services are separated from individual hardware devices. Rather than merely authenticating the device on which content can be viewed, identity can be bound to a smart card (a Java Card or a SIM card, for example) for personalisation in DRM systems. So the content rights are bound to individuals (or roles) rather than devices.

Providing an open, standards-based framework for building interoperable, vendor-neutral DRM/CAS implementations. The DReaM solution can work with virtually any type of content needed, including documents, images, audio, and video, spanning a wide range of device types and operating systems. It also works with multiple file formats and codecs. It can control access to content independent of the delivery medium—whether it is a physical or a digital connection, the Internet, CD-ROM, TV broadcast, DVD, Flash memory etc. and it supports a range of business models, including subscription-based or fee-based service models, providing flexibility for service providers.

Providing security without obscurity. Historically, proprietary end-to-end architectures have relied upon obscurity to avoid being cracked. These systems are based upon a false foundation of security promises; they have been cracked and will continue to be breached. DReaM promotes the view that open system architectures will present greater opportunities for review and discussion of technology choices so that shortcomings can be better evaluated and corrected ("review & repair" versus "hope & pray") to provide the greatest protection possible.

Avoiding onerous licensing fees. Project DReaM is designed to be royalty free in order to encourage development and ongoing innovation. In addition to employing CDDL licensing terms Project DReaM will rely on other models for assuring royalty-free usage such as employing a Patent Commons approach.

Also a generic Digital Asset workflow based on an Open Architecture will include the following components; that includes Acquisition (multiple content providers leads to Identity and Federation needs), Content Processing (appropriate AuthN/AuthZ and roles required for users who are operators), Digital Asset management (requires Identity based rights management and encryption), Distribution and Consumption (Identity head ends, access networks, devices etc.). In each of these five steps and Identity System offers functionality from one perspective or the other.

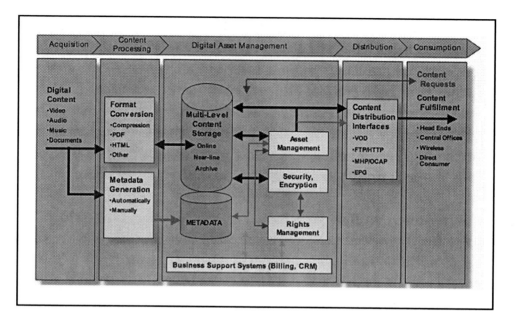

Figure 10.2: Asset Workflow

10.2.1 Rationale (& Value Proposition) for IDS & DRM Alignment

- DRM Silos—content specific to wireless, tied to devices, etc. (they are network/device agnostic and user specific DRM),
- Federated and Interoperable DRM (delivery of content from multiple content providing entities that belong to a federated COT with interoperable DRM standards),
- User Centric DRM workflow (users intervention to allow access on demand, delegation of rights, transfer of rights etc. are problematic),
- DRM for Content created by users is not addressed (medical records, books, academic content, legal documents, etc.),
- Tied to specific Service to Content interaction (content is not agnostic to service).

10.2.1.1 Breaking current DRM Silos

Today's DRM specifications and standards are content specific and access network such as wireless specific (e.g. OMA's DRM), tied to devices etc. However an all encompassing DRM system in an IP/Network Converged environment where it is relevant to consumers on the move, however where the content is distributed in multiple enterprise networks and enterprise systems, current SILO approach to DRM solution will not work. This is even more true when the DRM system must be all encompassing and address all types of content, including, infotainment content, business content (enterprises) and life model.

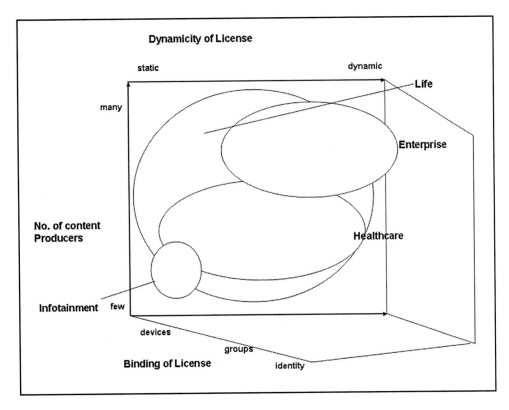

Figure 10.3: All encompassing DRM model

Traditional DRM systems addressed only either one of these three models or in many cases only a subset within the life model, business content model or infotainment model.

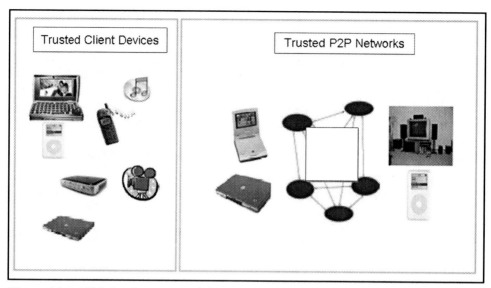

Figure 10.4: All Infotainment model

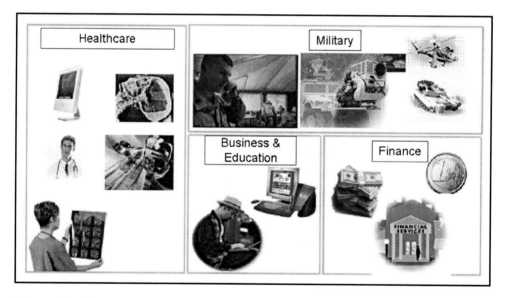

Figure 10.5: Business Apps/Content model

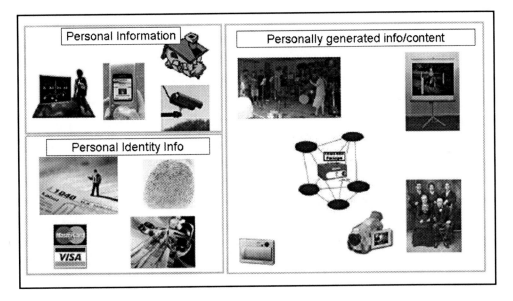

Figure 10.6: Life model

Given these three content and service delivery models and IP Network Convergence—several thousand use cases are possible (such as a virtual doctor's visit over a multi-media session between a patient and a specialist doctor across continents -not just visually communicating, but also sharing recent patient's hospital records, sharing descriptions of current medications, sharing data from embedded sensor devices etc., all within the same session) wherein, content stored in specific enterprise networks and personal networks are shared near real-time between individuals with licensing granted and revoked within that session based on owner intervention etc. The majority of these scenarios already involve an Identity System—such as an Identity enabled ILM (information life cycle management) for enterprises and identity enabled content delivery systems not just for user authentication but also for access control to content and information. This also requires a disintermediation and interoperability as well as agnosticism (agnostic to device, access network, content type, service, etc.) and a user centric model.

10.1.2.2 Federated DRM

Delivery of content from multiple content providing entities that belong to federated COT with interoperable DRM standards requires linking multiple DRM systems, a user centric content rights repository, ability to negotiate for licenses, interoperability between content packaging and encryption systems, ability to manage rights for any type of content, ability to deliver timeline dependent content to multiple content consumers and more. This type of disintermediation and federated access is relevant to Content Aggregation Scenarios, converged communication services scenarios, and more.

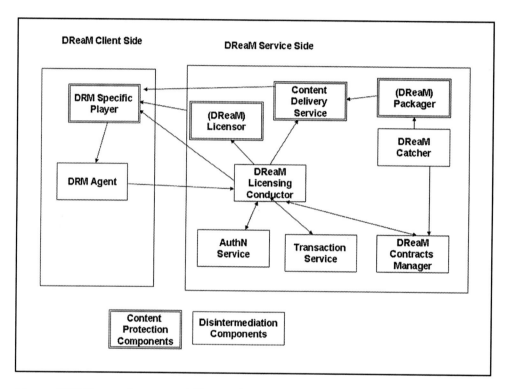

Figure 10.7: Dream Interoperability Architecture

The DRM specific player might support any specific SILO DRM standard, such as, Opera, Coral, CAS or others such as OMA DRM, wherein the content specific components include, the player, licensor and packager. The components that are not content protection specific and ones that ensures inter-operability with proprietary external DRM systems include, the disintermediation agent, conductor, catcher, licensing conductor, contracts manager, authentication services (in a federated model), transaction systems and content delivery systems. This disintermediation between client specific, content specific DRM systems allows for interoperability between multiple DRM standards such as:

CORAL,
ISMAcryp,
DVB's Symulcrypt,
DReaM CAS,
DReaM MMI,
OMA 1.0 and 2.0 DRM
Mobile Entertainment Forum's mDRM
Microsoft Media DRM
XRML
And more.

How does Disintermediation (D15N) work?

These are the steps for d15n to work. The beauty of this solution is that disintermediation can take place in a federated model, due to integration with an Identity System.

1. Content packaged with D15N redirect information agent
2. DReaM agent installed on user device
3. User requests rights for content which gets redirected to D15N server/conductor through DReaM agent
4. DReaM licensing conductor processes request
5. Authenticate user
6. Evaluates rights
7. Processes transaction
8. Signals license server to deliver licenses to device License server delivers license
9. User device receives license (rights and keys)
10. User device can now consume content (content type maybe converted, based on device needs

This architecture allows for multiple SILO proprietary or standards based licensing and packaging implementations from multiple vendors inter-operate via the disintermediation components. However this implies the subscriber databases, entitlement service user repositories etc., are accessible in a federated manner, so appropriate levels of user authentication can take place. Authentication can be independent of the DRM implementation as well. The notion of federation, establishment of circles of trust, federated profile sharing etc. are expected out of the different participating business entities (content providers subscriber information, access network provider's subscriber information, service provider's subscriber information, such as HBO, Cox Cable, Verizon, and more), via an established Identity Service Provider.

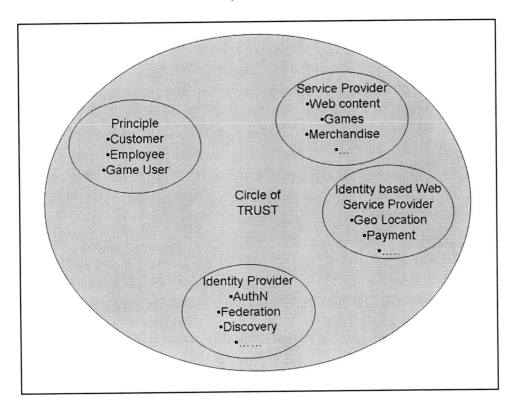

Figure 10.8 Federation for Inter-operable DRM

10.2.1.3 User Centric DRM Workflows

The majority of today's DRM solutions do not offer the users the flexibility to manage their digital access rights and privileges, however, today's users require the capabilities such as:

- users intervention to allow access on demand
- delegation of rights (temporary and short term)
- transfer of rights (long term)
- legitimate access to content based on user defined policy
- user defined rights management etc.

With the advent of IMS (IP Multi-media Subsystem), IPTV, IPTV IMS interoperability extensible alignment between communication services and digital rights of content is required. For example, a user could allow access to his or her medial records from recent hospitalisation, that are available on the net to a specialist doctor while having a virtual consultation session (over multi-media communication services). This requires the DRM system to be identity enabled and policy driven wherein a user allows temporary rights for this session. Also a user could have bought 6 drm licenses for a VOD service and since he is out of town - might delegate the DRM privileges to a different household member. A parent might allow content access to kids within certain timeframes or for specific customer premises equipment, policies defined by the owner to limit access. One might want transfer rights to a digital library of books to an adopted child.

These scenarios are becoming more and more relevant today due to the digitisation of content such as books, music, movies, pictures, home albums and more (accessed while the user is on the move).

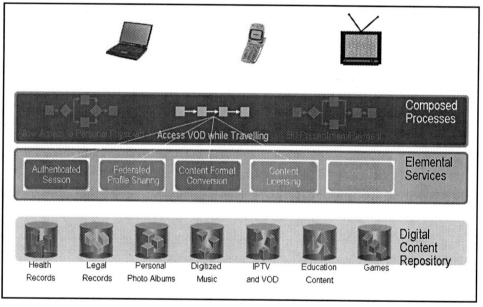

Figure 10.9 User centric DRM workflow (accessing content on the move)

10.2.1.4 DRM for Content created by users

The internet today is a Read/Write Internet. There is an enormous amount of content created by users themselves, self published books, short stretch non-professional movies, digital art work, music, nature pictures and more. Even though majority of this content is expected to be accessed freely or shared through an identity infrastructure there are requirements to leverage simple DRM systems such as CAS to wrap restrictions around these content.

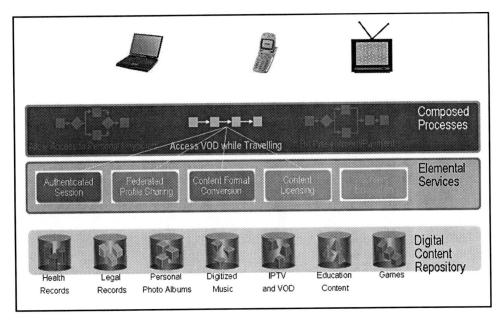

Figure 10.10 User created content (allowing access to a new physician)

10.2.1.5 Content agnostic to Services

The most interesting development since 2005 is the notion of access device agnostic and access network agnostic service delivery. This implies true "service mobility" wherein the services that were traditionally accessed from a silo access network" such as a voice call from PSTN networks, TV services from cable networks and Internet Services (traditional data services) from Wifi LANs, etc., can now be accessed from any type of access network.

Along these same lines the Service layer has to be agnostic to the content layer as well. For example, a video mpeg (or any other format) file created is not expected to be accessed and played by a real media service and client alone. The mpeg file could be played by a media service in isolation and in conjunction with other services as well—such as multi-media communication services. For example, it should be downloadable and playable by a client device that is not attached to the network all the time, could be attached to an e-mail for a different user (who has the transferred access rights) to be used playing a different service. This implies that content is tied to a user's identity and is service agnostic as well. This is probably one of the primary reasons why Telecom companies are investing heavily in Identity initiatives as well as Service broker initiatives all around the globe—for federated identity management, federated DRM and federated orchestration (a.k.a. Choreography) and disintermediation of DRM services.

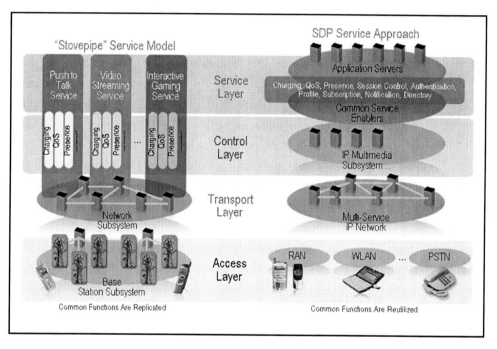

Figure 10.11 IDS and ESB in there respective layers.

10.3 Conclusion

While an Identity Broker manages the full life cycle associated with identities (user, identity of things, service identifiers, profile etc.), an ESB manages parts of the full life cycle associated with Services. However, both are tightly aligned as they are the core middleware infrastructure solutions that sit between Services and Users - in a device and network agnostic manner. Both are infrastructure service building blocks that typically act as the "Glue Code" between Service, Networks,

Devices and Users. Services include business services, communication services, media/entertainment services, converged services and networks include core IP network, access networks, service networks and content grids.

- Convergence of telecommunications Service Brokers with ESB (intelligent brokering)
- Converged Services that leverage a virtual consolidated registry (federated)
- Contextual and user defined preference, profile and policy based service delivery
- Telecom SDP leverages SOA principles (XML, Identity based Integration)
- Converged IP Networks makes Services device and access networks agnostic (breaking network silos) and allows for e2e near real-time auditing.

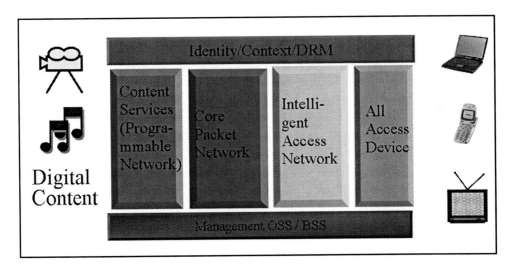

Figure 10.12 IDS and ESB - pervasive across all services.

Both an ESB and an Identity System are distributed across Services, Data and Networks, allowing for a converged NG services;

- A KM Service can be invoked from within a VOIP Call between a customer and a customer

- support person
- A Patient can allow access to his medical record with recent hospitalisation for a Specialist Doctor over the network while completing a virtual visit/checkup
- An IM, email or voice mail notification can be sent based on presence, when a meeting is cancelled in a Calendar Service
- A team of procurement personnel can view the entire supply chain inventory cycle while on a video conference
- A husband can send live video feed of a scenic location in Europe while on vacation with a video call and share the moment with his spouse and children (between a handheld in his hand and a STB/TV at home).

All this require Identity based Intelligent Service Brokering.

11. Identity enabled Devices

11.1 Introduction and Overview

Until now (chapter 10) we have seen how developments such as 4G Networks, IMS etc. allow mobile workers and consumers, increasingly numerous ways to access these networks - via data-enabled and multi-media enabled:

- cell phones,
- smart-phones,
- PDAs,
- ultra-mobile personal computers (UMPCs), and,
- notebook computers.

In many cases, these same devices can also access the thousands of Wifi hotspots which are in every major metropolitan area. The near term benefit underlying the increasing use of smart-phones and data-enabled/multi-media enabled cell phones is high-speed data access which can be used to browse the public Internet, connect back to a corporate network or even watch television. This access creates huge security concerns for both consumers and the IT managers tasked with guarding their companies' confidential information. Over time, this increased access will have an impact on the type of information/data content which is exchanged on a daily basis - i.e., that content will increase in utility and value. Electronic financial transactions conducted via mobile devices will become a norm rather than the current exception, for example. This shift will, in turn, require ever greater platform integrity and protection for that content. Other than the reach of an

Identity System and its related services, there are no existing security solutions in hardware or software - which can support security in this type of cross-network and cross-device environment. Also consider that today the vast majority of white collar mobile workers carry at least two types of mobile devices - primarily cell phones and notebook computers. The use of smart-phones and similar devices is increasing, but overall usage is still low as compared to cell phones. Indeed, only about six percent of the handsets shipped worldwide in 2005 were smart-phones - that is approximately 51 million smart-phones versus 809 million new cell phone shipments. By 2010, iGR expects smart-phones to comprise approximately 21 percent of all mobile handsets shipped worldwide. In this world of mobile broadband, IT managers have several primary concerns about wireless security. They want to make certain that their current, wired networks remain secure, and they want to ensure that only authorised and authenticated users are accessing that network. Finally, IT managers are concerned about the security of the data saved on those wireless devices—be they laptops, PDAs, cell phones or smart-phones. There are also concerns around device behaviour (virus checks, patch updates, client side firewall and more), device reputation and device centric policies (that get pushed to the devices). The fear, of course, is that the mobile devices will become compromised and either mined for confidential information or used as a base from which to launch an attack on a corporate network. Despite the existence of malicious software (malware) which can cause mobile devices to fail or bog down a mobile operator's network, the real security threats surrounding the increasing use of smart-phones, data-enabled handsets and other multi-media mobile devices are rather pedestrian: loss and theft. There are several factors to consider when a device is lost or stolen:

- Lost productivity until device and data is replaced
- Replacement cost of the lost/stolen device.
- Cost of restoring data to the device - i.e., the time it takes for the IT staffer to reconfigure the device.
- Possible compromise of confidential data (personal and/or company), which could be almost anything depending on the device lost and the data kept on it - e.g. customer records (any industry),

patient information (health care) etc.
- Possible breach in the security of the network to which the wireless device connects -
- e.g., if network passwords are stored on the device, then an unauthorised user could gain access to the network via an authorised device.

Telecom companies (mostly wireless companies) and operators around the world are also gravely concerned about wireless security. They need to ensure that their subscribers are using secure devices both because it's good for their business - i.e., they can more readily launch mobile commerce related services - and because compromised handsets are a potential threat to the smooth functioning of their networks. Mobile operators are also always looking for ways to protect themselves from the revenue losses associated with cloned devices i.e. stolen mobile phones which are illegally resold.

There are numerous software-based ways to safeguard mobile devices —virtual private networks (VPNs), firewalls, on-device data encryption software and device management solutions, to name just a few. These types of solutions typically protect the data and/or operating systems of the devices from attacks, but do little to protect the unique identity of a device such as a cell phone e.g. the International Mobile Equipment Identity (IMEI) number. These software-based solutions also should ensure the integrity and/or authenticity of the hardware platform on which they are running (SIM cards, TPM, Bio-metric embedded in client devices etc.). This chapter will provide an overview of the security threats facing mobile devices and the existing solutions for shoring up those security holes. It will also provide a look at a new technical specification from the Trusted Computing Group (TCG) which has been developed to address the specific global needs of wireless and mobile security from both a consumer and enterprise perspective. These needs include:

- A solution that can address the Device validation, Device behavior and Device reputation
- A solution that can push device centric policies based on param-

eters such as (time of day, location, presence and more).

- A hardware-based approach to mobile device security is significantly stronger than a software-based approach. Software approaches tend to be limited in scope and do not, to date, enable interoperability between different security applications, device platforms and/or data networks.
- A cross-platform and open security standard given the wide array of networks, devices, operating systems and services in the converging world of wired and wireless data. Support for open standards for any IP devices (such as TS69).
- A solution which simultaneously provides protection for the user's information, the device itself, and the network operator's assets. (Bio metric combination, JSR 279 and more).

11.2 Advances in Device and their functionality

Today the mobile devices have evolved to a point where they perform many functions over and above a mobile phone. These devices are used in myriad ways, over and above voice communication to provide a broad array of communication, entertainment and business-centric functionality, such as:

JME capable phones also support RFID and the phones are in a position to display responses based on events in a sensor environment that request services. Similar to the Smart Home services along with i-Control offered by AT&T with the Cingular cell phones as the remote control.

Identity enabled devices with payment services and RFID also act as digital wallets for micro payments.

Rich features and function: Devices today are loaded with features - everything from AM/FM radios and Wifi / GSM roaming to i-Tunes players and TV players (such as IPTV, mobi-TV, you-tube and more).

Advanced form factors: Flip phones and smart-phones with larger color screens, QWERTY keyboards, better battery life, faster processors, more memory and slots for removable cards. Handset manufacturers are also taking the flip phone form factors to new levels with slide and rotating designs. Not all of these designs make sense for mobile workers, but some are applicable in particular industries - e.g. Real Estate, where realtors might more highly value a camera-oriented smartphone.

Advanced operating systems: The emergence of devices with greater memory, better processors and more storage has increased interest in bringing the traditional OS into the mobile space. As well as smartphone operating systems from Palm, Microsoft, Symbian and ZTE other companies now offer new operating systems for feature phones. A good example is Savaje with its Java-based OS. There is also much discussion of Linux in mobile handsets, in 2007.

Wifi/WWAN/WiMAX connectivity: Devices with integrated WLAN capabilities are of greatest interest to corporate users, since many companies have WLANs in place in their offices. It is likely that mobile devices with integrated Wifi will enter into WiMAX as well in a few years.

More services and applications: The emergence of Java on handsets has opened up the market for innovative services and applications. To date, these development environments have enabled content and game creators to make more interesting games and applications, but these environments can also be leveraged by independent software vendors such as Salesforce.com who want to port their applications to mobile devices.

Multimedia: Cameras are now included on a wide range of mobile devices to the point that there is little market differentiation to be gained by including a camera and image capability. Indeed, the reverse may be true (not including a camera), given corporate paranoia and industrial espionage. Full multimedia capabilities, including video (for messaging or possibly for conferencing or SWIS - "see what I see") will be the next major differentiators. Clearly, 3G and 4G networks are required to take full advantage of video - in addition to devices with longer battery life, more memory and higher processing power.

Office productivity and presentation tools are available in smart-phones along with miniaturised gadgets such as a micro projector, keyboard etc. This would potentially replace the requirements to carry laptop like devices in the future.

11.3 Security Requirements for Devices

With the understanding of the advances in device functionality and the access networks, device security, then, implies the creation of security policies on how to use wireless devices, what types of corporate-related information can be stored on them, and the implementation of technology which:

- Ensures the validity of the Device, its behaviour and reputation.
- Push device centric policies to the client based on parameters.
- Software Security framework that ties a device back to an IDP (Identity Service Provider).
- Encrypts data transmissions to and from the device.
- Encrypts data on the devices themselves.
- Protects the identity (IMEI, MSIDN, unique identifiers, etc.) of the device from being changed (i.e., cloning the device for illegal resale and use).
- Measures the trustworthiness of the hardware, OS and applications to detect an unauthorised configuration (in some cases performed by an Identity enabled NAC appliance).
- Allows IT staffers to de-activate, lock and/or wipe devices which have been stolen or lost. This is a feature of many device management software products and will be part of an overall Identity enable OAM&P environment
- Provides strong user authentication both to activate the device and to access the network. In the case of loss/theft, user authentication can slow or halt an attacker entirely. (Bio-metric embedded in device screens, SIM/Java Card technology etc.).
- Management functions on the device and on the back-end which allow IT staffers to centrally create, rollout, change and enforce their

security policies. These management functions are only feasible to the extent to which a device itself can be authenticated and its own integrity ensured (trust digital like services).

- Password protection on all devices at power-on. Most mobile devices ship with this feature; device management software products can allow IT staffers to enforce the use of this feature (which many users never activate).

The relative ease with which smartphones and PDAs can be stolen or lost should also encourage enterprises to put in place security policies and best practices which govern the use of those devices. Obviously, these policies will vary across companies and industries. Doctors using PDAs or smartphones to hold patient data need to be extra careful so as to protect their patients from inadvertent (or malicious) HIPAA violations. Similarly, mobile workers in the financial services industry might need more security on his/her device than a cable service technician using a phone to speak with his/her dispatcher.

According to iGR as compared to laptop or desktop computers, achieving these objectives with mobile devices is different for several reasons:

There are more operating systems to support: Symbian, Palm, Windows Mobile etc. The OS and product offerings from RIM, Good Technology and others incorporate their own security which is not reliant on third-party solutions.

Mobile operators may control the WWANs, but they have no dominion over the public Internet. Data traffic that leaves a mobile operator's network is "in the clear" unless the user (or enterprise) has some security in place (e.g. a VPN or application-level security).

Mobile operators also control what applications are loaded onto smartphones and cell phones which function on their networks. All applications and content available for purchase through a mobile operator's Web portal, for example, goes through a stringent approval process. They have somewhat less control over the applications used on a PDA with a WWAN data card and the emergence of smart-phones with expandable memory slots has also created the potential for unapproved content to be loaded onto those phones. That said, if the mobile operator has the proper tools in place, it can prevent certain applications from running over their network—e.g. VoIP, software on a laptop or PDA. A mobile operator would prevent these types of applications from running if the operator were not involved in the revenue chain associated with that service.

The smart-phone devices themselves have comparatively short battery lives, slow CPUs and less memory than laptops and/or desktop computers although their performance improves with each new generation of devices. Lower performance as compared to laptop or desktop computers can limit the types of security applications that can effectively be run on mobile devices. On the positive side, however, the disparity in performance has encouraged innovative solutions to mobile device security.

There are numerous software-based ways to protect mobile devices - e.g. anti-virus software, virtual private networks (VPNs) and firewalls. Another type of software solution is individual file, folder and/or hard drive. Once installed and configured, this type of software encrypts and decrypts any data on the device specified by the user in real-time. So, email and SMS can be encrypted, as well as contact information and Microsoft Office files.

Some of these products can also encrypt and decrypt information stored on removable media. File decryption can only be done by an authenticated user—a process which can be made transparent to the user. That is, the user logs into the phone and then has access to all his/her files.

Many scenarios, in which device centric policies can be involved, include:

- Turn off camera mode when within a premises (aligning logical and physical access control).

- Strong AuthN required when accessing from Access Network types A and B and not a requirement when accessing from type C or D.
- An AuthN Session is a mandatory with an IDP when the device accesses specific services.
- Device behaviour and reputation requires to be logged with a DRA (device reputation authority).
- Device Identifier correlation and Dev ID management has to be handled by an IDP (device identifiers to user identifiers to services), especially when families or teams of users with specific roles are allowed access with a given set of devices etc.
- Password protection on all devices at power-on (at least); password enforcement software should be used to make sure users are not disabling that requirement. The number of password attempts should also be restricted.
- Some companies might want to use two-factor or multi-factor authentication for additional security.
- When the devices connect to the corporate desktop/laptop, the wireless port(s) should be disabled on the device.
- All devices must have AV software and be scanned for viruses before connecting to the corporate network.
- The devices should run personal firewall software to protect against intrusions.
- The devices can only connect to the corporate network via a VPN.
- Sensitive corporate information cannot be stored on the mobile device unless it is encrypted. This encryption could occur per file, per directory or the entire hard drive (really only applicable to devices with hard drives).
- All devices must have the latest security patches installed. The onus here is on the IT department; they need tools that help them determine which devices can run what software and what version that software is on to then update the software appropriately.
- All devices must have a unique identity and a mechanism to demonstrate trust in their integrity claims.

11.4 The Five areas of Synergy and Alignment for Identity enabled Devices

11.4.1 Solution that can address the Device validation, Device behavior and Device reputation.

Validating a device is essentially the mechanisms such as bootstrap information, SIM card, client device based AuthN etc., with which the identity of a device gets validated in the network, wither in conjunction with a User or without one. Device behaviour is essentially having the potential to understand the device features and capabilities, and how the device could potentially behave with the network and services stemming from the network (for e.g. a GPS enabled device can also offer location data to the network so that services can be delivered accordingly). This ensures that when the user access services from the network the appropriate devices features are available along with software patches, updates, JVM and more. Device reputation is about validating that the device has a reputation and history of good behaviour and therefore can be trusted in the network –especially when security sensitive services are accessed. A DRA (such as the solution from iOvation) focuses on the reputation of the user's devices (such as a PC, pocketPC, smart-phone, etc.).

Conceptually with a DRA, one can use a device specific biometric mechanism (such as an infrared scanner reading the eye retina or a finger print detection mechanism), the DRA identifies the IP enabled device, using a multitude of hardware, software and network information to build a reputation for the specific device. The devices are associated with specific users (using and Identity System or and IDP). The DRA maintains the relationships between the devices and user accounts along with fact based fraud evidence entered against each device and user account. When a device (IP device) is uniquely recognised it becomes possible to establish a reputation for it, for example, devices associated with a chargeback fraud, have a reputation that may be materially different, than devices associated with predatory behaviour.

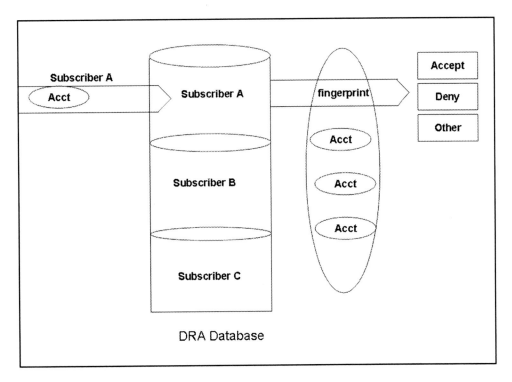

Figure 11.1: Sample DRA solution linked with an IDP

11.4.2 Solution that can push device centric policies based on parameters such as (time of day, location, presence, and more).

As these IP Devices gain more sophistication in terms of features, functions and its capabilities and are able to transcend from one access network to another seamlessly (WiMAX, Wifi, 3.5G,and more), to access services from a Communication Service provider as well as multiple enterprise networks and the web services offered by the Enterprise Networks via a Circle of Trust and a Federation model, it also becomes important to have the capability to PUSH device centric policies that leverage an Identity System (or an IDP) and identity based services such as location, presence, AuthN levels, session and profile management. This includes policies for both mobile device security and mobile edge perimeter security.

Policy based device and perimeter security in conjunction with an IDP (which stores these device centric policies as well as user centric and network centric and resource centric policies) ensures the following;

313

Central Policy Management: integrating with your existing (network) Directory infrastructure ensures that the appropriate groups and users receive security policies to ensure best practices, standardisation of device use and limit enterprise liabilities.

Granularity of Controls: provides a level of granularity to provide the flexibility you need to appropriately secure PDAs and smart-phones. End User Transparency: ensures true transparency—access to phone calls without a password, administrative settings that control when passwords are requested, "zero" latency on login due to encryption, background encryption/decryption without user intervention.
Network and Device Independent: makes your security decision separate from your changing carrier, sync, network and device environment.

Day-Zero Mal-ware Protection: trusted applications architecture ensures that protected data is only accessed by policy-approved applications.

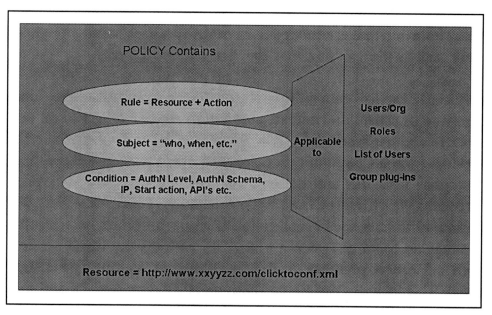

Figure 11.2 Device Centric Policies maintained by an IDP

11.4.3 A hardware-based approach to mobile device security

The Trusted Computing Group (TCG) has developed a specification to address the specific needs of wireless and mobile security. The goal of TCG has been to define a much stronger security solution based on hardware protection rather than more vulnerable software approaches. The specification also focuses on global interoperability between handsets and other platforms and will allow independent software vendors (ISVs) to leverage hardware-based security solutions in their products. This approach compliments the Identity System implementations and the existing Telecom companies acting as IDPs. The cross-industry experience from TCG also helps improve cross-device functionality as it is applied to mobile devices. Although the first iteration of the TCG's specification only applies to mobile phones, in the future it could be extended to encompass other mobile devices such as laptops or UMPCs. There are a large number of companies involved in creating the mobile specification, which include ARM, AuthenTec, Ericsson, France Telecom, Freescale, Hewlett Packard, IBM, Infineon, Intel, Lenovo, Motorola, Nokia, Philips, Samsung, Sony, Sun Microsystems, Texas Instruments, VeriSign, Vodafone and Wave Systems. Note that the TCG is not developing applications or hardware, but a specification which defines the fundamental hardware functions and transactions that are key components of a trusted mobile computing model. Original equipment manufacturers (OEMs), silicon vendors and/or ISVs can then take that specification and develop specific hardware and software solutions to leverage the strengths of the TCG-developed specification. With cooperation among the multiple vendors supporting the specification, the ultimate goal of the TCG mobile security specification is threefold:

- Significantly increase the overall strength of the security provided in mobile phones, including new protection for the handset itself (augmenting User and Service centric Identity Systems),
- Provide interoperability between competing hardware/software solutions, and
- Provide end users with a trusted mobile computing ecosystem.

Many TCG compliant ISV's building Software for device security, NAC, XML firewalls (see next chapter) also leverage an Identity System. This approach can also form the basis for Open DRA solutions.

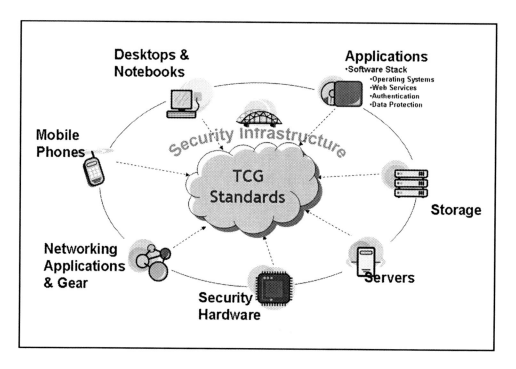

Figure 11.3 Trusted mobile device

11.4.4 A cross-platform and open security standard given the wide array of networks, devices, operating systems and services in the converging world

Customer premises equipment could include multiple devices such as a STB (set top boxes), ADSL or Cable modem and more. As we see wire-line and wireless convergence, there is a need for a common security framework that is cross-platform (in terms of client devices) that can handle both CPE Identity management and mobile device identity management (any IP end device). The same Identity System can be leveraged to implement device centric identity management solutions (such as TR69 from ADSL), wherein a centralised Policy repository and PEP (policy enforcement point) is leveraged for all CPE across all access networks including mobile devices. With combo phones that act as a PDA while mobile and a home phone over Wifi while within the premises etc., all require such an approach.

This aligns with Device convergence wherein, all devices are IP enabled and are data and multi-media capable, including the small (cell phone), medium (laptop) and large (STB/TV) screens. These and many more devices identity management solution can leverage IDS as a common SBB similar to leveraging a number management service or an ENUM service. This approach ensures that an IDS is leveraged for the convergence of device identity management across mobile devices, CPE and NE – to ensure convergence in multiple dimensions as described in chapter one is feasible. Without the alignment in Security by Identity enabling devices, security in a convergence will be difficult.

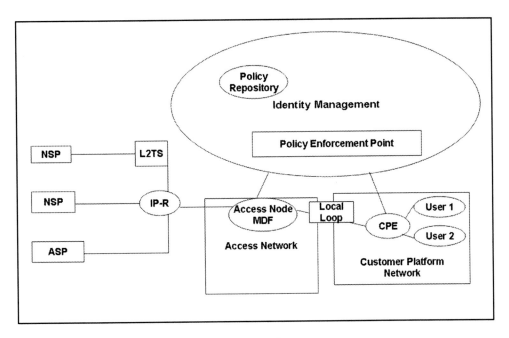

Figure 11.4 IDM for Mobile Devices, CPE and NE

11.4.5 A solution which simultaneously provides protection for the user's information, the device itself and the network operator's assets. (Bio metric combination, JSR 279 and more.)

The power of an Identity System is its pervasive nature in terms of aligning with many security tools out there so that a common solution can be leveraged simultaneously to provide protection for user's information, device (CPE) and network equipment (NE). The AuthN Service for example can be device dependent or device independent. Biometric AuthN can be another level of AuthN service. Policies centrally managed can be distributed to devices, edge network equipment, core network and more. For example with JSR 279 and SATSA (Security and Trust Services) supported by NEPs like Ericsson, Nokia and others) a high-level Service Connection API for JavaTM ME that supports a simple GCF (generic connection framework) -like model for application interaction with services, is possible from mobile devices. This JSR's API also covers the configuration needed to bootstrap interaction with service frameworks. SATSA is supported in the NetBeans Mobility pack as well. The very same security framework for JME/CDC devices and development environment can be deployed in any JME compatible device (including, mobile phones, set top box and other PDA devices). If this seems like it's deviating from the IMS control layer – it's not necessarily so, with NEP support for SATSA and JSR 279, it can be extended via the IMS/HSS route as well, treating the HSS as an IDP, prior to accessing Services, or hoping a step via a HSS to an IDSP. For all practical purposes with the integration of Federation Manager into an IMS/HSS environment the HSS in itself acts as an IDP for the IMS network layer.

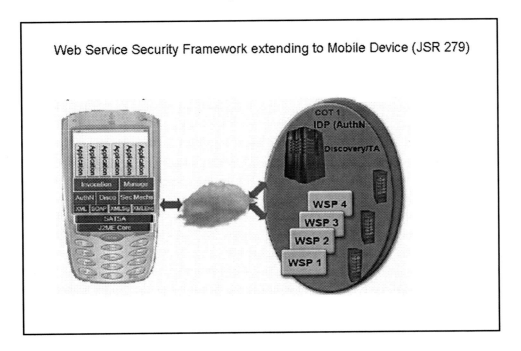

Figure 11.5: JSR 279 and SATSA for mobile devices

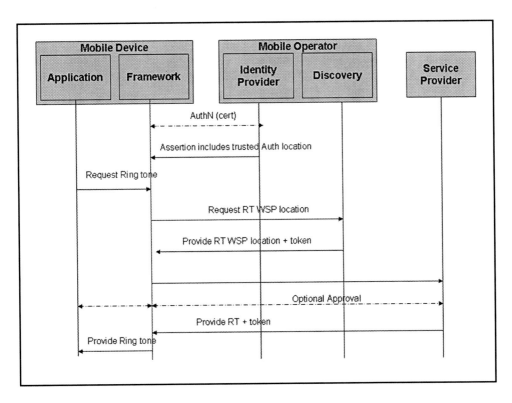

Figure 11.6: Sequence diagram for JSR 279

Using biometric authentication leveraging Sun's partner Bio-Bex that offers a interoperable middleware for multi-modal bio-metric deployment that are tied to devices or device independent as well. Combining this with biometric enabled Java Card's will offer the option of ensuring a) who you are (physical characteristics), b) what you have (ID card) and what you know (key generated password).

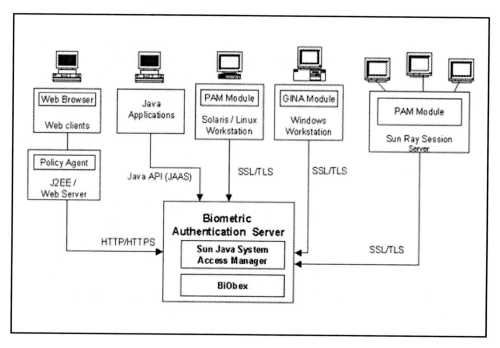

Figure 11. 7: Biometric AuthN integrated

11.5 Conclusion

"Identity enabled Devices" is essentially a loose integration approach where, DRA solutions, Policy Pushing solutions, hardware based security mechanism such as TPM (trusted platform module) from TCG, device management solutions and others leverage a common Identity System as the foundation to correlate users to devices, device reputation back to users, pushing device centric polices from a central policy repository and more, for the security alignment required for this converged NGN.

Wireless security is a key pain point for mobile operators and enterprises worldwide, due to the common belief that wireless networks are inherently less secure than wired networks. In fact, wireless networks and mobile handsets and smart-phones can be made every bit as secure as wired networks and the equipment which runs on them, with the appropriate security mechanisms in place in devices, CPE and NE, which is highlighted in this chapter. Achieving this high level of wireless network edge and device security today means relying on point solutions which are either proprietary and/or limited in scope. What is needed is an industry-wide, standardised and interoperable wireless/mobile security solution that does not limit the ability of either application developers or OEMs to innovate and compete effectively in the marketplace. This type of solution would also, of course, enable mobile operators and enterprise to address the security requirements of their subscribers and end users. The TCG specification provides that underlying platform on which the industry can build robust wireless security solutions in a trust framework which is appropriate to the disparate platforms and endpoints of the converged network, in conjunction with exiting Identity System deployments and IDPs.

Identity and Security

12. Identity enabled Service Containers

12.1 Introduction and Overview

This chapter aligns the developments in terms of Identity System's integration with the Enterprise Network, trusted computing platforms and virtualised computing systems.

According to John Olstik from Enterprise Consulting Group as a member of TCG:

"One way to address this ever-growing issue is to turn the model upside down. Rather than base security on a "black list" approach that tries to identify and block things that should happen, why not utilise a "white list" model that defines the behaviour that actually is allowed and blocks everything else? ESG believes that a "white list" or trusted enterprise model is far more compelling given IT complexity and constant flux. "Trusted" security has been used effectively on a limited basis but to extend this model and make it a foundation for enterprise security, IT technologies must:

- Include the concept of identity. To prevent IT components from gaining malicious or accidental access to restricted areas, all technology piece parts need an identity - a unique and standard name proving that they are who they say they are. In the physical world, U.S. citizens have a unique Social Security number that has been used as a form of individual identity (author's note: the issues around Social Security Number theft and fraud are intentionally avoided in this analogy). IT devices, systems and applications need this same type of system based upon unique identities.

- Build upon identity with strong authentication. To make identity a building block of security, it must be supported with a failsafe method of authentication where one entity can identify another entity with absolute certainty. This kind of authentication must be tamperproof to ensure that identities cannot be stolen, copied or falsified.

- Allow organisations to create trust relationships. Once technologies have unique secure identities that can be authenticated, large companies must have the ability to map technology entities together to form trust relationships. For example, entity A and B could be grouped into an exclusive trust relationship based upon their identities. In this example, no other identity is trusted by either A or B and are therefore restricted from communicating with both. By defining who can participate in an activity, trust relationships preclude malicious outsider from gaining access to an IT asset and thus lower the risk of an accidental or intentional compromise.

- Guarantee information confidentiality and integrity. Once a trust relationship between entities is established, all subsequent communication passed back and forth must be protected against prying eyes. In addition, a receiver must have assurance that the information received actually came from the sending party and was not altered in any way while in transmission. "

This statement clearly shows the value proposition of integrating an Identity System that supports, identifiers, AuthN, AuthZ, Federation, Session, SSO and auditing with the TPM that TCG has developed to achieve Secure Enterprise Computing. This security model is not new; this type of infrastructure is based upon security technologies like Private Key Infrastructure (PKI), digital certificates, encryption and hashing. The technologies described above are readily available but they can be difficult and expensive to implement and operate limiting them to ultra-secure organisations like law enforcement, intelligence, and defense agencies. Why? Since technologies were never "instrumented" for security, establishing individual identities would require IT to retrofit every device, system and application - a daunting, if not impossible task.

Fortunately, there may be a solution to this untenable situation on the horizon from a:

- the Trusted Computing Group, an industry standards body formed in 2003 to develop, define, and promote open standards for robust security technologies and trusted computing across multiple platforms, and,
- Sun Microsystems with its ECC like initiatives tied back to dedicated CPU cores for security in their CMT solutions (supporting Industry Standards as well).

In this chapter after recognising the security requirements of Enterprise Network computing we identify five areas of Synergy in terms of Security functionality developments and an Identity System. These include;

- Identity enabled TPM, Trusted Computing and Trusted network connect
- Identity enabled NAC appliances
- Identity enabled NG Enterprise Network Security Services
- Identity enabled Network Polices
- And Identity enabled Enterprise Rights Management

12.2 Generic Enterprise Computing Security Requirements

Heterogeneity and Openness

The Identity System should not place any restriction on the use of any specific underlying network technology, computer hardware, operating systems, programming languages or other hardware or software entities other than the expected operation involving the use of HTTP protocol in regular and secure forms. This concern is based on the ability of IDS to provide identity services to web applications that could be developed in any programming language, be hosted on any web or application server, deployed on any operating system that utilises any underlying hardware and network facilities. An Enterprise Network Computing Infrastructure is expected to be completely heterogeneous in terms of platforms, operating systems, database technologies, application environments and more. The IDS is expected to be compatible and integratable with all this heterogeneity.

Security and Confidentiality

User information associated with authentication and user sessions should be handled by ID system in a secure and confidential manner, allowing only the privileged administrators to access it where necessary in limited ways. This concern is the basis for sharing core identity services across multiple applications to establish trust in a transparent yet secure manner.

Scalability

The ID system should be able to scale up to the necessary levels in order to include more and more web application as well as more and more users. This concern is based on the premise that there should not be any limit to the number of web applications that can participate in SSO within this system or any limit to the number of users catered within this system as long as the underlying hardware and software components can accommodate such load and bandwidth requirements.

Distribution Transparencies

Services provided within the environment should have sufficient address, location, distribution, replication (caching) and concurrency transparencies to accommodate the invocation from anywhere within the deployment by different types of clients such as web applications or SSO agents. This concern is the basis for ensuring ease of use, operation, and configuration of network elements and is also necessary to ensure sufficient availability of the services offered by this system.

Extensible Architecture

The ID system should allow the creation and integration of custom identity services that can be added to the system to enhance its overall usability. This concern is based on the need to enable system integrators and other developers to provide more functionality via Federation and SSO than what is provided by default.

Use of Standard Protocols

The ID system must only rely on the use of standard protocols such as HTTP in order to function correctly. This requirement is based on the constraints that will be placed around an IDS deployment within secure production environments or other environments where firewalls are present between various network elements within the system.

12.3 The Five areas of Alignment

12.3.1 Identity based Trusted Platform Model

The TCG model is based upon standards such as the Trusted Platform Module (TPM) and the Trusted Computing Module Software Stack (see Figure 1). TPM/TSS will not be layered on top of existing systems like most of today's security solutions. Rather, these standards will be added directly into IT assets as they are instrumented into Integrated Circuits (ICs), systems and applications. TPMs from a number of semi-conductor vendors are included today on new PCs and laptops, integrated into the motherboards of virtually all enterprise systems from leading companies like Acer, Dell, Fujitsu, Hewlett-Packard, Lenovo, Toshiba and others. As of the beginning of 2006, approximately 50 million TPM-based PCs have been shipped.

Just what does TPM/TSS do? Simply stated, TPM instruments hardware and software with core security technologies that can generate and store keys securely for use in digital certificates and encryption. These operations are accessed and controlled through standard TSS interfaces and readily available to security. management software for file/folder encryption, secure e-mail, identity and access management and remote access. TPM is inherently more secure that current software-based key management because the keys are stored in hardware in an encrypted format. In a PKI environment, private keys are never exposed to anyone. In this way, TPM's are virtually tamperproof. Compromising at TPM would require expert knowledge of microprocessors and a brute force attack on a sophisticated encryption algorithm. Even in this unlikely scenario, the world's most powerful supercomputers would require thousands of years to "guess" the value of an actual key.

TPM also supports the concept of "attestation" a method for measuring or fingerprinting the state of a system (i.e. describing the hardware and software that is or isn't installed on the system). Through attestation, one system can check the health of another to make sure that it conforms to security policy and does not contain any suspicious or unknown code. An IDS can essentially be part of the TSS.

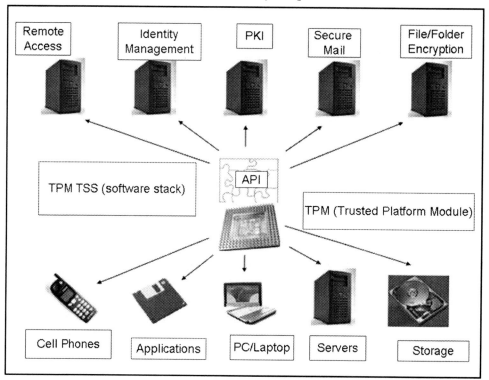

Figure 12.1: Identity enabled TPM

12.3.2 Identity enabled NAC appliances

Network Admission Control appliances are prevalent in the market since late 2005, with multiple large scale vendors such as Cisco and Nortel, supporting such appliances along with many startup companies that specialise in this space. These NAC appliances integrate with an Identity System for allowing an AuthN Session of a user after performing its role around admission control into the enterprise network. The NAC appliances essentially quarantines a User's computing device in a secure VLAN and checks the device for Virus/malware, Spyware/adware, Spam, Hackers, Trojans, Rootkits and other potential attacks.

While performing these admission control mechanisms the NAC appliance can also consult an Identity enabled DRA (device reputation authority) to understand the device's past behaviours and reputation. By default they do integrate with an Identity System for User AuthN and offering access based on anonymity or pre-defined roles associated with the user. The majority of the NAC appliance vendors who integrate with an IDS also support TCG and TPM. The authN session with IDS implies capabilities to have trust relationships and federation. NAC appliances perform preventive functions and therefore are integrated with IPS (intrusion prevention tools) as well.

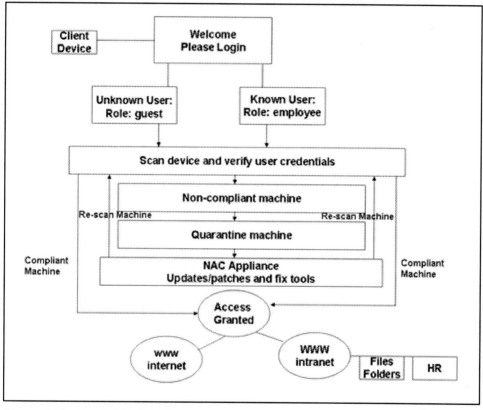

Figure 12.2: Cisco's NAC Architecture

12.3.3 Identity enabled NG enterprise network security services

This section talks to how an Identity enabled XML firewall, XML accelerators; XML router/gateway augments an Enterprise Network that embracing SOA. Cisco for example is building solutions around SONA (service oriented network architecture). In our earlier chapters we've discussed Service Delivery Networks that specialise in delivering Services based on SOA as well. Here the idea is simply one where when a lot of XML traffic is generated, by internal Services and Web Services. Sun's partner Reactivity for example leverages Sun identity systems for performing its function in conjunction with an Identity System and relevant AuthN sessions. As major corporations initiate services-oriented architecture (SOA) and Web Services projects Reactivity's XML gateways, XML routers and XML accelerators are fast becoming a critical piece of the network infrastructure. These solutions often referred as XML enabled Networking are also Identity enabled as well – leading to Identity & SOA (XML) enabled Networks. A well aligned solution that augments Sun's existing Identity Systems and Java CAPS customers (see chapter on Identity enabled ESB as well). These solutions are relevant for B2B Integration XML Threats exists, such as XML DOS attacks. They also include Access Enforcement, where, Identification of requesting systems and users is conducted and enforcing appropriate access to web services, is made possible. Real-time Portals where Identity Brokering Cross Platform Services is key to the solution, can execute policies to transform between credential types and more. Secure integration implies a myriad of potential authentication methods, data-formats, and transport protocols can create a complex environment for architects, developers, security managers and operations (server and network) to manage.

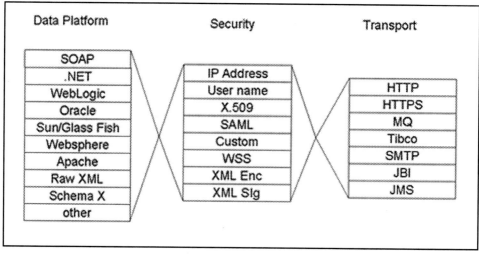

Figure 12.3: Secure Integration with XML gateways and routers

Also in such intensively integrated environments unparalleled auditing capabilities for web services messages are needed for governance and compliance purposes as well. Performance requirements are met by accelerating authentication, schema validation, transformation, new policy deployment, WS Security operations and end-to-end web service performance. This in turn leads to better service performance and service level agreement compliance, as well.

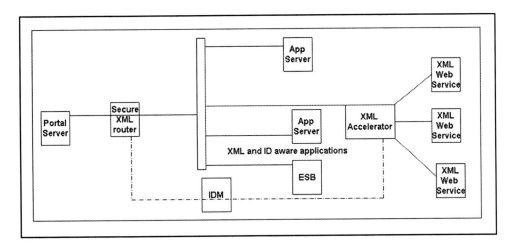

Figure 12.4: Reactivity's Secure XML router, accelerator and XML gateways/routers that are Identity enabled

12.3.4 Identity enabled Network Polices

Similar to how Identity enabled Device Management allows for the pushing of policies centered on a device and edge perimeter network equipment to the respective device (CPE or NE), an Identity enabled Enterprise Network allows for the integration of user centric policies with enterprise network centric policies that revolve around resources such as computing elements and the switching gear. Along with the support from large NEPs there are many startups also specialising in this level of integration with their policy engines (such as ID-engines). Some NAC appliance vendors also support this level of policy integration, with the policy hierarchy available in a Identity System. These systems also integrate with an IDS for correlating AuthN, Session management and policy alignment. Through this level of integration the following benefits are achieved.

- *Faster time to policy deployment with a centralised policy management system* - there is no longer a need for network administrators or application developers to set up individual user accounts or policies on individual devices or applications.
- *Effective and efficient use of the wide range of network devices that organszations already own,* by easily defining and managing policies through a centralised management appliance.
- *Reduced administrative cost;* a network administrator can update authorisation policies for entire groups of people, automatically deploying across an enterprise-class network within minutes, instead of having to spend up to several days manually updating each control point.
- *Reduced IT and help desk costs for guest network access* as non-technical workers may provision guest users while maintaining the same audit and reporting capabilities available for employees.
- *Immediate and secure access granted to new users, with the appropriate level of access to network services and applications,* as soon as they are added to company directories.
- *Improved security and compliance with government regulations* such as Sarbanes-Oxley, Gramm-Leach-Bliley and Health Insurance Portability and Accountability (HIPAA) Acts.
- *Phased deployment of the system,* allowing network administrators to trial the system in one or two areas before rolling it out across the organisation.
- *No additional investment in network devices,* as Ignition uses the capabilities of and allows for multiple protocols that are already built into the enterprise's existing access points and switches.

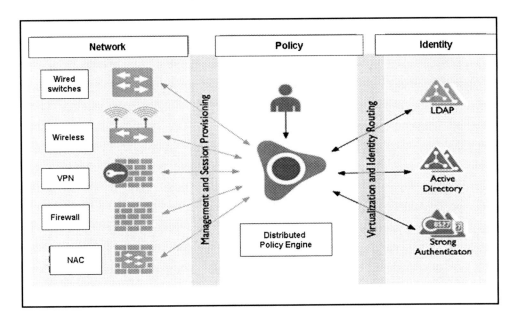

Figure 12.5: Identity enabled Network centric policies

12.3.5 Identity enabled Enterprise Rights Management

Enterprise Rights Management (ERM) refers to the use of DRM technology to control access to corporate documents (Microsoft Word, PDF, TIFF, AutoCAD files etc.), rather than consumer playable media. The technology usually requires an Identity System (as a Policy Server) to authenticate users' rights to access certain (software/code as well) Corporate resources. ERM vendors include Microsoft, Adobe Systems, EMC Corporation/Authentica and several smaller companies. There are open source implementations as well. EDRM is generally intended to apply to trade secrets, which are much different from copyrighted material (though there is sometimes an overlap as some material is both copyrighted and a trade secret — e.g., the source code for some proprietary software), and for whom the primary issue is industrial or corporate espionage or inadvertent release. By Identity enabling ERM services we can expect alignment of rights management at the User level, Enterprise level and Digital Content level. The underlying operating systems (like Solaris 10) also should support Identity based User Rights management. Rights management at all levels perform the roles to rules to resource alignment through policies and addressing alignment of rights management at levels will allow legitimate users to access digital content, enterprise content or user specific files without having to validate the identity again (when the appropriate AuthN level is achieved). This approach will allow a user to access whatever he or she is entitled to. Therefore an Identity enabled NAC appliance can also allow users access to the right resources within an Enterprise network, by integrating with an ERM system since an identity system permeates to the client device, NAC appliance, TPM, DRM, ESB, ERM and network centric policy engines as well.

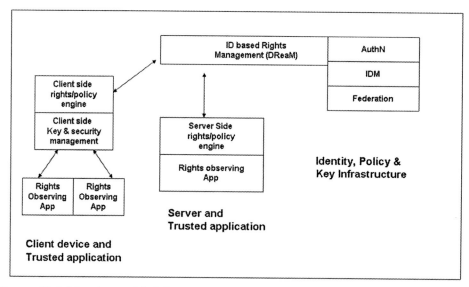

Figure 12.6: Identity enabled ERM

12.4 Conclusion

In order to achieve systemic security in an Enterprise, that is evolving its Enterprise Architecture towards a SOA, and aligning the same with NG Networks to offer mobility to its employees, partners and customer, traditional Enterprise Security mechanisms, such as, establishing a DMZ, Firewall Ridges, Intrusion Prevention Systems and User centric Identity Systems ought to be augmented with NAC appliances, integrated network policy engines, DRA, XML routers/gateways/firewalls, ERM and Trusted Computing Group's TPM and trusted network connect. This approach to systemic security for an enterprise must be aligned with Telecom companies networks (such as IMS, Access Networks, etc.) as well, since the enterprise network constantly interacts with Service provider networks for additional services. Also an Identity System plays a major role in virtualised environments where Service Containers (Secure execution environments) exist, with the support for identifier and label for System Containers.

13. Identity enabled ILM

13.1 Introduction and Overview

Information Lifecycle Management (sometimes abbreviated ILM) is the practice of applying certain policies to the effective management of information throughout its useful life. This practice has been used by Records and Information Management (RIM) Professionals for over three decades and had its basis in the management of information in paper or other physical forms (microfilm, negatives, photographs, audio or video recordings and other assets). ILM includes every phase of a "record" from its beginning to its end. And while it is generally applied to information that rises to the classic definition of a record (Records management), it applies to any and all informational assets. During its existence, information can become a record by being identified as documenting a business transaction or as satisfying a business need. And while most records are thought of as having a relationship to business, not all do. Much recorded information may not serve a business need of any sort, but still serves to document a critical point in history or to document an event. Examples of these are birth, death, medical/health and educational records. Functionality in ILM includes;

Creation and Receipt deals with records from their point of origination. This could include their creation by a member of an organisation at varying levels or receipt of information from an external source. It includes correspondence, forms, reports, drawings, computer input/output or other sources.

Distribution is the process of managing the information once it has been created or received. This includes both internal and external distribution, as information that leaves an organisation becomes a record of a transaction with others.

Use takes place after information is distributed internally, and can generate business decisions, document further actions, or serve other purposes.

Maintenance is the management of information. This can include processes such as filing, retrieval and transfers. While the connotation of 'filing' presumes the placing of information in a prescribed container and leaving it there, there is much more involved. Filing is actually the process of arranging information in a predetermined sequence and creating a system to manage it for its useful existence within an organisation. Failure to establish a sound method for filing information makes its retrieval and use nearly impossible. Transferring information refers to the process of responding to requests, retrieval from files and providing access to users authorised by the organisation to have access to the information. While removed from the files, the information is tracked by the use of various processes to ensure it is returned and/or available to others who may need access to it.

Disposition is the practice of handling information that is less frequently accessed or has met its assigned retention periods. Less frequently accessed records may be considered for relocation to an 'inactive records facility' until they have met their assigned retention period. Retention periods are based on the creation of an organisation-specific retention schedule, based on research of the regulatory, statutory and legal requirements for management of information for the industry in which the organisation operates. Additional items to consider when establishing a retention period are any business needs that may exceed those requirements and consideration of the potential historic, intrinsic or enduring value of the information. If the information has met all of these needs and is no longer considered to be valuable, it should be disposed of by means appropriate for the content. This may include ensuring that others cannot obtain access to outdated or obsolete information as well as measures for protection privacy and confidentiality.

Long-term records are those that are identified to have a continuing value to an organisation. Based on the period assigned in the retention schedule, these may be held for periods of 25 years or longer, or may even be assigned a retention period of "indefinite" or "permanent". The term "permanent" is used much less frequently outside of the Federal Government, as it is impossible to establish a requirement for such a retention period. There is a need to ensure records of a continuing value are managed using methods that ensure they remain persistently accessible for length of the time they are retained. While this is relatively easy to accomplish with paper or microfilm based records by providing appropriate environmental conditions and adequate protection from potential hazards, it is less simple for electronic format records. There are unique concerns related to ensuring the format they are generated/captured in remains viable and the media they are stored on remains accessible. Media is subject to both degradation and obsolescence over its lifespan, and therefore, policies and procedures must be established for the periodic conversion and migration of information stored electronically to ensure it remains accessible for its required retention periods. Information Lifecycle Management (ILM) has become well known in the last several years. But organisations are finding that simply adopting ILM is not enough. To provide more secure, cost-effective access to data, the next phase in ILM maturity is the development of "Identity-Enabled" ILM. Identity -Enabled ILM links data access to specific roles within an organisation. It adds the idea of a user lifecycle to that of the information lifecycle. Users will require access to different information as they move to different positions within an organisation. Parts of the Identity System solutions, such as the Identify Management and Automated Data Manager software, can link these roles to appropriate data automatically. Identity -Enabled ILM also addresses the need to bring data back from archival media (after encryption and decryption) to "active duty." Increasingly, data is not sent to the archives to die; it may need to be accessed for business or audit purposes at any time. This bi-directionality is an important new data management concept. This chapter introduces Identity-Enabled ILM, in terms of how today's organisations face a myriad of

IT challenges, including managing data growth, protecting data, and simplifying data management; all while attempting to reduce IT costs. Most ILM approaches focus on static tiers of storage, and do not take into account the dynamic, bidirectional nature of data access. Perhaps more importantly, today's ILM methodologies do not have enough emphasis on data security. Any discussion of security focuses on encrypting data, but there is no emphasis on effectively controlling access to data throughout its entire lifecycle and Aligning:

ILM (Information lifecycle management) with
IdLM (Identity lifecycle management) and
SLM (Service lifecycle management).

Enterprises can address these problems with Identity -Enabled Information Lifecycle Management, in conjunction with Identity enabled SOA. Identity -Enabled ILM is designed to make data management more cost-effective and compliant while making sure that data is secure and available. It makes sense for today's data-intensive enterprises, introducing an identity-driven approach to controlling and accessing data throughout its lifecycle.

The five areas of Synergy in terms of Identity enabling ILM include;

- IdLM acting as the Meta Layer between SLM and ILM
- Streamlined automated Data control over long periods of time
- Value to Storage Environments and Storage Networks
- Value created for Auditing and Reporting
- Alignment of Access Rights

13.2 Security requirements for ILM

Some of the Best Practices in ILM Security include;

13.2.1 Physical Security

Physical security, from an ILM perspective, relates to the safeguarding of data in all its forms and states. This includes securing data both while it is "in flight" and "at rest." The security of media, hardware devices, and data centres, plus the data flowing between each of these, all must be considered. At the media level, loss and corruption are the biggest risks. While loss of removable media (whether tapes, removable disks, or some other format) is a risk, physically transporting data can offer security as well as other advantages over network data transmission. Encryption can be added to any of these techniques, offering additional safety but typically increased cost and complexity. Media with write once, read many (WORM) capabilities provide another means of achieving physical security. Hardware devices also require physical security commensurate with the data they may contain over time. The concept of creating logical "gaps" between storage devices used for different purposes is worthy of consideration, despite the additional costs and productivity hindrances they may produce. Gaps created to separate different levels of use are less likely to create productivity issues. For example, having a gap between a data warehouse (central repository) and more accessible — and thus exposed — data marts (distributed functional copies of data) can improve security. At the data centre level, perimeter security is of primary concern. However, with current technologies the concept of a "perimeter" can be vague. Physical security and access control at remote or disaster recovery sites must be as rigorous as at primary data centres. These sites must be periodically inspected for compliance with security policies. Historically, storage networks have been difficult to secure. Because data cannot be fully secure unless the storage network environment is secure, this has meant avoiding the use of networks for sensitive data or limiting their use to encrypted data. Recently, however, great strides have been made to improve the security of physical networks.

While all of these layers of physical security reduce risk, active monitoring is required to provide fully effective physical security. However, analysing alerts and investigating incidents is very labour-intensive and is often not done. More intelligent tools and processes are needed to facilitate effective monitoring and improve overall physical security.

13.2.2 Access Control

Access control can be defined as the rules that govern who can see or modify information. There are many different potential users of an organisation's data, including customers, partners and suppliers, regulators, auditors and prospects. The "castle defense" mentality that assumes anyone within the organisation can be trusted and all others cannot has no place in today's business environment. Role-and policy-based identity management enables the building of robust rules that allow various types of access to different classes of data, assuring security and providing affordable productivity. Basic access controls restrict read, write, and delete privileges based on a user's identity and successful authentication. Access controls restrict basic access to an object and can be implemented in the file system or database system. Third-party products, applications and some storage and operating systems can provide the manageability advantages of role-based access controls. Note that access controls protect an object only within controlled systems. Once data is downloaded or otherwise moved outside the controlled system, other identity management tools or techniques must be adopted to maintain control. Logical controls further enhance content security and support access controls, especially in structured data systems and applications. Security can be significantly enhanced through proper database and application design, and effective use of structured database management system (DBMS) features. For example, referential integrity supports the soundness of the data and enhances access controls. All major DBMS products allow administrators to assign restrictive access to tables while granting wider access to table views, an essential security mechanism. DBMS products include additional vendor-specific security features, such as data labeling for multilevel security, triggers, and row-level access controls, but applying these to established databases may impact performance.

13.2.3 Encryption

Encryption is a process of transforming data into a format that only the intended recipient can understand. Should unauthorised access occur, encryption would prevent the intruder from reading or manipulating the data. Encryption converts data into cipher-text, which can only be accessed through appropriate credentials or keys. This technique is particularly useful in situations where it is impractical to prevent unauthorised access to data — for instance, while it is in transit across distrusted or hostile networks or stored in unacceptably vulnerable environments. There are three commonly accepted layers and approaches to encryption. Each layer approach delivers an encrypted solution in a different manner and addresses different requirements:

- Application Layer
- Database or File Layer
- Storage Layer

Implementing encryption in the application layer is known to require extensive coding changes, create inconsistencies across systems and produce ongoing maintenance headaches. Database level encryption allows enterprises to secure as it is written to read and from a database. Database-layer encryption will also secure data in the file system that the database is using to store the database information. Ideally this type of deployment is done at the column level within a database table and, if coupled with database security and access controls, it forms a sound policy to prevent theft of critical data. Database-layer encryption secures structured data against a wide range of threats, including storage media theft, database-layer attacks and compromised database administrator access.

Storage-layer encryption enables enterprises to encrypt data either at the file layer (in network-attached storage or direct-attached storage) or at the block level in storage area networks. This type of encryption is well suited for encrypting files, directories, storage blocks and tape media. In today's large storage environments, storage-layer encryption addresses a requirement to secure data without using logical unit number masking or zoning. Enterprise digital rights management (DRM) as part of identity management uses encryption to provide granular controls tied to the individual object. Unlike basic encryption, enterprise DRM follows the object throughout its life cycle and allows deep integration within the business infrastructure. Example controls include read, edit, forward, copy, paste, delete, or expires the file after a set time.

13.3 The Five areas of Synergy in terms of Identity enabling ILM include

As described earlier there are five major synergies associated with Identity enabling ILM.

13.3.1 IdLM acting as the Meta Layer between SLM and ILM

In many chapters this particular idea has been discussed, including the alignment between an Identity Centric Architecture with an SOA in chapter 1, Identity based Registry Repository for an ESB in the chapter on Identity enabled ESB, Identity enabled NG Network Security Services and more. An Identity System as a meta-layer can provider secure access to meta-data that maps and aligns information life cycle management with service lifecycle management.

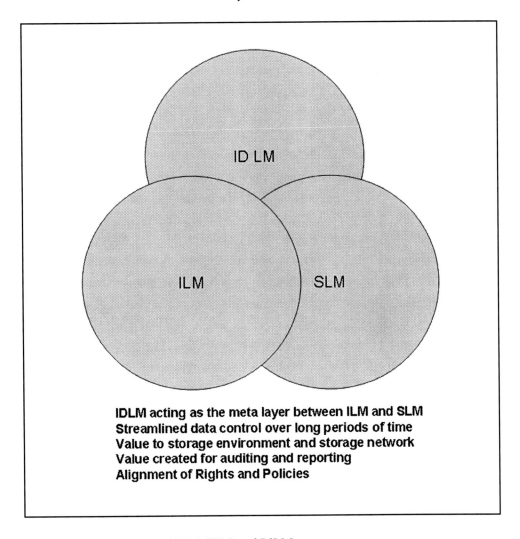

IDLM acting as the meta layer between ILM and SLM
Streamlined data control over long periods of time
Value to storage environment and storage network
Value created for auditing and reporting
Alignment of Rights and Policies

Figure 13.1: Alignment of ILM, SLM and IdLM

13.3.2 Streamlined automated Data control over long periods of time

ILM was originally created in response to a valid need; namely that data should be managed differently at different phases of its lifecycle. While it has vastly improved data management, traditional ILM has limitations, focusing on data storage and migrations. Automatic provisioning of user access rights and storage allocation can happen at the application level, file system level and device level to streamline access management, simplify compliance and improve data security. Identity enabled ILM allows policies to be set so that data is moved to appropriate tiers of storage as it ages. Newly created data is kept on primary disk for fastest access, while older data is migrated to secondary storage or archived in long-term storage. This strategy is effective in reducing storage costs, allowing older data to remain accessible without using expensive primary disk to store it. Identity -Enabled ILM addresses bidirectional data flow with storage archive and management software. With this technology (such as SAMFS and ZFS), data is migrated to secondary storage as it ages and is brought back into disk cache whenever it's recalled. Just the act of accessing data allows authorised users to changes the data's classification from "dormant" to "active." When data files move into disk cache, the lifecycle clock is reset, and the file is subject to the same migration policies as other active data. Thus, allowing customers to manage information based on its ever-changing value to the business.

This approach is very strategic for enterprises that are participating in the Web 2.0 space and the read write internet. It's also important for those enterprises that require efficiencies in its business processes (supply chain to Customer facing business processes).

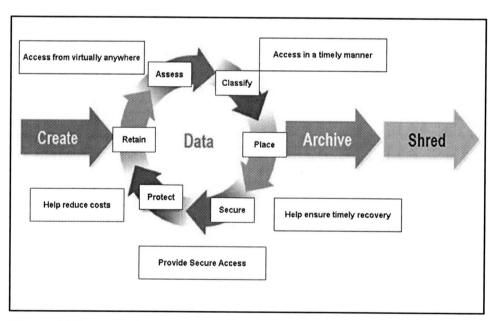

Figure 13.2 From creation to management to archiving to shredding

13.3.3 Value to Storage Environments and Storage Networks

Identity and TPM enabled Storage environments are also another key area of synergy for Identity enabled ILM. The root of trust for storage (RTS) manages a small amount of volatile memory where keys are held while performing signing and decryption operations. In Mark Dixon's blog on Discovering Identity he recalled, Sun's recent announcement of Device-Level Encryption on the Sun StorageTek T10000 Tape Drive. If data on a tape is encrypted, it must be decrypted to be used. Decryption implies authentication and authorisation, which should be part of a cohesive Identity Management system. This is yet another example of how Identity Management is not only an essential function whenever we consider secure, personalised information services, but is an enabler to new, innovative business opportunities. This approach aligns with Identity enabled Enterprise Computing since there are support for TPM (trusted platform module) for computing platforms, client devices and network connections as well.

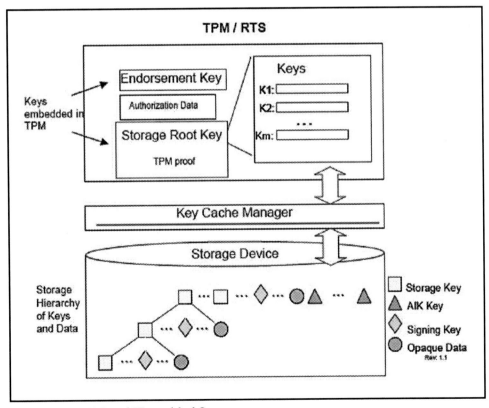

Figure 13.3 TPM and ID enabled Storage

13.3.4 Value created for Auditing and Reporting

Identity Manager Solutions in conjunction with Information Management solutions combine the capabilities of provisioning and auditing, with AuthN and AuthZ, Administration and synchronisation, Retention and retrieval, storage tiering and more, controlling the cost of compliance, with the ability to collaborate safely in a Converged NGN. Alignment of the two IDM and ILM allows for addressing the overlapping functionalities offered by the two and hence streamline the auditing and reporting processes for compliance with regulatory requirements.

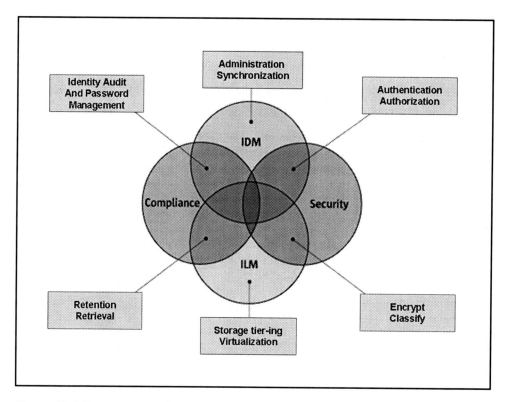

Figure 13.4 Convergence of IDM and ILM

13.3.5 Alignment of Access Rights

Everything boils down to bits and bytes, whether it is data (information, content, files, etc.) or code (application, services, OS etc.). The rights to access to these bits and bytes by users whether they are consumers, partners, employees or others involve Identity Lifecycle Management. The granular levels of rights (whether its User Rights management at the OS level, Digital Rights Management for the content or Enterprise Rights Management for enterprise resources and artifacts) when identity enabled can be mapped to a policy hierarchy that support roles, rules and resource framework. Also aligning these with the right levels of encryption (application level, database or file level and storage level) requires Identity System integrated with Enterprise Storage Managements as well. The figure below depicts how the security and compliance layer (in the form of IDS) transcends customer applications, enterprise storage management, storage devices and storage networks and more.

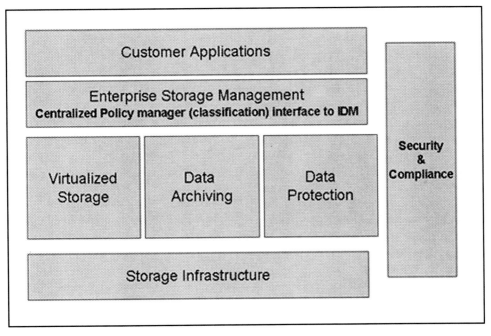

Figure 13.5 Alignment of Rights Management

13.4 Conclusion

Sun's Bill Vass states that today, ILM have helped numerous organisations balance storages costs against data access needs. But with the increasing importance of data security and regulatory compliance, ILM based solely on time retention policies is no longer enough. Storage systems require identity intelligence because data value doesn't always erode on a predictable path. Identity-enabled ILM seeks to examine user lifecycles in order to take actions on storage and data management that makes sense for the people who create, store, and access the data. In the future, it is only by integrating identity management and ILM capabilities that organisations will be able to cost-effectively manage the challenges posed by data security and regulatory compliance.

14. Conclusion & Future

The main thrust of this book is about integrating an Identity System for AuthN, AuthZ, Policy Mangement, Session Management, SSO, Federation and more with external elements such as, Networks and Network Services. There are many more areas of Integration that is possible, due to the pervasive nature of an Identity System and its role in making "The Network a Computer". Instead of dedicating a chapter each, majority of these areas are discussed here in the concluding chapter, in brief.

Identity enabled Multi-xxx Meta System

Integrating an Identity Systems, with ISVs, for functional alignment. Here is a list of 14 such integration efforts and their specific additional functionality.

- *Actividentity* for integrating logical and physical asset security with the Identity System.
- *Approva* for integrating, streamlining and automating compliant provisioning processes with the Identity System.
- *Bridgestream* for integrating roles management solution with the Identity System.
- *Bonsai Networks* for integrating Wifi (& Wimax) Service Managers with the Identity System.
- *Consul* for integrating privileged user monitoring and auditing with the Identity System.
- *Leapstone* for integrating Service Brokering and Subscriber information with the Identity System.

- *Locationnet platform* for GIS engine and location application engine integration with the Identity System.
- *Lucents VOIP* platform integration with Identity (& Directory) System.
- *Mobicents* SLEE and other SLEE platforms integration for policies, profiles, etc., with the Identity System.
- *Passlogix* for integrating simplified enterprise & desktop SSO (non web applications) with the Identity System.
- *Pronto Networks* for integrating wireless SDP (service delivery platform) with the Identity System.
- *Vaau* for integrating role engineering, identity auditing and identity certification with the Identity System.
- *Verimatrix* for integrating with OMC DRM via disintermediation (d15n- implied) with the Identity System.
- *Virsa* for integrating continuous compliance and real time insights with the Identity System.

Through these integration efforts, as well as successful integration with network facing Identity Systems (such as HSS, HLR, RADIUS, TACACS, AAA, GUP, ENUM, and more), deployments of these joint solutions into the network (access network, core network, service network and content network) has already morphed an identity system into a meta-layer, to a certain extent, that offers,

- multi-repository,
- multi-modal,
- multi-media,
- multi-channel,
- multi-factor

capabilities. Of course with Identity System's support for standards coming from OASIS, Liberty and others, including support for Microsoft's environment and existing network facing ID systems, it has morphed to a meta-system already (using the existing implementations rather than competing with them).

Identity enabled Compliance

Continuously throughout the year, Enterprises have to ensure compliance with multiple regulations, including:

- HSPD 12 (new standard for secure, reliable identification issued for Federal employees and contractors)
- Gramm-Leach-Bliley (GLB - Privacy and Secuirty Requirements)
- Sarbanne Oxley (to address financial control and financial reporting issues)
- HIPPA (Protection of health care information and access to information systems)
- Identity enabled extensible SW Architecture

The notion of a markup language has tremendous value (like in html) and the notion of extensible markup language has exponential value. Simply look at the various dialects of XML that are being proposed today; ebXML, XACML, XML Signature, XSLT, XKMS, XRI/XDI, and many more. If you take industry specific XML developments there are several hundreds more (e.g., MOML and MSML for media markup languages based on XML). XML capable of describing many sets of data along with, XSD an instance of an XML schema written in XML schema—that can be custom XML private between two parties as well —makes this value exponential. XSD is extensively used by Identity Systems to share data/profile (about location, preference, identifiers, payment, presence, devices and just about any data) securely between trusted entities. XSD is the secret sauce that allows for the exchange of intelligence within the network.

Adding Java technologies to the picture (such as JBI) we have a programming paradigm (logic extensibility) that is flexible and extensible and a markup language (data extensibility) that is flexible and extensible as well, ensuring the goal of achieving business agility with SOA. A list of Appendices is added that talks as to how Sun Microsystems has opened up its Identity System Architecture into Services themselves and how they can work (the internals of AuthN, Session Management etc.) , so that the next level of integration can take place. Appendix 1 to

9 is essentially the internals on How an Identity System works and can be leveraged as a Core Service Building Block.

Identity enabled extensible Data Exchanges

There was a research paper written a few years ago around the secure and extensible exchange of URI based -XRI/XDI - of identity related data, such as profiles; my driving record, my credit record, my medical history, my device reputation, my education history and many more — that talks to XML based object orientation. Relating this paper to today's SPML v2 and EPP (for extensible provisioning protocol) one can clearly see the value proposition of an Identity System way beyond sharing AuthN context, identifiers, etc., reaching out to sharing profiles securely and later supporting a federated AuthZ and entitlement model -XACML.

Identity enabled Service Registry

An ESB (Enterprise Service Bus) and a Registry are two foundation infrastructure software for the implementation of an SOA. A Service Registry is expected to support multiple XML standards, including (these are requirements specific to a registry):

- ebXML Registry 3.0
- UDDI 3.0
- XACML 1.0 for Role Based Access Control Policies
- SOAP 1.1 with Attachments
- WSDL 1.1
- XML Signature 1.0
- XSLT 1.0
- Web Services Security: SOAP Message Security 1.0
- Web Services Security: SOAP Message with Attachments (SwA) Profile 1.0
- WS-I: Basic Security Profile 1.0
- WS-I: Basic Profile 1.1
- SAML 2.0

Its a fundamental requirement for both the ESB and the Registry to be tightly aligned with an Identity System, especially when Business are expected to deliver information beyond boundaries to employees, partners, suppliers and consumers.

Identity enabled Data Quality

Identity addresses the Quality of a Query Result. Security is generally measured in terms of confidentiality, integrity, authentication and authorisation. Integrity in this context means that data is not replaced or modified without authorisation in transport or storage. Ensuring the integrity of the data is one perspective of Identity enabled ILM. Additionally Identity enabling ILM adds Intelligence to data storage and there is more to it when we consider the notion of a meta-layer between "services" in a SOA and the information resources the Services need to access, in the form of an Identity enabled Registry/Repository. It adds the contextual layer within a Storage Network as well and is quintessential for aligning the Identity life cycle management with the Information life cycle management. It also becomes a requirement when Regulation is taken into account.

Identity enabled SSL

The next Killer App will be the one that is built with Security from scratch at the same time with technologies that ensure that performance penalties are minimised even with Security built into the core of these applications. K-SSL stands for both Kernel SSL (on the server side) that is part of Solaris 10 (plus it has JES support) and Kilo-byte SSL (on the client side) that is part of JME's client-side-only implementation of SSL for handheld and wireless devices (of the previous generation that ran WAP/WTLS). Of course both Solaris and JME are offered via an open-source license from Sun and of course "Security" is the killer attribute in every App. Both Kernel and Kilo-byte SSL can be Identity enabled, as well.

Identity enabled Convergence

Identity Manager solution combines the capabilities of provisioning and auditing. There is also a good paper that discusses;

- Controlling the Cost of Compliance
- Ability to Collaborate Safely
- Converged & Combined Capabilities of Provisioning with Auditing

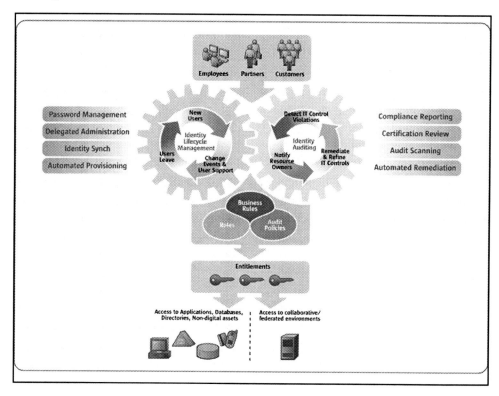

Figure 14.1 Convergence of Provisioning and Auditing

Identity enabled Throughput Computing = Trusted Computing

All these three topics on Throughput, Threading and Trust are key to Sun and are intertwined in many ways. With the advances in Access Networks and the proliferation of broad-band all over the world; including global WiMAX rollouts, BPL (broadband over power-line) rollouts, Wifi Mesh networks, Cable and Fibre to the home, we are seeing access networks that can support 100MBps bandwidth and more. This in conjunction with powerful client devices is causing innovation in three areas within Sun to ensure that the Network can sustain the next wave of users and services offered.

Throughput (both network and compute) is Sun's forte today in the form of Niagara 1 and 2 chips, blades (ATCA compliant blades ready for 4GRAN, IMS/HSS, etc.) and systems. **Threading** is another major plus with these throughput systems (where Niagara supports four hardware threads per core today and eight hardware threads per core next year) and in good alignment with Java/Solaris software threading model.

What does all this have to do with Identity and **Trust** (see picture that depicts how trust is established)? Cryptographic operation and smart card communication establishes security and trust however without the performance penalty when the combination of Throughput and Threading is applied to Trust—and that's what I call Addressing Tradeoff - One can have High-end Security and Superior Performance at the same time saving costs (energy, physical space and administrative costs).

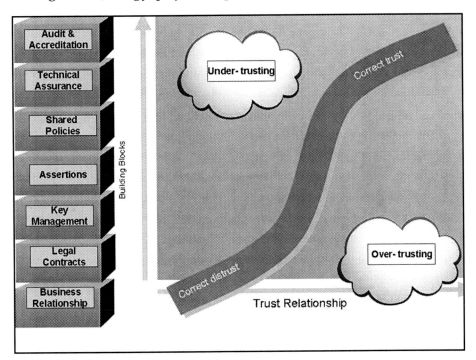

Figure 14.2 Identity and Trust Relationships

Identity enabled e-Governance

One of the most important value proposition of an Identity enabled Network or a Network Identity Platform that is standards based is the foundation framework it creates for countries to participate in a Global Economy. Enterprises doing business in different countries of the world are able to be part of the value chain (from suppliers to consumers in each industry) in a global marketplace. I'm reminded of a great quote made by a saint from India "each country is but a room in the mansion of god". Countries strong in specific industries are able to act as the supplier for the entire world for products and services produced within that industry (like flowers from the Netherlands and Spices from India- supplied to the entire world). This concept when abstracted to today's complex products and industries from bio-tech, computing, aviation, electronics, e-Gov, pharmaceuticals etc., for enterprises and governments to participate in this highly intertwined world more effectively and efficiently a foundation framework is mandatory for a federated model to flourish. Government in each country is typically the largest service provider of that country and a National Identity program that will allow for a federated world is practical necessity.

To this end there is an upcoming event sponsored by Sun for Security in a Federated World in October 2006. This is actually part of an excellent Executive Master's Program on eGOV.
This was also the topic that I presented at eGOV India 2006 (on a National Identity Program).

Identity enabled e-Connectivity

In a series of papers I covered the topic of eGOV, eConnectivity and PURA (providing urban amenities to rural areas). Since then I met with several folks and leaders in New Delhi who are addressing this issue, around digital divide and electronic connectivity. Another fantastic option other than Wifi and WiMAX (that also compliments wireless networks) is BPL (broadband over power line), which has the potential to provide electronic connectivity to rural areas in Asia, Africa and the Americas. I met the CEO of Corinex at New Delhi (a company that specialises in BPL) who advised me more on the inner workings of this technology and how it can address e-connectivity in rural india as a 3rd pipe beyond cable and dsl, especially after the new FCC policy supporting this technology even for rural areas in the US.

This in conjunction with renewable energy sources producing 3000MW by 2010 in India- there is potential to meet and reach the energy needs for the entire country, hopefully ensuring round the clock supply of electricity (a must for e-Connectivity as well), Solar energy or Wind energy supplies electricity, similar, to solar powered access controllers offering a mesh network.

Identity enabled Call/Application Control Sessions

I recently viewed this press release from Appium, Sun's Service Delivery Platform partner, showing the value proposition of a SIP based Call Control Sessions in a Cool-thread Chip.

"Key results included the performance of 16 million Busy Hour Call Attempts (BHCA) and 59,800 SIP messages per second, using telecoms applications such as Find-Me. These were implemented with call duration of 10 seconds with a response time of less than 15ms using 50,000 active sessions and with no failed calls on a resilient hardware configuration that included three T1000 and one T2000 for executing the sessions that were being generated by a separate traffic generation system". This is indeed impressive when the BHCA number ranges in the 600,000 for class 5 switch (end user calls) and 1.5 million for a class 4 switch (trunking) systems. The integration value (systemic security for services) of this Service Delivery Platform (which is an SOA based approach for the Telecom, Media and Entertainment Industry) with Identity and Access Management Systems is discussed here, by Anthony Robinson from Accenture.

Identity enabled SIP Signaling

As SIP evolves into the Open Signaling Protocol for the Next Generation Converged Network and SAML is leveraged extensively for Vertical Integration of multiple Identity Systems, Aligning Assertion Arti-facts within the Signaling Domain becomes critical for Open yet Secure Communication and Collaboration.

There is a paper at *http://www.softarmor.com/wgdb/docs/draft-tschofenig-sip-saml-04.html*, explaining, SAML for SIP that illustrates the strength and significance of an Identity System in the Network. This is another context within which Identity enabling Communication Profile ser-vices (such as ENUM) become relevant, profiles -combining protocols, bindings and assertions for a given use case.

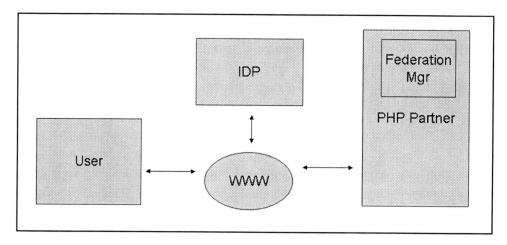

Figure 14.3 SIP Signaling

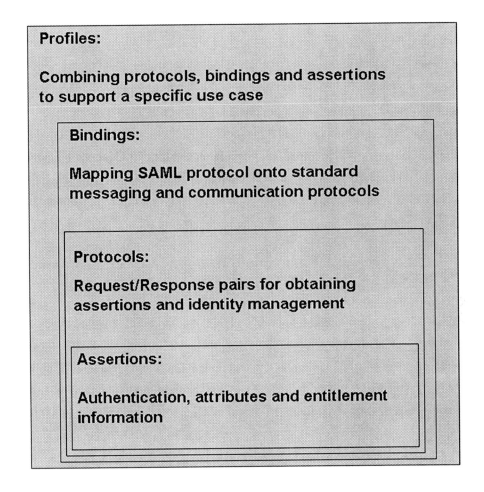

Figure 14.4 SAML Profiles, Bindings, Protocols and Assertions

Identity enabled IDE

Sun released NetBeans IDE 5.5 recently, an integrated development environment to develop Identity enabled SOA. This is the home page for the Integration of Identity Management suite of products as modules in Netbeans IDE. This video also has a demo on how the integrated development environment offered by NetBeans enables you to easily add SAML-based authentication to your Java EE application, using Web Service Client and Provider Security. Using this IDE developer can build identity enabled web services and web application for deployment on the Java EE Container. NetBeans also offers a rich environment for the development of any CLDC and CDC apps for any

JME compatible device (handheld, PDA, Cell phone, STB, DVR/DVD payer, etc.). It is great to have an Identity enabled IDE!!

Now that a programming abstraction is available for identity-enabled Web services in general and ID-WSF in particular, how do all the pieces come together? Just perform two tasks, with an IDE:

- Register the newly created Web service with the Discovery Service so that Web-service consumers can find it.
- Deploy the service into a container so that Web-service consumers can invoke it.

And that is where Java Studio Enterprise comes in. From a wizard in that IDE, you can create Web-service providers. New capabilities currently being prototyped will prompt you for the location of the Discovery Service and other relevant information as you deploy the Web service. As soon as the service is deployed, Java Studio Enterprise registers it with the Discovery Service through a Discovery Update operation. You're then ready to run the client. In the following example, ABC purchasing clerk Alice, who has a $1,300 purchasing limit, authenticates at the ABC portal, fills her shopping cart with chips, and checks out. At this point, ABC's purchasing application invokes the CMT Web service. Since the total cost falls within Alice's purchasing limit (as expressed in the SAML assertion that is included as a SOAP header with the Web-service invocation), the checkout operation succeeds.

Identity enabled IT Service Management

OGC is updating ITIL and ITSM from version 2 to version 3 and Sun leveraged ITSM (with several hundred Certified Practitioners and Managers) in its Managed Services group, in conjunction with partners such as BMC. This is even more significant as ITIL forms the basis for IT Service Management for SOA and facilitates the implementation of Services based on SOA. Identity System plays a key role as well in the form of Identity enabled IT Service Management.

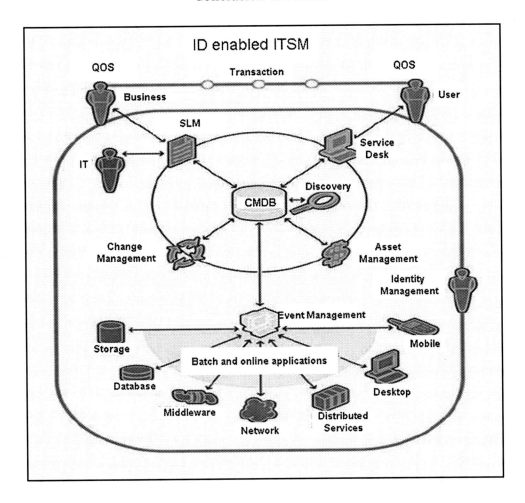

Figure 14.5 Identity enabled ITSM

Identity 2.0, Open ID & Project Light-bulb

In the Identity 2.0 space there are multiple new emerging standards such as, SXIP, DIX, LID, Open-ID, OpenSSO, I-names and more all of which emphasise on user centric, XRI/XDI or URI based, distributed identity system for the developer community. For customers there are multiple options that open-up to address the multiple spectrums of requirements in the identity space - primarily as a profile, preference and information sharing tool - in a simple and secure manner. We can expect to see Industry specific identity initiatives as well - such as E-NUM for Telco, E-HR for Healthcare, and more that uses unique identifiers and industry specific profile (identity schema) that leverages one or more of these Identity 2.0 standards, based on requirements.

Here identity discovery services such as YADIS that facilitates inter-operability between i-names, open-id, sxip, and more, are quite significant as these options that offer the opportunity to address the many facets of an individual's identity are also inter-operable as composite application execution is relevant in all business processes. For example, in a virtual doctor's visit between a patient and a doctor, using IMS networks, certain services such as payment can be using a specific identity 2.0 standard or can stem from an established IDSP (identity service provider), while others such as viewing the latest hospital records may use a different identity 2.0 standard or can stem from an existing COT (circle of trust) established, including the referral service that the doctor offers to a specialist that uses a 3rd identity 2.0 standard or a IDSP or a COT (all within a AUTHENTICATED SESSION). Here, identity discovery services will allow for the alignment of the web services (such as a payment service, hospital record view service and referral service) with the appropriate identity services (which in itself could be a web service as well) all acting as a SBB (Service Building Block) in a SOA (Service Oriented Architecture).

Pat Patterson from Sun has done some work to combine YADIS/XRI Identifier Resolution (as in OpenID) with SAML 2.0 Web Browser SSO Profile. The user experience is:

- I go to a service provider (relying party)
- I enter my identifier (URL or i-name)
- I authenticate at my identity provider
- I can access services at the service provider

The magic takes place between steps 2 and 3: the service provider resolves the user's identifier, which might be a URL or an i-name, to the location of a SAML 2.0 identity provider. The service provider can now do vanilla SAML 2.0 with the identity provider. The service provider is implemented on top of Project Lightbulb (this section is referenced from Project Lightbulb).

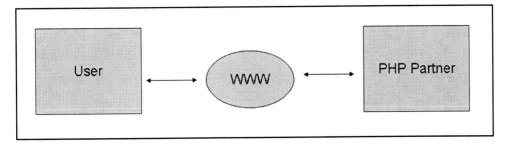

Figure 14.6 Direct User Access

Consider a hypothetical PHP web site – PHPartner. This website currently requires users to authenticate to access some subset of its resources. PHPartner provides services to a variety of individual users. Some of those users access the site on their own behalf, but many access the site in the context of some other relationship; perhaps they access the site to perform work on behalf of their employer, or to access services provided by virtue of the user's relationship with another third-party, such as an ISP. In many of these cases, the user must authenticate to their employer/ISP before accessing PHPartner. In fact, PHPartner is willing to delegate authentication to a number of identity providers (IdPs), allowing users who have authenticated at an IdP to access PHPartner resources without a further authentication. See Figure:

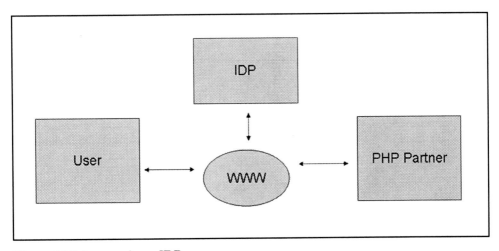

Figure 14.7 Access via an IDP:

To achieve this, PHPartner must implement a protocol for federated single sign-on. Specifically, PHPartner must either deploy a federation product alongside their existing PHP infrastructure or federation-enable the PHP infrastructure directly. See Figures below:

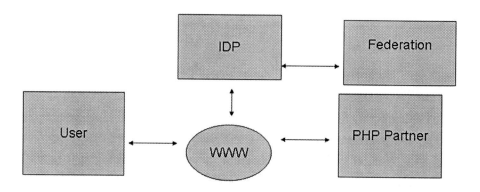

Figure 14.8 Adding a Federation module

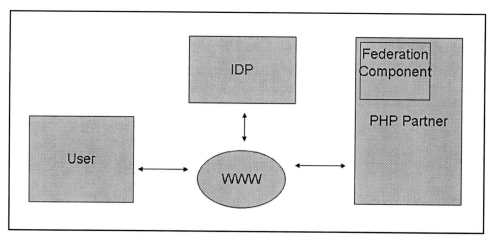

Figure 14.9 Directly Federation-enabling PHP

- Integrating with Federation Manager

Sun Java System Federation Manager (FM) is designed to federation-enable service providers. There is a number of deployment options depending on the degree of integration required. The advantage of using FM is that we can leverage a full federation infrastructure, including command line tools and a console for managing the CoT. FM is migrated to Sun's OpenSSO project over the next few months (by dec 2006), providing a full, open-source, federation solution. All of the discussion below concerning FM will equally apply to the federation-enabled OpenSSO. Where an existing application cannot be touched in any way, FM can be deployed in a 'hands-off' configuration, capturing and replaying passwords to give users federated single sign-on to the target application. See Figure below.

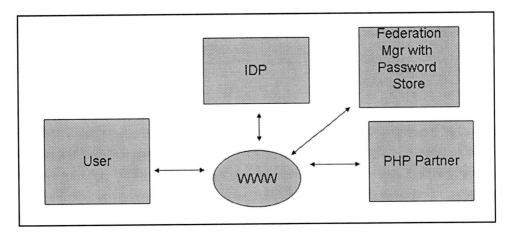

Figure 14.10 FM hands-off integration

This configuration mode has the benefit of not requiring any changes to an existing application at the cost of storing user passwords outside the target application. Password confidentiality can be provided by encryption, but there are always additional risks in storing passwords using reversible encryption as opposed to a one-way hash. There are also synchronisation issues – what happens when passwords change? For this reason, hands-off integration should be seen as a last resort, when there really is no way of customising the target application. Sun provides a wide range of policy agents that may be deployed into web containers as policy enforcement points. The policy agent acts as a filter on incoming requests, redirecting unauthenticated users to an authentication service and applying policy to authenticated users. In the case of a federated deployment, the authentication service is located remotely, at the IdP. See Figure:

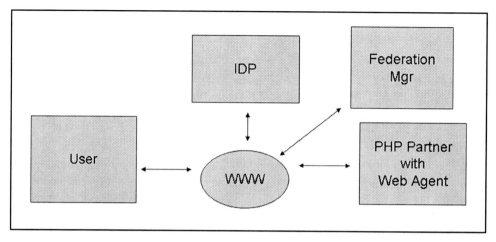

Figure 14.11 FM agent integration

Web agents are deployed into web servers such as Apache Web Server; J2EE agents protect J2EE application servers such as Apache Tomcat. Both types of agents are able to augment the request context with the authenticated user's identity, either by setting an HTTP header or by a deeper integration with J2EE Security. This approach requires that the target application be modified to accept the authenticated user's identity in this way either replacing or extending the previous authentication mechanism. The benefit of this approach is that the target application can completely delegate authentication of some or all users to the IdP. The service provider need not store passwords for these users at all.

Container Integration Although Agent Integration provides a number of benefits of federation, sometimes a still tighter integration is required. For example, using Agent Integration, the target application has no direct knowledge that it is participating in a CoT. Consider again our example service provider. PHPartner has entered into agreements with several IdPs but still allows users to have a direct relationship with PHPartner outside the context of an IdP. See Figure:

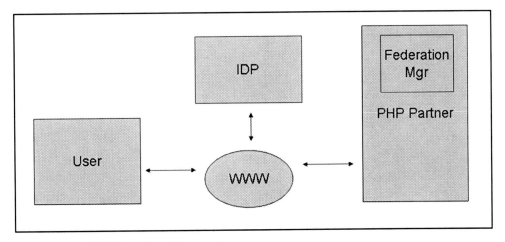

Figure 14.12 FM Container Integration

Now PHPartner needs to be able to allow users to choose their authentication mechanism and even to make or break the link between their PHPartner account and an IdP account, for example, when an employee leaves their employer but wishes to maintain their PHPartner account in their own right, or link it with a new employer account. FM can co-exist with Java web applications, sharing the Java VM and namespace. Servlets and Java Server Pages (JSPs) can invoke FM APIs to determine whether the user has been authenticated, and by whom, and to construct URLs to make and break account links etc.

This is all well and good for Java web applications, but leaves web applications developed in other languages out in the cold. Along these lines, Quercus is an implementation of PHP 5 in Java, running in the Caucho Resin application server. PHP web applications deployed on Quercus can create and manipulate Java objects in the underlying application server. Although this avenue seems promising, both the PHP application and FM must be deployed on Quercus/Resin. The former may not be possible for all PHP applications; the latter is not a tested or supported configuration as of this writing. We can use the open source PHP/Java Bridge to allow PHP web applications to invoke FM's API as if they were co-located Java web applications. See Figure below:

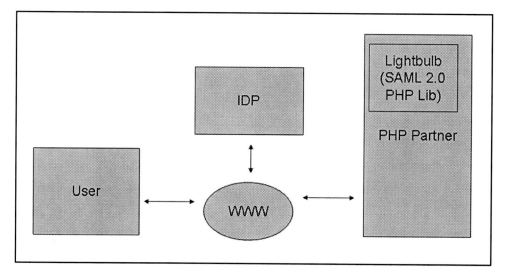

Figure 14.13 PHP/Java bridge and FM

The channel between the PHP/Java Bridge's front and back ends can be configured to be a named pipe (providing higher performance and restricting communication to processes in the same OS image) or a regular socket. The latter would require additional protection, such as SSH tunneling, for security.

Given the PHP/Java Bridge, we can abstract all of the Java specific PHP code to a header file to be included in the PHP code, allowing a PHP app to act as a service provider by simply using the provided objects and functions. This code will be open-sourced as part of the Lightbulb project (a sub-project of OpenSSO). Lightbulb's mission is to federation enable LAMP and MARS applications (Lightbulb fits into LAMP). Using FM for federation enabling PHP web applications has one major drawback – the service provider must deploy an additional web container (or at least, an additional web container instance, if the PHP application happens to be hosted in a container supported by FM). In some environments this may not be desirable or even possible. In such environments, a direct PHP implementation of SAML 2.0 is required. Using Rob Richards' PHP XML Security library as a basis, we have implemented a SAML 2.0 single sign-on directly in PHP.

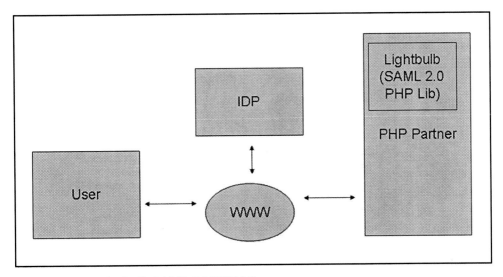

Figure 14.14 Light-bulb SAML 2.0 PHP Library

Again, this code will be open-sourced as part of Light-bulb.

- End to end correlated alignment for Vertical Integration using an Identity System

As of December 2006, the Identity System market is fragmented with multiple Identity Systems Consume that specialises, for example, in User Identity Management & Provisioning, User and Service centric Identity systems, Device centric Identity Systems, Network centric Identity Systems, Object centric Identity Systems etc. Vertical Integration of these systems would be quite simple if all these systems systems tie back to user identities. However in many cases that is not so. Therefore Vertical Integration of these fragmented Identity Systems can potentially be achieved via a mechanism that involves an extensible identity and identifier markup language based on XRI (extensible resource identifiers) that has mappings to these fragmented identity systems based on a user's definition.

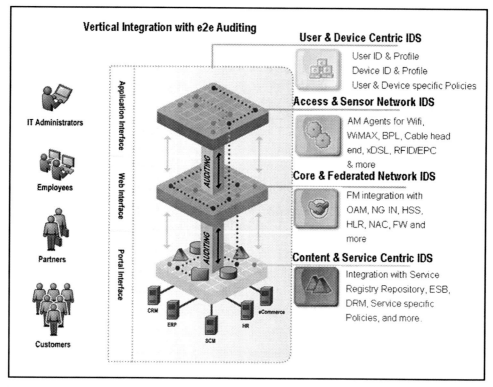

Figure 14.15 Vertical integration

For example a consumer might be a subscriber of:

1. A specific telecom carrier's plan (e.g. Sprint's family plan) and have four handheld/PDA's for each member of the family,

2. Have an ISP (e.g., Comcast) and Cable TV provider - with a Cable Modem Device and 2 Set-top-Box (and Comcast could have a relationship with Sprint),

3. Let's say the same user has three Cars with three VIN (vehicle ID numbers) and eSurance (+ driving record) as the Insurance Provider,

4. There are multiple Identities as an employee (of Sun Microsystems), SS#, Drivers License Numbers, United Healthcare (health record), consumer (ENUM, telephone number, fax), etc., and

5. Multiple consumer devices with there own identities also exist-Sprinkler System with a device ID (Bio Turf as Service provider for the sprinkler), Kitchen appliances (GE as a Service provider, Electronics (Best Buy as a Service provider), etc.

All these are handled by different standards -distributed in the network (as SILOs and not integrated end to end – some bi-directional integration exists between one or two specific standards). TS69 (an ADSL standard for any customer equipment device identity, such as a ADSL modem, a Set Top Box, a PDA/handheld, and more), XRI/XDI (Extensible Resource Identifier –used to map multiple user Identities), ENUM (an e.164 number that maps to multiple user identities in a telecom network), iName/iNumber (an implementation of the XRI specs), SAML (an Oasis standard for AuthN levels and federated user identities), Federation (and potential federation identity- liberty specifications that supports SAML and more between users and services), RFID (an Identifier that is associated with things from a sensor network that attach to the Internet as well), IMEI (international mobile equipment identity), EIR (equipment identity registrar – that maintains network equipment identities – such as base stations, mobile stations, head-end, access controllers, service controllers and more –primarily in Access Networks –such as WiMAX and BPL – and can also include IMS networks), TNC (standards for computing equipment identities), UCI (Content identifier), SI (Service identifier based on public key and X500), CSID (communication service identifier), VIN (unique vehicle identification number), SCID (potential Service Container Identity – for Virtual Servers), SPID (Service Providers Identity) and many more.

Even XNS based XRI and XDI solve the problem of integrating multiple user identities (such as iName and iNumber) but are not extensive and end-to-end in terms of there reach to: Users, Devices, Access Networks, Core Networks, Sensor Networks, Programmable (Virtual) Networks, Service Networks, Content Networks and more.

When we take into account the three trends in the network towards IP convergence - Core IMS control layer, Sensor Networks (affecting all business and user processes) and Programmable (virtual) networks - a Cohesive Integration approach is required so Users can be delivered Services -based on vertical identity Integration (not just federation of user identities). Aligning user identities distributed in the Network has already been accomplished with Federation standards such as SAML and Liberty and User controlled standards such as XRI/XDI.

However as a User and as a Network Service Provider there are also requirements around aligning User Identities with Device Identities (User Equipment), things (such as a Car and Refrigerator), Service Provider Identity and Service Identities, unique Content identifiers, Device (network equipment) identities and more. We propose XiiML as a standard is intended to address this particular problem referred to as "Vertical Identity Integration".

This section describes a method that will leverage XML (extensible markup language) similar to XRI – defined as "XiiML" (for extensible identity & identifier Markup Language) – that will allow both users on the client side and the service providers on the network side to align and correlate user identities with object identities, component identities, customer equipment identities and more. Each correlated security space can be offered as an association policy - wherein the customer implementation has to specify or input:

1. identifiers, (SS#, VIN, Alien#, Passport Number and many more)
2. identity specs under use (WS-PP, ENUM etc.)
3. identity ranges as necessary - (for devices and RFID)
4. selection of identity integration mechanism (trailing, virtual mapping, correlation, federation and aggregation)
5. and the activation of an associating policy made based on data fed real-time (temporary identifier –for example of a Service Container or a Virtual Server) and non-real time (by a Service Provider and/or User) or input manually (role is to correlate with Service Identities, Service Container Identities, Network Element identities in their path, etc. that is predefined in the network). This makes a (authenticated) session with a token id (federate-able) traverse multiple domains, networks (including sensor network's data), multiple SP etc., while limiting it for a valid user with valid devices and valid access to specific services.

For example: I go to my Carrier (Sprint) - feed the data about my sprinkler system (including its unique id number), my Service Contract identity number with Bio Turf, my notification id and my device id's) - I'm on vacation - my Sprinkler system fails in peak summer - notifies a problem with the network - network recognises the Service Provider -sends me a notification -that I approve and - problem is fixed - since I approve access to my gate/premises (even though I'm not there) - to the specific Bio Turf individual Service technician (with unique bio metrics) for a duration (lets say 10 to 11am July 5th 2007) via ADT as my Physical Security provider. Based on the user's input and the user's selected policies – he or she only gets notified via a set of devices that the user carries, and allows the sprinkler system to complain about its problem to my SP, only with pre-provisioning of one user to be allowed with his/her specific id etc. There could be thousands of use cases similar to this - the idea is the network is programmed by the end user to behave in certain ways -based on his/her inputs. This application includes nine subsections; for "Vertical Identity Integration using XiiML", across many identity layers.

- Identity based Correlated Security for Consumer Personal Devices
- Identity based Correlated Security for Consumer Home Devices
- Identity based Correlated Security for Sensor Networks
- Identity based Correlated Security for Services (Service ID correlation)
- Identity based Correlated Security for Service to Device (within a Session)
- Identity based Correlated Security for Network Devices and Network Elements
- Identity based Correlated Security for Device to Service Container
- Identity based Correlated Security for Service to Service Container (within a Session)
- Identity based Correlated Security end-to-end device, network and services

Sun, through its leadership in the Identity space (project liberty and OASIS) and market penetration (major telecom customers, integration with multiple NEP's products etc.), is in a unique position to implement these techniques as product features (easily implementable and practical) or partner ISV functions and differentiate itself further more as the leader in the Network ID systems market. Each correlated security space can be offered as an association policy -wherein the customer implementation has to specify or input the identifiers, identity specs and identity ranges as necessary—and an associating policy is activated based on data fed real-time or input manually. As a proposed OASIS standard or Liberty Standard multiple vendors can take the same approach and ensure interoperability between there Identity Systems.

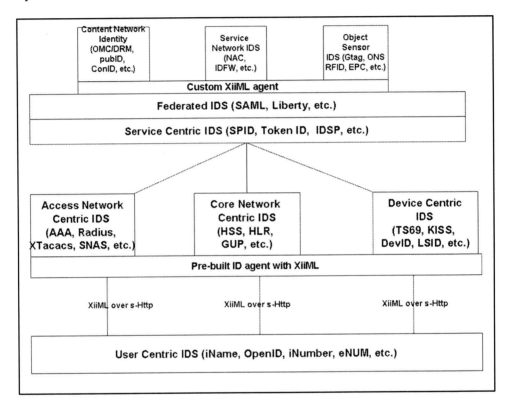

Figure 14.16 Vertical Integration using XiiML

"XiiML" can be an OASIS defined standard such as XRI (and could extend the developments in the XDI space) or a Liberty Specification– that extends beyond user identities and service identities – and can potentially be implemented by vendors such as Sun, leveraging the XSD – XML Schema Definition tool built into the current generation Identity System – with a predefined data model definition mechanism.

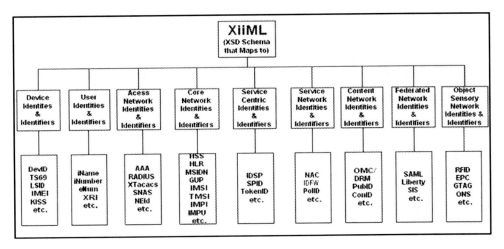

Figure 14.17 Sample use of XiiML specifications

This will potentially be the mechanism to link—for example a Device Reputation Authority (such as iOvation) with a User Reputation Authority (such as HSS within IMS) and a user IDSP (liberty based implementation at Sprint) and a Sensor Network operator (for a hospital) all linked with the Hospital Authority. The diagram above depicts how an XiiML artifact can extend from User's to Devices to the Network and the Network of things, by extending and integrating the Identity and Identifier standards within each realm. The patient or an authorised Individual enters RFID/EPC associated with the patients gadgetry (heart monitor, bp monitor etc), with a Patient history data provider (profile identity) with the set of allowed Doctors as users (user identities), with specific communication service identities to use and more. XiiML as a Macro extensible Markup Language that ties together multiple implementations of XML for identification – such as XRI, SAML, DevID, ONS, and more. XiiML will allow users to define their related identities and identifiers in the networks and select form a list of policies the ones that they need – in essence -defining there expectation of service behaviour in the network. For example:

- Stating that Find-me service will direct all office calls to cell phone and then home office phone until 6pm and after 6pm will direct it to voice mail.
- Stating that each time any of the Vehicles owned by an individual speeds beyond 10mile over the speed limit a notification in the form

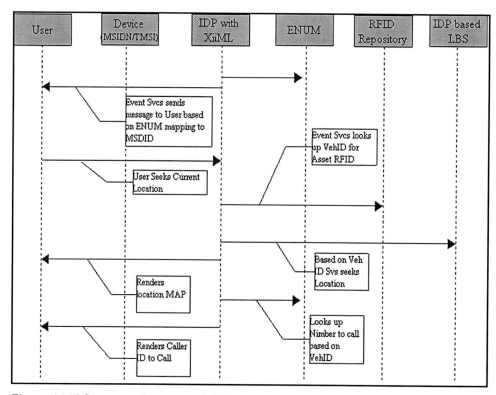

Figure 14.18 Sequence Diagram with XiiML

of a message is sent to the presence enable communication service

- Stating that a user with a certain credential be allowed via the Gate and the main door at a certain point in time (3 to 4 PM on 12/01/06), while the activity is viewed from a camera phone
- and more.
- Using XiiML we can have an artifact (similar to the SAML artifact on AuthN Levels) that allows for automated linking and connections to multiple identity and identifier repositories, including a RFID repository, a Service Registry repository, a Device Reputation Registry repository, XML Fire-wall repository, Sensor Smart Home device repository, SNAS (secure network access switch) repository and more -regardless of the underlying repository technology (XMLDB, RDBMS, LDAP/Directory, File System, Real-time DB, and more). For example, an XSD based XiiML implementation using an Identity System is abstracted from the underlying repository technology. The sequence diagram below depicts how an IDP that manages a Users XiiML artifact acts as the intermediary between User, Device, ENUM, RFID and another IDP. Even though an XiiML artifact may contain more pointers and links to identities and identifiers (see XiiML sample schema) only a subset is revealed based on services that are invoked on behalf of the user.

```
<?xml version="1.0" encoding="UTF-8"?>

<xs:schema  targetNamespace="urn:oasis:names:tc:XiiML:1.0:ac:class-
es:compositeid&idf"
  xmlns:xs="http://www.w3.org/2001/XMLSchema"
  xmlns="urn:oasis:names:tc:XiiML:1.0:ac:classes:compositeid&idf"
  finalDefault="extension"
  blockDefault="substitution"
  version="1.0">


    <xs:redefine   schemaLocation="XiiML-schema-id-context-types-
1.0.xsd">


  <xs:annotation>
   <xs:documentation>
          Class  identifier:  urn:oasis:names:tc:XiiML:1.0:ac:classes:
compositeid&idf
   Document identifier: XiiML-schema-authn-context-compositeid&idf-
1.0
      Location: http://docs.oasis-open.org/security/XiiML/v1.0/
      Revision history:
       V1.0 (March, 2007):
        New authentication context class schema for XiiML V1.0.
     </xs:documentation>
    </xs:annotation>


  <xs:complexType name="AuthnContextDeclarationBaseType">
   <xs:complexContent>
    <xs:restriction base="AuthnContextDeclarationBaseType">
     <xs:sequence>
      <xs:element ref="Identification" minOccurs="0"/>
      <xs:element ref="TechnicalProtection" minOccurs="0"/>
      <xs:element ref="OperationalProtection" minOccurs="0"/>
      <xs:element ref="AuthnMethod"/>
      <xs:element ref="GoverningAgreements" minOccurs="0"/>
                  <xs:element  ref="Extension"  minOccurs="0"
maxOccurs="unbounded"/>
```

```
    </xs:sequence>
    <xs:attribute name="ID" type="xs:ID" use="optional"/>
   </xs:restriction>
  </xs:complexContent>
 </xs:complexType>


 <xs:complexType name="AuthnMethodBaseType">
  <xs:complexContent>
   <xs:restriction base="AuthnMethodBaseType">
    <xs:sequence>
     <xs:element ref="PrincipalAuthenticationMechanism" minOc-
curs="0"/>
      <xs:element ref="Authenticator"/>
      <xs:element ref="AuthenticatorTransportProtocol"/>
                    <xs:element  ref="Extension"  minOccurs="0"
maxOccurs="unbounded"/>
     </xs:sequence>
    </xs:restriction>
   </xs:complexContent>
  </xs:complexType>


 <xs:complexType name="AuthenticatorBaseType">
  <xs:complexContent>
   <xs:restriction base="AuthenticatorBaseType">
    <xs:sequence>
     <xs:element ref="Subscriber.e.164Number"/>
           <xs:element ref="SubscriberMSIDNumber"/>
           <xs:element ref="SubscriberLineNumber"/>
           <xs:element ref="SubscriberIDP1Identifier"/>
           <xs:element ref="SubscriberIDP2Identifier"/>
           <xs:element ref="SubscriberOpenIDiNumber"/>
           <xs:element ref="SubscriberOpenIDiName"/>
           <xs:element ref="SubscriberDevID"/>
           <xs:element ref="SubscriberVI1Number"/>
           <xs:element ref="SubscriberVI2Number"/>
           <xs:element ref="SubscriberObject1RFID"/>
           <xs:element ref="SubscriberObject2RFID"/>
```

```
    </xs:sequence>
   </xs:restriction>
  </xs:complexContent>
 </xs:complexType>

 <xs:complexType name="AuthenticatorTransportProtocolType">
  <xs:complexContent>
   <xs:restriction base="AuthenticatorTransportProtocolType">
    <xs:sequence>
     <xs:choice>
      <xs:element ref="PSTN"/>
      <xs:element ref="ISDN"/>
      <xs:element ref="ADSL"/>
           <xs:element ref="Cable"/>
      <xs:element ref="FDDI"/>
      <xs:element ref="Wifi"/>
           <xs:element ref="WiMAX"/>
      <xs:element ref="BPL"/>
      <xs:element ref="MetroEth"/>
     </xs:choice>
                    <xs:element  ref="Extension"  minOccurs="0"
maxOccurs="unbounded"/>
    </xs:sequence>
   </xs:restriction>
  </xs:complexContent>
 </xs:complexType>

 </xs:redefine>

</xs:schema>
```

Figure 14.19 Sample XiiML Schema (as a SAML Artifact)

Dr. Ramarao Kanneganti and Prasad Chodavarapu, in their 2007 Book titled "SOA Security in Action" (highly recommended for SOA Security Architects) highlight the following (excerpts from the 1st chapter):

Basic issues in application security

Security management in IT can be broadly classified into network security, platform security and application security. Of these, the first two have little to no relationship with SOA Security conceptually. Hence, the issues we introduce in this section are limited to the ones needed in application security. In this section, we will briefly discuss the security issues that an application should address. Of course, not all applications need to take care of all these issues. Typically, any application that is available to multiple users as a shared resource has to address at least a few of these issues. A web application catering to different users with different privileges is a good example you can consider when trying to understand each of the security issues described below.

Verifying identity of users

Applications need to verify that only legitimate users are trying to use them. The burden of proving identity rests with the users. Users may prove their identity in multiple ways, each with their own pros and cons.

1. Users may present one or more secrets that the service expects them to know. For example, users may present username and password that they previously registered with. Alternatively, users may have to respond to a challenge question that can be only be answered correctly by those who know the secret.
2. Users may prove that they are indeed in possession of something the service expects them to have. For example, the service may challenge the user to present a number currently being displayed on a RSA token she should possess.
3. Users may present proof of who they are by presenting biometric evidence such as a digitised finger print or retina scan.

The process of verifying identity of users is referred to as "authentication" in security literature.

Granting access to users

Once a user is authenticated, the application needs to determine if the identified user is allowed to access the functionality he is requesting. The decision to grant access may depend on multiple criteria such as the action that is being requested, the resource on which the action is being requested, the groups to which the user belongs to and the roles that the user plays. For example, the super-user or the administrator may access all the files in a system, but the user belonging to HR group can access only those files that are allowed for that group. The process of making this determination is referred to as "authorisation" in security literature and we shall refer to it in that way through out the book. Novice engineers often use the term "authorisation" when they mean "authentication" and vice-versa. It is critical to not make this mistake as both refer to quite different aspects of security. You may remember it this way: Authentication establishes who you are. Authorisation determines what you are allowed to do. Your photo id may establish who you are. Your age and local laws may determine whether you can legally take a drink.

Keeping data confidential with Encryption

Data exchanged over the network as well as data stored by applications needs to be safeguarded from prying eyes. There are applications that can sniff out the packets that go over the wire. Using these applications, rogue users can gain access to data that we are exchanging with legitimate users. The standard technique to keep data confidential is encryption. Without encryption, web commerce would never have succeeded as it would have been unsafe to transmit credit card information on the wire. The encrypted data can be understood only by the intended party and nobody else.

Guaranteeing data integrity and Non-repudiation

Keeping the data confidential is not sufficient. When the receiver gets a message, neither the sender nor the receiver should be able to repudiate it - that is deny the authenticity of the message. As you can see, there are two aspects to non-repudiation: from the perspective of the senders and the receivers.

Suppose you authorised withdrawal of certain amount from your bank account for purchases at an online merchant. How can you be sure that the merchant or even the bank did not modify the amount in your authorisation? Looking at the aspect of data integrity from a recipient's point of view, how can you protect yourself as a merchant against customers that falsely report fraud claims against you? As a recipient of a sensitive email, how can you be sure that the message was indeed sent by the person whose address appears in the mail headers? These concerns can only be addressed by techniques that guarantee integrity of data in transit. "Digital Signature" is a common mechanism to guarantee data integrity.

Thwarting common attack strategies

Quite a few common attack strategies are identified and named in security literature. For example, attacks that seek to take advantage of fatal bugs such as "buffer overflows" in application code or attacks that effectively cause a "Denial of Service" (DOS) to legitimate users by bombarding a service with invalid requests cannot be completely avoided using the techniques described in this book. However, the risk posed by them can definitely be mitigated by adopting appropriate security architectures and deployment strategies described in Part III of this book. There are a few other security threats that are common. For example, suppose you sent a message authorising the recipient to withdraw a certain amount of money from the bank. Can someone else other than the recipient pose as the recipient and intercept your messages? How do you prevent the recipient herself from submitting the message multiple times to withdraw more money than you intended to authorise?

Guarding Privacy

Service providers are often obligated to guard the privacy of users by law or by business policy. First let us understand what we mean by privacy. According to law, privacy places restrictions on disclosure of personal information to others. There are two aspects to it from application perspective. One is that of information kept in the applications and how it is dispensed. The other is about how services themselves expose the personal information of the users. Let us consider the first aspect. We often hear about breaches in security exposing user information kept in applications and databases to unauthorised people. These can be several reasons for these breaches. Some of the security issues such as buffer overflow happen to be in the implementation of applications. The second aspect of privacy is about how applications divulge information on users. For example, consider the simple scenario of identifying the sender of a message. Even if we disable all possible ways of linking a message to a sender, we might still be not doing enough. If user identity can be narrowed down to a small enough set in anyway, user's anonymity is clearly diluted. For example, if it can be gathered from multiple messages that their sender is living in a particular town, is working for a particular bank, is a security guard and works on night shift during weekends, the user's identity can be narrowed down very quickly to a small set.

All these security issues are well understood. However, all of them typically deal with security of single applications (by which we mean standalone as well as n-tier distributed applications) or two-party interactions such as a client-server interaction. When we are designing a system in which multiple applications are brought together (to execute business processes, for example), most of those books, code, libraries, and frameworks do not help as much. What we see is that integration, which is a necessity in large enterprises, makes security issues lot more complex than single application or point to point interactions.

(Loose) Integration complicates security

Before proceeding further, let us understand what integration means. Integration is the act of bringing together data and/or capabilities from two or more independent applications, within the same enterprise or across multiple enterprises. For example, in a brokerage firm, there may be two different systems, one keeping track of savings account and another investment account. If we need to devise an application that provides a unified view of the information, or transferring money from one account into another, we need to integrate two applications. The level of integration between applications could be different. Not all applications can be cleanly be integrated. Consider the scenario of the investment account where money can be transferred from one fund to another. If we want to integrate with another application, that reports all the monetary activities, we would need the internal transfer information.

Of course, easy way of integrating is to rewrite the applications, which is not a choice most of the times. Instead, we use several different techniques to integrate the applications. Here are a few:

- File transfer (most commonly used in EDI - a very popular B2B integration standard)
- Point-to-point message exchange: over synchronous transport protocols such as HTTP (as in AS2 - a B2B integration protocol) or asynchronous transports such as Message Queues (MQ)
- Multicast messaging using a publish-subscribe protocol (such as TIBCO RV)
- Distributed computing using Remote procedure calls (RPC), Microsoft DCOM or CORBA For full details on the history of integration, please refer to the Appendix A.

Integration comes with several challenges: it is costly; it can be error prone; it can be inflexible; above all - it can be a security nightmare.

Despite all those headaches, we still have to integrate applications. Large companies are able to realize good ROI when applications are integrated across the enterprises. For example, automobile companies integrate their supply chain with their suppliers to reduce the inventory sizes. Even within an enterprise, integration is highly valuable. There is a reason why integration is a must in any large enterprise. Even though we are building more technically complex applications than before, any enterprise still has several applications serving its needs. For example, a manufacturing facility may have an enterprise application managing personnel, another dealing with supply chain, and yet another providing business analytics. To build each of these applications, it takes deep understanding of the domain and cumulative experience of the users. Thus, corporations are forced to use diverse applications, often from different vendors. In summary, commerce grows with integration. Integration brings forth new possibilities and business opportunities. Integration enhances convenience for customers and drives down business costs. Integration allows for incremental solutions that leverage existing applications. It lets us build best of breed systems. All these benefits come at additional complexities, one of which is security.

Complexity of security issues that can arise with integration is itself not very well understood. Consider the example of a web portal such as My Yahoo or an enterprise web portal you may have used at work. A web portal collates information from multiple applications and hence, is a good example of integration in action. When you login into a portal, how does the portal application pass on your credentials to each of the applications from which it needs to pull your data? In the simple case, all of the applications portal integrates with may be using the exact same password store to authenticate users. In a more complex case, each application may rely on its own password store. How do we deal with such complexity?

In fact there are several such issues with security in application integration. To understand all those, let us study a few real or near real world examples. In the next two sub-sections, we present two such examples. Subsequently, we will return to the basic security issues we discussed in the previous section and discuss how they become complex in integration scenarios.

These scenarios are common in integration of applications.

Authentication

Individual investors, for example, that are directly placing orders with a service need to identify themselves, possibly with a username and password combination. Corporate customers might need multiple "signatures" authorising their orders. Smaller brokerages that wish to route orders from their customers to the larger brokerage need to some how prove that the orders are emanating from their customers. They may do so by attaching signed "assertions" about the identity of their customers placing the order. Institutional clients need signatures on their orders as well.

Consider examples around RFID. Here, applications need to serve users about whom they may not have prior information. In this scenario, no single application has access to all the username and password information. What these scenarios point to is that there are several different kinds of authentication systems possible within the enterprise. If we are building authentication for one application, we can keep the username and password within the local store and manage user logins. We can even implement more sophisticated authentication schemes based on technologies such as digital certificates. However, if we want to share the same user credentials with other applications, we have to make sure that the credentials are available to those applications. If we make that data available, especially to applications that do not belong to the same enterprise, how can we make sure that data is not abused?

Authorisation

In a single application, the authentication and authorisation are essentially one single step, though engineering practices may make them into different modules. That is, the application can determine who should have access to which resource. However, in an integration scenario, the user authentication can be separate from authorisation. This situation calls for keeping authorization information separate, available for all applications. What complicates this decision is that there may not be a uniform model for authorisation. In a single enterprise, we may force users into groups and assign rights to groups. As groups proliferate, it can lead to a manageability problem. In a multi-enterprise integration example like in RFID, we may not be able to do even that. Ultimately, the complexity is in mapping the permissions in one system to permissions in another system. This issue comes up because we are integrating multiple applications.

"In any identity-centric architecture, the two (AuthN and AuthZ) must be separated. Authentication is a 'closed question'; it gives a yes-or-no answer: 'do I trust these credentials, or not?'. Authorisation is not; it's a process of matching various user attributes to entitlements which express a resource access policy.

If your business application does not require you to make that distinction, then you don't have any real justification for an identity-centric architecture (and you might as well just adopt a simpler approach more aligned with the application design itself)".

Data Confidentiality

In point to point communication, the technology for guaranteeing data confidentiality is well known. This is not the case when multiple parties/applications are involved in message exchange; different parts of a message may be intended for different recipients. For example, as shown in figure 1.7, part of a request to use bank funds for an order is intended for the bank but is forwarded via the brokerage. Thus, that who can play which role in an application? How do we keep track of the role changes for a person? How do we take care of it when corporations merge?

Data Integrity and Non-repudiation

In a two party situation, where there is only one sender and one receiver, we can meet data integrity and non-repudiation requirements using digital signatures. A receiver can make sure that the message was not tampered with along the way by checking the sender's signature in the message. The receiver can also prove that nobody else other than the signing sender could have sent the message. The situation gets complex when there are several senders and receivers. As the message goes through multiple applications, each of them may add some information to the message. They need to vouch for only that part of the information. While technically it is not difficult, it can be difficult to manage without clear standards. Applications will have to clearly understand who is signing what part of the message.

"Digital signature alone is not enough; for non-repudiation you are likely to need an ACID protocol which guarantees that both parties either agree to the transaction in question, or mutually roll it back. Obviously, for non-repudiation purposes, you cannot afford to have one party think the transaction has concluded, and the other think that it has not".

Privacy

If we have only a sender and a receiver, the threat to privacy of the involved parties can only come from the sender or the receiver. As long as the message exchanges is done on a secure channel and the receiver takes good care of the information provided by the sender, privacy of the sender is somewhat easy to guard. When there are several senders and receivers, the threat to privacy can come from anywhere. Each system can contain some information about the particular investor, which by itself is not a threat to his privacy. When we add up all these pieces of information, it can reveal more information than it is supposed to by law. These legal restrictions may impose constraints on how we can integrate applications. Technically, it is difficult to model privacy requirements in a complex integration scenario.

"Privacy" is the hot button at the moment. It's a lot like "security" was 10-15 years ago: people think it can be bolted on after the system is in place. We need to be evangelising the fact that it needs to be part of the design from the outset: *if it is not, then the requirements statement is deficient*.

Man-in-the-middle and Replay Attack

If we have one sender and one receiver, the only possibility of man-in-the-middle is somebody who is listening over the wire. By suitable encryption at transport level, we can avoid giving away any information on the message to such attacker. To prevent message replay, we can resort to several techniques, including timestamps, message sequence numbers and so on. When integrating multiple applications, any application can play man-in-the-middle role. That is, potentially, one of the applications in the integration can be the attacker. Since that application has access to the message, it can replay the attack easily enough, unless we take extra precaution. Thus, the need for protecting from un-trusted applications makes defending against man-in-the middle attacks difficult.

Manageability and Traceability

There are some issues which are easy to manage if there is no integration involved. Manageability of security is one such issue. How does integration complicate manageability? To be sure, any security management is difficult. I f there are several applications in the enterprise, managing user names and passwords can be a nightmare. Even when all the applications use a centralised directory for username and passwords, managing security policy can be complex. How do we make sure who can play which role in an application? How do we keep track of the role changes for a person? How do we take care of it when corporations merge? These questions become even more complex with integration. In integration, applications will have to deal with not only end users, but also other applications and its end users. As more and more applications participate in integration, potentially, applications may not have much idea of which user they are dealing with. Any changes in either an application, or user directories, may cause wide repercussions, which are difficult to understand. Thus, any manageability solution must cope with this kind of complexity. In addition to manageability, the other issue often comes up in integration is traceability. Since a message can go through several applications, for regulatory purposes, we may have to keep an audit trail. In addition, to tune and manage the applications, we may have to trace the data and actions to their full path through the systems".

This book (From Dr. Ramarao) further describes Techniques such as;

- Applying security at the Message level,
- Security as a Service,
- Declarative and policy based security and more.

Its is a classic text that highlights the significance of an Identity System as a distributed security system, to address the security concerns especially for loose integration approaches for AuthN, AuthZ, privacy, Data integrity and more, in conjunction with Integration software such as an ESB.

Gelnn Brunette, Sun's CTO for Security, Distinguished Engineer and a security expert identifies five properties for Systemic Security;

- Self Preservation—that every element within the environment should be able to protect itself from attack
- Defense and depth

- Mutual reinforcing layered security controls
- Compartmentalisation
- Least privileges to contain and limit exposure

These are discussed in the chapter on Identity enabled Programmable Network. However, these principles are important to keep in mind in order to address systemic security concerns when an Identity System is used as a foundation infrastructure for all security services in the core network, service network and access networks—acting more as an eigenvector for systemic security. Self preservation characteristics are in Identity enabled Network Admission Control, Identity enabled ESB, Identity enabled Devices (CPE/NE), and Identity enabled Storage and more. Defense in Depth is addressed via Identity enabled XML firewalls, XML accelerators, etc., Identity enabled OS Containers, Identity enabled Computing (TPM), Identity based Encryption, and more. Mutual reinforced layered security controls are achieved via the push and pull model of policies, making and identity system a distributed contextual firewall depending on the entity (device, a car, resource, etc.). Compartmentalisation characteristics can be seen with Identity enable IMS/HSS, Identity enabled Web Services etc., wherein the provisioning of services is compartmentalised for specific roles, Identity enabled Enterprise Networks and Service Network-policy engines that allow an authenticated session only into specific areas of a LAN, and more. Least privileges to contain and limit exposure is the basis for the notion of AuthN levels and AuthN context, Roles-Rules-Resources combination, alignment of User Vs Enterprise Vs Content rights management and more.

Hence an Identity System and its Integration in multiple areas essentially augments the notion of "Systemic Security", in an open Network.

Chapters 1 to 14 by now have addressed the nine pain points discussed in chapter 1. Chapter 2, 3 and 4 are aligned with each other due to the sensor and programmable characteristics that can be expected to be found in the evolving 4G Networks. 4G Networks are expected to be augmented with the common converged control layer offered by the

IMS and to support this NGN, both NG IN and NG OAMP Services are required. Both chapters 6 and 7 that talk to IN Services and OAM&P Services can essentially leverage the concepts in chapter 8 since they can be implemented as Web Services as well. Chapters 9 and 10 on ESB and DRM talk to how these form the core infrastructure service aligned with an Identity System for SOA. The common thread in chapters 11, 12 and 13 is the notion of Identity enabled TPM found in devices, computing elements and storage elements that form the trusted network at the hardware layer in conjunction with Trusted Network connect or other similar approaches. Identity enabling all three devices, computing and ILM helps establish a COT at the application and user layer. There are many interrelationships between chapters in this book for example Identity enabled Devices and a DRA Service can itself be an Identity enabled Web Service. Identity enabling ENUM, NG DHCP and NG DNS can also act as the NG IN services, and many more such examples are there.

Since this book is on "Identity and Security" and is on the topic of Integrating an Identity System with different network, services, network elements and service elements, a very good understanding of an Identity System and its internal workings is required, especially to understand how they address the security concerns such as trust, privacy, SSO, federation, distributed policies, session management and more (that was identified as core security concerns for loosely coupled integration). Therefore the author recommend 9 white papers from Sun Engineering on the internal workings of an Identity System (AuthN, Policy, Session, SSO and Federation). Each of these whitepapers from Sun Microsystems covers how all of the Identity System's Services are opened up, such as Open SSO, Open Federation, Session Management and more. Majority of these were released in December 2006. The opening up of the Identity System's services as services in a SOA approach and the Open sourcing of the Identity system, based on projects such as Light-bulb, Open SSO, Open Federation and more, simply implies that Integration is going to grow at an exponential pace moving forward. The 9 pain areas discussed in chapter 1 is the main focus moving forward (2006 and later) that can be addressed with the 9 step methodology that treats an Identity System as the meta layer that makes the "Network a Computer", by Identity enabling end to end and establishing an end to end trust framework.

These are available at the Open SSO project site that includes
https://opensso.dev.java.net/servlets/ProjectDocumentList
https://opensso.dev.java.net/public/use/docs/index.html

Acknowledgements

This book would not be possible if not for the contribution of many Sun Microsystems employees and our partner companies. I thank Badri Sriraman (from Unisys), Mike Wookey (Sun), Dr. Ramaswamy Rangarajan (Sprint), Ali Tafreshi (Sprint), Thomas Deffet (Sprint), Dennis Baker (Sun) and others who had co-authored many Sun White papers, with me, which are key to many of the chapters in this Book. I thank Pat Patterson (Sun), Rajeev Angal (Sun), Srividhya (Vidhya) Narayanan (Sun), Pirasenna Velandai Thiyagarajan (Sun), & Marina Sum (Sun), who were the contributing authors for chapter 8 on Identity enabled Web Services. I thank my boss at Sun Shawn Malaney and the Telco Architect team that includes Nimish Radia, Kathy Green, Guanghwa Ho, Andreas Frank and others (what a TEAM!!). I thank the reviewers of the Book Kirk Brown (Global CTO Identity Practice at Sun), Dr. James Baty (CTO Sun GSO), Glenn Brunnette (CSO at Sun), Ramesh Radhakrishnan (Sun), Mark Dixon (Sun), Robin Wilton (Sun) and Scott Stillabower (Sun) who reviewed and have sent in there valuable comments as well. The majority of these reviewers are Sun Distinguished Engineers and CTO's and there time is extremely valuable, hence I appreciate the importance they have given to this material. Thank You. Once Again.

I thank the authors of the 50+ papers that were referenced in this Book. I thank Sun Authors like Adrian Cockroff, Brian Wong, Hal Stern, Dan Berg and John Crupi, who were my motivation to Author a Book since 1999.

Finally I thank almighty God for making this Book a reality and my parents as well as my wife Meena and my three boys Arjun, Trinith and Tushar for all their cooperation. I also thank my three Brothers and Sister who have encouraged me all along.

Glossary of Keywords

SOA: Service Oriented Architectures is an Enterprise's Architecture is developed in a Service Driven approach, where each service is autonomous and can be considered to be a Service Building Block (SBB). Using an analogy between the concept of service and a business process, in SOA, loosely coupled SBB are orchestrated into business processes that support customer goals and/or organization's business goals. More than just a component of reusable code, a SBB becomes part of a running program that can be invoked by a client without having to incorporate the code itself. A SBB by definition is reusable and replaceable, that is, one SBB's service is reused again and again by other services for the functionality it provides and SBB's service (provider implementation) can be replaced by another (another providers implementation). In SOA – the SBB's themselves can be categorized into basic/foundation services, management services, security services, business services, portal services, etc. It should also be noted that a SBB is offering a specific functionality for an Enterprise and transcends projects, i.e., a Digital Rights Management Service (DRM) as a SBB is only implemented once in an enterprise architecture and can be reused across projects that deal with delivering content, services, multi-media, etc. In SOA the communication flow is closed to new unforeseen inputs once the communication flow has started, i.e., they are typically well defined and the boundaries well set.

CBA: Component Based Architecture, the basis for distributed component architecture embraces mechanisms and techniques for developing coarse yet reusable business/technical implementation units that is environment/container aware, which decomposes a service of SBB, into multiple plug-able and distributable parts associated with presentation logic, business logic, resource access logic, integration logic, network event logic, security logic and more. A component based approach evolves from object oriented design principles (encapsulation, polymorphism, inheritance, etc.), and leverages a foundation set of infrastructure technologies (based on JEE/J2ME/JAIN or .NET/OSA/Parlay) for seamless integration. Component Based Architecture (CBA) fundamentally modularizes large scale (monolithic) systems into multiple coarse-grained, durable and reusable technical units that could be implemented by multiple vendors yet integrated into a larger enterprise system. CBA typically engenders designing the internals of these coarse-grained, business-aligned component boundaries, through finer-grained object-orientation. Lately the capabilities to instrument components with service contracts around security and SLA's, has made component based design even more powerful.

EDA: Event Driven Architecture, embraces mechanisms for coordinating the callers and providers of service, producers and consumers of data, sensors and responders of software events with variable level of communication coupling, with variable spectrum of message correlation and with variable options to deliver quality of service. EDA engenders a network that listens to thousands of incoming events from different sources, wherein complex event processing results in intended system response. EDA supports dynamic, parallel, asynchronous flows of messages and hence reacts to external inputs that can be unpredictable in nature. For example EDA approach can enable a caller invoke a provider SBB using events without knowing who provides it or what address the provider uses, what choice amongst multiple providers exists, while load balancing across them and selecting amongst these providers with varying levels of qualities of service based on the caller's requirements. Meanwhile the same software event that represents the request or the events generated by the service in response can be of interest to other SBB in the network, opening a channel for value-add to the customer and business. An EDA can coordinate synchronously or asynchronously between software endpoints, and possibly provide both synchronous and asynchronous access between the same participants. In EDA, simultaneous streams of execution can run independently of each other to fulfill a customer request or system responsibility, typically an event bus serves as a platform to manage integration and/or choreograph a larger process.

MDA: Model Driven Architecture, modeling an enterprises system (data, systems, and model of your data model) in conjunction with meta-data, which keeps a record of an enterprise's architecture in-terms of data, information, application, services, technology and implementation (platform specifics) is the basis. There are three basic tools used in an MDA as defined by OMG (Object Manage-ment Group) – (see http://www.omg.org/mda): Meta-Object Facility (MOF)- The MOF defines a standard repository for meta-models and, therefore, models (since a meta-model is just a special case of a mod-el). XML Meta-Data Interchange (XMI) - XMI defines an XML-based interchange format for UML meta-models and models; by standard-izing XML document formats and DTD (document type definitions). In so doing, it also defines a mapping from UML to XML. Common Warehouse Meta-model (CWM) - The CWM standardizes a complete, comprehensive meta-model that enables data mining across database boundaries at an enterprise and goes well beyond. Like a UML profile but in data space instead of application space, it forms the MDA map-ping to database schemas.

UCA: Utility Compute Architectures (UCA), computing is accom-plished via a service provisioning model in which a service provider makes computing resources and infrastructure management available to the customer as needed, and charges them for specific usage rather than a flat rate. The utility model seeks to maximize the efficient use of resources and/or minimize associated costs. Here the word utility is used to make an analogy to other services, such as electrical power, that seek to meet fluctuating customer needs, and charge for the re-sources based on usage rather than on a flat-rate basis. This approach, sometimes known as pay-per-use or metered services is becoming increasingly common in enterprise computing and is sometimes used for the consumer market as well, for Internet service, Web site access, file sharing, and other applications. It should be noted that another version of utility computing is carried out within an enterprise. In a shared pool utility model, an enterprise centralizes its comput-ing resources to serve a larger number of users without unnecessary redundancy, where the IT division charges the rest of the Enterprise division for its services. From a technology perspective UCA leverag-es advances in Grid Computing (dynamic grids), service provisioning technologies, consolidation (networks/compute/storage) and auto-discovery mechanisms (such as JINI).

ICA: Identity Centric Architecture is the discipline of designing systems that put the concepts of secure, distributed, open and owner controlled digital identity at the center." ICA implementations may use various systems, such as: I-name/I-number, XRI/XDI, SXIP, LID, Open-ID, SAML, Liberty, XACML, etc." ICA also ensure the alignment of Network Facing Identity Systems with Service Centric Identity Systems via Vertical Integration of multiple fragmented Identity Systems

NGN: Next Generation Network is a broad term to describe some key architectural evolutions in telecommunication core and access networks that will be deployed over the next 5-10 years. The general idea behind NGN is that one network transports all information and services (voice, data, and all sorts of media such as video) by encapsulating these into packets, like it is on the Internet. NGNs are commonly built around the Internet Protocol, and therefore the term "all-IP" is also sometimes used to describe the transformation towards NGN.

4G Networks: The 4G will be a fully IP-based integrated system of systems and network of networks achieved after the convergence of wired and wireless networks as well as computer, consumer electronics, communication technology, and several other convergences that will be capable of providing 100 Mbps and 1Gbps, respectively, in outdoor and indoor environments with end-to-end QoS and high security, offering any kind of services anytime, anywhere, at affordable cost and one billing

Administrator
The Administrator is a privileged user who is responsible for configuring the system so that it can achieve SSO

Authentication
The process by which the identity of a user or administrator is established within the system. This process may involve explicit user interaction with the system outside the scope of any of the web applications that participate in SSO

Authentication Client
A client library for authentication service

Authentication Service
A service that facilitates the authentication of users and administra-

tors within the system

Client
An entity that accesses a service within the system

Client Library
A specialized component that provides programmatic access to a set of services within the system by acting as a client on behalf of the subsystem that uses it. A client library abstracts the underlying communication and other implementation details necessary to efficiently access the service from within the system

Cluster
In the context of OpenSSO, a cluster is a system where more than one installation of OpenSSO services are available which operate together as a single logical installation

Cookie
A mechanism that allows a web server to store some data on the browser that accesses that server

Domain
A suffix used in fully qualified host names that allows the logical grouping of hosts

Firewall
An entity that limits access to and from a network based on the configured security policies

Federation Termination
Termination of Identity Federation

HTTP
Short name for Hypertext Transfer Protocol. This is an open standards based protocol used for exchange of information between web browsers and web servers

Liberty
Refers to the Liberty Alliance Project (*http://www.project-liberty.org/*) that provides standards specifications for protocols and frameworks to facilitate network identity based services

Logging Client
A client library for logging service

Logging Service
A service that allows a client to create log messages in order to form an audit trail of important events within the system

Naming Client
A client library for naming service

Naming Service
A service that allows a client to locate other services available within the system

OpenSSO
Alias for the Open Web Single Sign-On project. This project is an open source initiative of Sun Microsystems Inc., that provides the foundation of identity services for the web platform

SAML
Abbreviation for Security Assertion Markup Language. SAML is an XML based framework for exchanging security information

Service
In the context of OpenSSO, a service is an abstraction that represents functionality provided by a subsystem which can be accessed any-where within the network using appropriate request and response message constructs

Session Client
A client library for session service

Session Service
A service that provides the ability to associate a user session with a particular user once that user has successfully authenticated

Session time-out
A preset interval of time after which the user session is considered invalidated. A session time-out can be a hard time-out or an idle time-out value depending upon the configuration of the system.

SSL
Abbreviation for Secure Socket Layer. SSL provides a means to encrypt communication between two entities in such a way that it becomes illegible to any other entity.

SSO
Abbreviation for Single Sign-On. SSO is defined as the ability of a user to authenticate once and gain access to a variety of web application resources that otherwise would have required individual authentication, with each authentication potentially requiring different set of credentials.

SSO Agent
A minimally intrusive transparent software component that can be added to the access path of a web application to allow it to participate in SSO.

System
In the context of OpenSSO, the System represents a complete deployment where various web applications participate in an SSO environment using the identity services provided by OpenSSO.

System Stakeholder
A set of people who interact with the system at various stages and in different capacities. The system stakeholders could be individuals, teams or organizations

UML
Abbreviation for Unified Modelling Language. UML is a well known modelling language used for expressing architecture, design and implementation details

URL
The user of the system is an end user who is interested in accessing one or more web applications that participate in SSO. This user has no administrative privileges and cannot change the behavior of the system for other users. This user may be able to change the behavior of system as experienced by self to the extent allowed by the Administrator. Abbreviation for Uniform Resource Locator. A URL contains the necessary information regarding the address and access mechanism needed to access a resource available on the network

User

An interval of time for which a user is considered authenticated and the associated identity information is available to all participating web applications in SSO. A user session begins with the successful authentication of the user and ends with the invalidation of session either by a direct action of the user such as an explicit logout, or by indirect means such as configured session time-out or being invalidated by an administrator

User Session

An interval of time for which a user is considered authenticated and the associated identity information is available to all participating web applications in SSO. A user session begins with the successful authentication of the user and ends with the invalidation of session either by a direct action of the user such as an explicit logout, or by indirect means such as configured session time-out or being

Web Application

An application hosted on either a Web Server or an Application server and is accessible via the web using a traditional browser

Web Service

The W3C defines a Web service[1] as a software system designed to support interoperable machine-to-machine interaction over a network. Web services are frequently just application programming interfaces (API) that can be accessed over a network, such as the Internet, and executed on a remote system hosting the requested services. The W3C Web service definition encompasses many different systems, but in common usage the term refers to those services that use SOAP-formatted XML envelopes and have their interfaces described by WSDL. For example, WS-I only recognizes Web services in the context of these specifications

XML

Short name for Extensible Markup Language. XML is an open standards based data markup language used for representing structured data.

References

The topic of unifying and consolidating Architectural Approaches has been discussed and written by multiple industry groups and bodies and this thought process is substantiated by

i. Integration Consortium at: *www.integrationconsortium.org/uploads/members/fiorano%20software%20inc./bca_unifying_soa_and_eda.pdf* —discussing how Component based Architecture unifies SOA and EDA.

ii. Also ITU RM-ODP references CBA, EDA, SOA and MDA and related approaches –for open distributed processing. Architectural practices/approaches and RM-ODP, use of MDA concepts and mechanisms for ODP system specifications; use of other modeling languages for ODP system specification and implementation; and relationship and integration of RM-ODP with other architectural practices (e.g., IEEE Std. 1471, RUP) and architectural approaches (e.g., SOA, CBA, or EDA). *http://www.lcc.uma.es/~av/wodpec2005/*

iii Tibco discusses how Real-time Business is made possible with SOA and EDA at *http://www.opengroup.org/projects/soa/uploads/40/8652/SOA_EDA_Chapter_FINAL_101404.pdf*

iv. IBM's web site on SOA talks to MDA and SOA synergies "As you can see, change and the ability of the SOA system to adapt to it are the most important elements here. For developers, such changes can occur within their context of work or outside of it, depending upon if there are changes needed as to how the interfaces are defined and how they interact to each other. Rather than the developer's, it is the role of the architect to engender most changes to a SOA model. This division of labor, whereby the developer focuses on creating functional units defined as services, and the architect and modeler focus on how the units fit together, has been around for over a decade, represented commonly in the Universal Modeling Language (UML) and described as a Model-Driven Architecture (MDA)". *http:// www.128.ibm.com/developerworks/webservices/newto/*

v. Another quote from Daniel Foody states "SOA (service oriented architecture) and MDA (model driven architecture) are, in many ways, orthogonal to each other. While SOA defines an architectural paradigm for how you use interconnected systems at a macro level, it says nothing about the tooling you use to go from high level architecture to working code. In contrast, MDA allows you to follow any type of architectural paradigm, but provides a well-defined approach to go from high level to code. SOA is a destination; MDA is a way to get to a destination. *http://expertanswercenter.techtarget.com/eac/ knowledgebaseAnswer/0,295199,sid63_gci1105612,00.html*

vi. A Gartner paper discussing the relationship between SOA and EDA *http://www.gartner.com/DisplayDocument?id=391595*

vii. Ramani Vaidyanathan of BEA describes how Agility commands the appropriate combinational use of SOA, MDA and EDA *http:// www.ftponline.com/channels/arch/reports/eas/2005/slides/16_vaidyanathan. pdf*

viii. The alignment between Web Service and SOA with Utility Grids is currently being addressed with working groups such as: Oasis Web Service Resource Framework. *http://www.oasis-open.org/committees/tc_ home.php?wg_abbrev=wsrfi*

ix. Globas Alliance with OGSA initiative. *http://www.glo- bus.org/ogsa/ and http://news.taborcommunications.com/msgget. jsp?mid=465579&xsl=story.xsl*

Other References
i. NGOSS & TT Hub Paper
http://www.sun.com/solutions/documents/white-papers/te_ngoss_tthub.pdf

ii. Sun SDP for IMS
http://www.imaworld.org/ima/Media/Sun.pdf

References

iii. Sun and Pronto whitepaper on OSS for NGN
http://www.prontonetworks.com/OSSWhitePaper.pdf

iv. Pronto & Sun Identity and Wifi
http://www.prontonetworks.com/SunProntoWiFiPaper.pdf

v. Sun White Paper on Common Mobility Architecture
http://www.sun.com/mobility/documents/cma_technical_whitepaper.pdf

vi. Sun White Paper on Model Driven Architecture enabling Service Oriented Architecture

vii. *http://www.opengroup.org/events/q405/mdasoa.pdf*

viii. Sun White Paper on Event Driven Architecture augmenting Service Oriented Architecture

ix. *http://www.opengroup.org/events/q405/edamdasoa.pdf*

x. Sun White Paper on Component based Architecture supplementing Service Oriented Architecture
http://www.opengroup.org/events/q405/cbaedamdasoa.pdf

xi. Sun White Paper on Utility Compute Architecture supporting Service Oriented Architecture
http://www.opengroup.org/events/q405/ucacbaedamdasoa.pdf

xii. Sun White Paper on Identity Centric Architecture extending Service Oriented Architecture
http://www.opengroup.org/events/q405/idesoa.pdf

xiii. Java RFID Software Architecture
http://www.sun.com/software/solutions/rfid/EPCNetArch_wp.pdf

xiv. A Sea Change – Standards for Open SOA and NGN
https://communications.dev.java.net/files/documents/510/28722/ASeaChange_d_fin.pdf

xv. Service Delivery Network Architecture
http://www.sun.com/service/sunps/architect/delivery/sdn-arch-overview.pdf

xvi. P2P Mobile Sensor Networks by David Clearly and Daryl Parker
http://csdl2.computer.org/comp/proceedings/hicss/2005/2268/09/22680324c.pdf

xvii. FAIN Active Network Architecture
http://www.ist-fain.org/deliverables/FAIN.paper.Vf.pdf

xviii. Active Network (FAIN) Strong Authentication
http://www.ee.ucl.ac.uk/~lcheng/Papers/Published/2003/SOFTCOM_2003.pdf

xix. Active Network (FAIN) Authentication
http://www.sun.com/service/sunps/architect/delivery/sdn-arch-overview.pdf

xx. How Wimax Works paper
http://computer.howstuffworks.com/wimax1.htm

xxi. A SLEE for all Seasons Open-cloud Paper
http://www.opencloud.com/downloads/asfas.pdf

xxii. Security for Sensor Mobile Networks
http://www.cs.berkeley.edu/~ckarlof/papers/senroute-adnj.pdf

xxiii. IMS Architecture –Ericsson
http://www.ericsson.com/technology/whitepapers/ims_ip_multimedia_sub-system.pdf

xxiv. Project DReaM white paper
http://openmediacommons.org/collateral/DReaM-Overview.pdf

xxv. How to implement Trusted computing
https://www.trustedcomputinggroup.org/news/Industry_Data/Implementing_Trusted_Computing_RK.pdf

xxvi. Securing Mobile devices on Converged Networks (TCG)
https://www.trustedcomputinggroup.org/groups/mobile/Final_iGR_mobile_security_white_paper_sept_2006.pdf

xxvii. TCG Architecture Overview
https://www.trustedcomputinggroup.org/groups/TCG_1_0_Architecture_Overview.pdf

References

xxviii. Transforming Service Delivery via IMS
http://www.telcordia.com/collateral/whitepapers/svc_delivery_ims.pdf

xxix. Identity enabling ILM Sun Paper
http://www.sun.com/storagetek/white-papers/identity_enabled_ilm.pdf

xxx. Best Practices for ILM Security
http://www.sun.com/storagetek/white-papers/ilm_security.pdf

xxxi. Powering the IP Media Subsystem
http://sun.systemnews.com/articles/91/4/opt-sysadmin/15100

xxxii. Wimax Security requirements
http://www.ieee802.org/16/tgd/contrib/C80216d-03_60.pdf

xxxiii. Extending Internet Connectivity to Smart-dust
http://research.sun.com/projects/crypto/Sizzle_4pager.pdf

xxxiv. ECC The NG of Internet Security
http://research.sun.com/projects/crypto/ECC-Whitepaper.pdf

xxxv. Sizzle: A standards based end 2 end Security Architecture for the embedded Internet
http://research.sun.com/projects/crypto/guptav_sizzle_pmc.pdf

xxxvi. Project Liberty Personal Identity
http://projectliberty.org/index.php/liberty/content/download/395/2744/file/Personal_Identity.pdf

xxxvii.A New Business Layer for IP Networks
http://www.ipsphereforum.org/Files/A%20New%20Business%20Layer%20for%20IP%20Networks%20-%20TN1.pdf

xxxviii. TrueOMF Target Service Management Applications
http://www.truebaseline.com/applications.html

xxxix. Towards Systemic Secure Architectures
http://www.sun.com/blueprints/0206/819-5605.pdf

xl. Project Liberty Social Identity
*http://projectliberty.org/index.php/liberty/content/download/387/2720/file/
Liberty_Federated_Social_Identity.pdf*

xli. Project Liberty Deployment Guidelines
*http://projectliberty.org/index.php/liberty/content/download/373/2678/file/
deployment_guidelinesv2_9.pdf*

xlii. Project Liberty Contact Book
*http://projectliberty.org/index.php/liberty/content/download/1051/7215/file/
draft-liberty-id-sis-contactbook-guidelines-v1.0-06.pdf*

xliii. Project Liberty Presence
*http://projectliberty.org/index.php/liberty/content/download/1053/7221/file/
draft-liberty-id-sis-presence-guidelines-v1.0-12.pdf*

xliv. Project Liberty Location
*http://projectliberty.org/index.php/liberty/content/download/1052/7218/file/
draft-liberty-id-sis-gl-guidelines-v1.0-15.pdf*

xlv. Project Liberty Web Services
*http://projectliberty.org/index.php/liberty/content/download/390/2729/file/
Liberty_ID-WSF_Web_Services_Framework.pdf*

LaVergne, TN USA
30 June 2010

187897LV00003B/20/A